New

Pilgrims

For Andrea,

& for the courage
the fortitude
the devotion
& the integrity
of the Pilgrims.

Pilgrims

a poem

Garrett Buhl Robinson

Poet in the Park
In Humanity I see Grace, Beauty and Dignity.

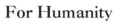

For Humanity

Table of Contents

Opening Notes

— 1620 —

— 1621 —

— 1624 —

— 1625 —

— Epilogue —

Appendixes

Bibliography

Opening Notes

The Julian and Gregorian Calendars

The Pilgrims used a different calendar from what is used in the contemporary era. The Julian Calendar was used in 17th Century England and today we use the Gregorian Calendar. For the Old Style of the Julian Calendar, the beginning of the year was March 25. For the New Style of the Gregorian Calendar, the beginning of the year is January 1.

For the designation of years in the poem, I begin each year on January 1 in the New Style. For example, in the Pilgrims' first winter at Plymouth, the Rendezvous catches fire on January 14. In the Old Style of the Julian Calendar, this would have been in the 11th month of 1620. However, using the New Style of the Gregorian Calendar, this occurs in the 1st month of 1621. Thus, in chapter 14, the episode of the Rendezvous catching fire occurs on January 14, 1621.

Also, there is a ten day difference between the Julian and Gregorian Calendars. The Pilgrims dated the signing of the Mayflower Compact on November 11. We would now date this as November 21 in the New Style. For the poem, I have left the specific days of the month the same as what was used by the Pilgrims. Thus, in chapter 7 of the poem, the signing of the Mayflower Compact occurs on November 11, 1620 which is the date the Pilgrims wrote on the document upon signing.

On the Composition of the Poem

Pilgrims was developed and composed during the Covid-19 Pandemic. I drafted and polished the book while sheltering alone in my studio apartment in New York City. I wanted to develop my own poetic portrayal of the events described by the few personal accounts of the settlement of Plymouth Colony in New England.

For this, I studied the writing of William Bradford and Edward Winslow primarily. I also gained insight from the letters of John Pory, Emmanuel Altham and Isaack de Rasieres as they are collected in *Three Visitors to Early Plymouth*. In the poem there is one phrase quoted from Azel Ames and about two dozen scattered phrases quoted from Bradford and Winslow, such as Winslow's phonetic rendering of the Algonquin dialect spoken by the Wampanoags.

The dating and sequencing of the events in the poem were provided by William Bradford and Edward Winslow principally. *Three Visitors to Early Plymouth* also provided more information for some specific dates. The log of the Mayflower published by Azel Ames was also helpful for events through April 5, 1621, which was the Mayflower's departure date from Plymouth Bay in New England. Some dates were also provided by editors of the primary sources such as William Bradford's marriage to Alice Carpenter Southworth in Plymouth on August 14, 1623.

Without question, the famous events at Plymouth Colony did happen. For example, there was a first Thanksgiving – although the Pilgrims would not have referred to it as such – which occurred in 1621 and Ousamequin, the Massasoit of the Wampanoags, attended with about 90 Sachems and Pnieses. This harvest festival at Plymouth transpired over 3 days. Edward Winslow gave a personal account of the event in *Mourt's Relation*. However, the manner by which the event is portrayed and brought to life is the art of the storyteller. *Pilgrims* is a poem, not a scholarly or historical text. I took liberties in depicting some events where there are few descriptive details in the primary sources. However, mindful of my poetic license, I took care to preserve the accuracy and spirit of this historic story.

For the bibliography, I decided to list the secondary sources I have read since composing the poem. The list is far from exhaustive. I list these titles in hopes that people will consult the expertise of these scholarly books to explore this fascinating and truly remarkable story. Extremely gifted and erudite scholars have devoted ponderous portions of their careers to these historic events. Their valuable scholarly work must be read, studied and revered. The story of the Pilgrims at Plymouth is not simply American History, but an important development in the History of Civilization.

Garrett Buhl Robinson
2022

To me, however, the question of the times resolved itself into a practical question of the conduct of life. How shall I live?

Ralph Waldo Emerson

1620

Chapter 1

Elder William Brewster's Sermon
September 1620

"Our swollen sails are filled for liberty
    to course across the vastness of the sea
and drive upon the fathoms of the deep
    to find a place to worship righteously.

"Escaping persecution of our past
    by steering into more adversity
we hold our sails uprightly as a mast
    and face the trials of life with our beliefs.

"Although we left the pain we knew before
    we steer our prow into uncertainty
as through our faith our lives have been reborn
    to build a reverent community.

"In England we were driven from our homes
    and shamed for peaceful ways we sought God's grace
and some gave up their lives before their souls
    when they were martyred by the magistrate.

"None from our church were spared from public scorn
    as we were ridiculed and scoffed and mocked
and from our quiet worship and accord
    we found our lives were locked in laughing stocks.

"Our peaceful, humble lives do not offend
    and we appeal upon the highest law.
We do not understand why we're condemned.
    We simply seek communion with our God.

"Yet at the times when we were pushed away,
　　we were obstructed so we couldn't leave
with bogus fees we had no means to pay
　　and held in anger for what we believe.

"Then when we were able to find a boat
　　sailed by an honest Captain and his crew
still even more misfortune struck our hopes
　　when we thought sanctuary within view.

"With half the group safe and secure on board
　　and waiting for the others to arrive
a falling ax severed our binding cord
　　and cut our group in half before our flight.

"The Captain weighed the anchor and set sail
　　with the approach of an armed company
and we watched helplessly from the ship's rail
　　at the harassment of our families.

"Our wives and children were stuck on the shore
　　and as the ship embarked to a safe haven
right when our spirits poised in hope to soar
　　we fell in chasms of our separation.

"Yet we were reunited through our love.
　　We never broke our sacred family bond
and with the truth we seek from up above
　　our love for one another is more strong.

"And as we face the cold indifference
　　of an unchartered span of wilderness
let us remember all the challenges
　　we overcame through faithful providence.

"The Netherlands received us when we came
    although their customs were foreign to us
and they all had their own lives to maintain
    and had no obligation unto us.

"The Dutch were kind to let us live our lives
    within abidance of permissiveness.
We huddled round the candle of our light
    within the stillness of their tolerance.

"Yet so we may fulfill the covenant
    in our acceptance of the Holy Spirit
we must sustain ourselves with sustenance
    and strive through sober work for earnest merit.

"In Amsterdam at bustling shipping yards
    we could not find a place to ply our trades.
Most of us are from humble country farms
    and do not know how oaken ships are made.

"So seeking work we could do in return
    we moved to Leyden, a small town nearby,
and then our church's pastor could converse
    with scholars at the University.

"And then together we moved to Leyden
    where all our skills and trades could be employed
and finding a place for our denizen
    we were appreciated and enjoyed.

"We proved our worth in which we were endowed
    through diligent reliability
and with our peaceful lives we were allowed
    to worship in our solemn sanctity.

"Yet in the laxity of smooth admission
    we felt the loss of our identity
to build upon our cultural tradition
    and make decisions for our legacy.

"And in the welcoming community
    where we had hoped to lift up high our faith,
set on a softened liberality
    we could not build upon a solid base.

"And as we strove to reach up overhead
    and lift a light into eternity,
we wandered along common river beds
    that pour erosion in the open sea.

"We do not seek to live our lives at ease.
    The vulgar call is not what beckons us.
We seek what is beyond what we conceive
    and find fulfillment in the arduous.

"We do not seek the spoils when others fall.
    We did not leave Holland in desperation.
We are committed to a higher call
    — a faith and courage for our liberation.

"We do not seek the glories of conquest
    to plunder El Dorado's treasury.
We have embarked upon a humble quest
    — a simple settlement of families.

"We worked with merchants and sold our estates
    to purchase the provisions for the venture
and then through seven years the shares we pay
    will settle the agreement we're indentured.

"We hope to find a way to live more pure,
    entrusted with our honest management
and cultivate our fruits from honest work
    with governance of faithful providence

"fulfilling every moment of our lives
    with a reliance on salvation's grace,
committed to the labors of our times
    and guided by the compass of our faith.

"And in the freezing chill of winter's ice,
    the trials and tribulations of each day,
through harshness of the rancor of dour strife
    our faithful compass truly guides the way.

"And when the clouds are covering the sky
    and overcast with ominous dismay
so shifty winds are howling through the night
    our faithful compass truly guides our way.

"And when the sea is tossing with unrest
    and when the waves are thrashing without break,
we bravely face the furious tempest
    and know our faithful compass is unchanged.

"And in the deepest pitch of the dark night
    so that our guiding compass can't be read,
in greatest trouble we may find more light
    by looking solemnly above our heads.

"And solitary we may find a star
    at where our compass guide is always bound
and if we watch, we see it is a star
    that all the other stars circle around.

"And as we journey through the lengths of life
    whether we go together or alone,
throughout the deepest darkness of the night
    this steady star can always lead us home."

So Elder Brewster gave his homily
    upon the *Mayflower* out on the deck
for all the gathered Pilgrim families
    within the church of their togetherness.

Chapter 2

The Belligerent Sailor
September 1620

In the release of being underway
   the *Mayflower* was cruising on the sea
with favorable winds through a clear day
   — the progress made was a welcome relief.

This was the third time they had set their sails.
   Before, each time they reached the open sea
alarms that came from the ship the *Speedwell*
   made them return to fix the seeping leaks.

They had to choose to leave the other boat
   and to reduce the numbers in their group
and ventured on the *Mayflower* alone
   like Gideon selecting his best troops.

There was a risk in sailing on their own
   without support of an accompaniment
yet it is safer without an escort
   then to be tied to tug a leaking ship.

The temperature was fair but time was short.
   The weather would not always be so mild.
They had to make their way to distant shores
   before the bite of winter time arrived.

A group of deacons stood upon the deck
   discussing matters of the venture's fare,
then paused to watch the matron deaconess
   lead children into the fresh open air.

Each day she nurtured their maturing growth
  and stirred and piqued their curiosity
as they were all confined upon the boat,
  she opened worlds of thoughtful inquiry.

The men discussed responsibilities,
  then paused to smile at the refreshing sight,
a break from weary practicality
  to watch the happiness of youth's delight.

And in the children rested all their hope,
  the yearning for a home they strove to find
as their devoted love would work to sow
  each generation's fresh rebirth of life.

Then suddenly their bliss turned into horror
  as Goodwife Brewster and the children cringed
while they were scolded by an angry sailor
  who burned and seethed with hot belligerence.

They did not know what had provoked attack,
  the children simply gazed upon the sea,
but as they slowly started walking back
  the sailor yelled at them ferociously.

The Governor John Carver was the first,
  and promptly he stepped forward in the lead
and then Myles Standish, always on alert,
  stood by to squelch any hostility.

Then Goodwife Brewster moved without a word,
  the kids were froze in a bewildered state.
She turned their fear from the enraged outburst
  and quickly huddled them safely away.

Then as the others gathered in reply
  to answer threats upon the families,
the Reverend Elder Brewster calmly tried
  to sooth the scene with rationality.

"Kind sir, I'm puzzled how we caused offense.
  We do not want to hinder you at work.
What wrong we've done, we'll carefully attend.
  The last thing that we want is to disturb."

The sailor looked up in resentfulness
  as if to wither Brewster's peaceful grace
then barked out brutish snarls of insolence
  through bitter sourness of his scowling face.

"Our boat was sweet before you came onboard
  but all you sickened people vomit filth.
Before we smelled of claret we had stored.
  You Puritans have filled our hull with bilge."

"We're sorry that some members have been sick.
  We're not accustomed to the rolling sea.
We are adjusting to the yaw and pitch
  and our infirmed recover steadily."

Then William Brewster carried on to say,
  "And although people call us Puritans
that is not anything that we proclaim.
  It is a term used in disparagement.

"We are devoted to a holy peace.
  We make no claim in having purity
and of the grace and beauty that we seek
  we hope to share with all humanity."

The sailor then condemned the Separatists
   with insults to provoke an altercation
but Elder Brewster could respond to this
   and tried providing more clarification.

"Some have referred to us as Separatists.
   The fact they burn us with so many brands
is probably the clearest evidence
   they do not take the time to understand.

"Our worship is not tiered in hierarchy.
   We seek communion in our simple church,
extolling praise and faith in unity
   while singing gospels of the sacred word."

For all the reasoning that Brewster gave
   in calm and gentle ways he could explain
from his attempts to cool the heated rage
   the sailor grew more angry all the same.

Our situations are all different
   and often this results in disagreement
where interactions become bickering
   so we become destructively egregious.

Yet in the blinding dust of confrontation
   where sensibility cannot be found
refreshing breezes of elucidation
   can help for recognizing common ground.

But when a situation is inflamed
   a cooling effort to communicate
can feed into the raging of the blaze
   and further stoke what one hoped to assuage.

And even Brewster's soothing countenance
could not extinguish or appease this fire
as the sailor continued to denounce
the passengers with vitriolic ire.

"Don't even try to skirt away the blame,
Governor Martin is who started this
and he abuses all of you the same
and I have heard you all remarking this.

"I'm sick of his complaints about the boat.
I listen to the Captain, not to him.
He needs to learn he doesn't know the ropes.
He needs to shut his mouth or learn to swim."

Here Brewster caught a sliver of insight,
"Now I can see the cause of the confusion
and in your debt from our mutual plight
I think there is a simple resolution.

"Christopher Martin had been Governor
and we cannot deny some problems rose
as we had arguments with one another
and Martin could not reconcile the throes.

"So when we had to leave the other ship,
consolidating on the *Mayflower*,
Chris Martin had his term of leadership
and now our Governor is Mr. Carver.

"If Mr. Martin says something again
we hope that you will let one of us know.
It is a matter we will promptly mend,
respectful of your duties on the boat."

The elder hoped the statement would resolve
   the sailor's spiteful animosity
but Brewster's calm was answered with a squall
   of dastardly irrationality.

"Tell him yourself!" The saucy sailor raved
   "the jackass acted like he was my boss
and now you all are doing just the same
   and then you wonder why I'm being cross!

"I don't expect your feeble group to last.
   I doubt that half of you will make the voyage
and while you die you'll listen to me laugh
   dumping your corpses in the ocean void.

"And then I'll merrily pilfer your things
   and plunder through your chests for all I want,
a pirate's spoiling fingers hooped with rings
   then burn it in a binge of drunken rot.

"I've never before seen such ignorance.
   You act like scholars but what have you learned!
You're lugging books into the wilderness
   and when you're starving you can eat your words!"

The Elder Brewster's hope turned soundly sad.
   He didn't want to cause a confrontation.
He felt he failed in any chance he had
   to find agreement through clear explanation.

Then barging forcefully into the scene
   just as the Pilgrim leaders turned away
the Captain of the ship came shoving in
   and suddenly they heard his stern voice say,

14

"What's going on? What's the commotion here?
  Get to your work sailor. Attend your job!
Don't even try to act like you don't hear
  or I'll command you with the flogging rod.

"Now Mr. Carver I must speak with you.
  Is your group causing problems on my ship?
If you are interfering with my crew
  then you must know I will not suffer this."

The Deacon Carver did not hesitate
  and stepped directly out front of the group,
as Governor he must fulfill his place
  and must respond for what his people do.

Then Mr. Carver with sincere respect
  as Governor of the community,
neatly articulated his address
  by speaking with refined diplomacy.

"Our pardon to the Captain and the crew.
  We will not interfere with your vocation.
There was an issue where we were confused
  for which the sailor gave an explanation.

"Make no exception on account of us
  and leave the worthy sailor to his work.
We trust your ship will soon deliver us.
  We'll be more careful as your passengers."

Then settled with resounding satisfaction,
  the stern Commander marched back to his cabin.
He had to plot his charts for navigation
  and focus on his duties as the Captain.

Then Mr. Carver turned to face the group
   so everyone could see the situation
and making certain he was understood
   the Governor gave them an explanation,

"We have a right to honest dignity.
   We paid our fares and chartered this long trip.
But there is also the reality —
   this is most certainly the Captain's ship.

"I won't deny that we have been abused
   but so has every person who has lived.
We gain the virtue of our fortitude
   and rise above offenses we forgive.

"Some people are determined to disrupt
   and only have a hope that others fail
but they're always dissatisfied because
   they never try to make something themselves.

"We do not know this sailor's situation.
   We have no place to judge or to assume.
Stay clear and let him do his occupation
   and we'll attend to see our families through.

"We're cramped for space and shoved in the dank holds
   and destined for an unknown wilderness.
Our love and worship are our only homes.
   We're merely passengers upon this ship.

"We have no interest fighting with the crew.
   We build our strength with what we can endure.
We have much bigger things that we must do.
   Beyond this ship, we're seeking a new world."

Chapter 3

Sea Burial
September 1620

Their journey was enjoying pleasant weather
   upon a little parting of the sea
and snug within the ship they sailed together,
   they cruised above the fathoms of the deep.

The spirit of the members of the group
   were higher than they had been for some time.
Like the full sails, their hearts were filled with hope
   and pulsed with waves that splashed in salty rime.

In retrospect, their lives had felt so small
   confined within their regular routines
while safely sheltered in their household walls
   of neighborly familiarity.

Some nights before they gazed up at the stars
   that floated in the distant mystery
but on the *Mayflower* from stern to spar
   they looked out at the vastness of the sea.

Yet in this space of possibility,
   extending off the navigation charts
where the horizons touch eternity
   they were confined upon a tiny barque.

The angry sailor was a hurtful problem,
   yet they had been inflicted worse before
but targeting the women and the children
   was something they especially abhorred.

They did their best avoiding confrontations
    but on the tiny boat they were confined
in every turn there was an aggravation
    crammed in the quarters they had been assigned.

The families were packed below the deck
    in common holding without privacy
and even with their mutual respect
    their jostled lives would rub abrasively.

There was a sense of the absurdity
    with talk of joyful hope and liberty
when all they saw was the reality
    of squatting in a squalid misery.

Then in an alteration of events
    Christopher Martin of the Merchants' men,
whose irritation and resentfulness
    had been the burden of beleaguerment,

was suddenly reborn a happy man
    and everyone could hear his jolly cheer
although some were concerned what was at hand
    as some men's joy are from other's despair.

The deacons gathered to inquire about
    what fortune of events had come to pass,
a remedy to cure the other's doubts
    and to confirm their faith in Providence.

With brightened eyes and a new sense of hope
    they stood to listen to what Martin said:
"The hateful sailor who had been our foe,
    I'm happy to report that sailor's dead!

"He had been deathly ill for several days
   and now the wheel of fortune has been turned
because last night his dour life slipped away
   and we see justice has been rightly served!"

Then Martin winced in grim astonishment
   as lofty hope dropped from each deacon's face,
he thought he brought the news of merriment
   and once again he was inflamed with rage:

"I cannot tolerate you Puritans!
   You people are completely ignorant!
If you're so smart, why can't you understand
   — you live in stinking filth beneath the deck."

Then Brewster turned to see the Governor
   and then John Carver nodded with his head,
this was of ecumenical nature
   and then the Reverend Brewster calmly said,

"We do not revel in another's death.
   We do not celebrate another's loss.
We have no interest in vindictiveness.
   We cannot weigh upon another's cross.

"There is no doubt there was an argument
   but there's no slights and barbs we want to share.
We strive to lift our lives from circumstance
   and try avoiding hateful snags and snares.

"We do not know about this sailor's life
   and what we do not know, we can't condemn.
We seek release from leaden weights of spite.
   We are a humble people who forgive."

Then Mr. Martin took another stand
    and shouted out another fierce rebuke
"How can you say you do not know this man
    when you received his threatening abuse?"

This time the Governor raised up his hand
    to signal Brewster he would take the lead
and try to help Chris Martin understand
    in giving answer civil mindedly:

"For once, I must explain for clarity,
    it's true the sailor offered us abuse,
however it had never been received,
    his outrage was decidedly refused.

"Another point is something you had said
    about the sailor being the group's foe
but I believe in this you are mislead
    because he helped to operate the boat.

"How could the sailor be our enemy
    while helping us to reach our destination?
Us deacons do not seek out rivalry
    and trusted him to his own occupation.

"And when we had our previous exchange
    of which the Captain and the crew all know,
the sailor made a comment that explained
    much of his ire — your griping had provoked.

"Now there is one less member of the crew
    with the ability to sail this ship.
Our lives depend upon the work they do
    and from this loss, none of us benefit."

Then Carver ended what he had to say
  and nothing more was needed to be said
and somberly the deacons turned away
  and in a line climbed up above the deck.

Upon the deck the Captain and the crew
  all stood together at the leeward rail.
They held the figure of a man they knew
  wrapped in a canvas tied like a furled sail.

The Pilgrim leaders in a line emerged
  and climbed up through the hatch above the hold,
and not a single sailor said a word
  as they watched the group solemnly approach.

The group advanced respectfully and slow
  and as the deacons lined up before them,
the Governor requested, "Captain Jones,
  may we make our peace with this worthy man?"

The Captain did not speak, there was no need,
  he simply turned and stepped off to the side.
Then setting his hand on the sailor's head
  the Elder Brewster prayed for his passed life.

And in the stiffness of the building gale
  and the conclusion of the elegy,
the body was set on the ship's side rail
  then dropped into the passage of the sea.

Then as the corpse sunk in the peaceful deep
  at the horizon clouds began to form
and flashing lightning struck upon the sea
  in the approach of equinoctial storms.

Chapter 4

The Broken Beam
October 1620

A group can stick with ideal principles
   and walk along a straight and narrow way
but something that is undeniable
   — the weather of the world will always change.

Before the sea was like a tender kiss
   that bubbled buoyant with a welcome glide
and softly parted with the passing ship
   in happy laughter splashing to the side.

But then the heavy sky came bearing down
   with swelling waves that rose in sharpened peaks
and with the frothy caps of windy howls
   the sea had then begun to show its teeth.

They had the fairness of the wind and sea
   to glide as if in flight for a whole month
but now their passage through tranquility
   was tossed on seas that turned tumultuous.

All of the petty squabbles that they had
   were recognized as silly lunacy.
The turning tides that swayed both good and bad
   were swallowed by the sea's immensity.

The deacons spoke with all the company
   so they would be prepared without alarm,
then everyone could bundle up their things
   to situate and brace before the storm.

The company was severed in two groups,
  although embarked upon the same endeavor,
and something none amongst them could dispute
  — all of them were on the same ship together.

The Pilgrims sought the means to build a church,
  the Merchants and their hires sought profit's gain
and often means and methods would diverge
  in how they thought the group should be maintained.

Yet there were times that their contentiousness
  was certainly a triviality,
the storm had no concern for argument
  because the ocean stomachs everything.

Their sole concern became the storm they shared,
  released to ride upon the ocean rolls
then see how well each one had been prepared
  and hope the ship was strong enough to hold.

The slimy boards that held the water back
  were drummed by rocking waves without relief
and every surge struck with a crashing wrack
  as salty water oozed between the seams.

The storm had made its way into the boat
  and dripped down from the deck above their heads
and every person was completed soaked
  while sloshing in a wash of filthiness.

All of the victuals became waterlogged.
  The scraps of meat were covered with a sludge
and biscuits they had joked were hard as rocks
  were soaked and had become a soppy mush.

And huddled in the hull through days and nights,
   they crested waves and plunged down deep again.
No sail was out as they were furled up tight.
   The ship was at the mercy of the wind.

The scudding ship continued through the blast
   yet no one heard a single person groan,
as crosswinds lashed against the bowing masts,
   they listened to the ship make dreadful moans.

And helplessly the ship would pitch and bob
   as waves were pounding on the hull's confines.
They were surrendered in the hand of God
   and could be crushed and sunk at any time.

Then falling from the crest of every wave,
   not knowing if they would come up again,
the boards began to moan like they would break
   and shuttered with the wallops of the wind.

Then riding up one steep slope of a wave
   the creaking of the boards began to crack
and teetering to tip the bearing strain
   there was the horror of a snapping wrack.

Water came pouring from the upper deck
   as if the boat had sunk into the sea
and waves were dumping down from overhead
   and people in the ship began to scream.

The deacons raced to the emergency
   to help the victims huddle to the side
and from the carnage of catastrophe
   they tried determining what had transpired.

They saw the swaying of the mid-ship mast,
    the massive pole constructed through the decks,
and as it shifted with the wind's hoarse rasp
    the boards were smashed and shattered in a wreck.

The winds had bowed the mast so that it wedged
    a buckle in the deck till a beam broke
then every wave that washed upon the deck
    was dumped on top of them huddled below.

And through the noise of the fierce tempest wails
    they watched the water pour into the boat
and heard the pilot yelling at the helm
    who rang the bell to let the whole crew know.

Then through the hatch the sailors clambered down.
    Some rushed below to operate the pumps
and Captain Jones ordered the crew around
    to dam the ocean less they would be sunk.

They carried boards and canvas stored below
    to nail a cover over the deck's breach,
a desperate patch that through the storm would hold
    to staunch the water temporarily.

Then when they had the crisis in control
    the Captain and the crew turned to survey
the full extent of damage from the hole
    and to determine if the ship was safe.

One of the beams was sagging with a break,
    a close review was able to reveal,
then overhead the deck collapsed and caved
    and broke the planks to compromise the seal.

At first there was a rancor with the crew
   — if they turned back they wouldn't earn their pay.
But others said they'd sacrifice their due
   — if they all drowned then nothing could be saved.

Then after he had sent away the sailors
   the Captain spoke with the whole company
and carefully explained to all the planters
   that he was confident they could proceed.

He was the Captain and the ship's part owner.
   The damage of the deck could be made safe.
The ship was strong and tight below the water.
   They simply would not over-press the sails.

The leaders all agreed they were committed.
   They suffered losses where they stayed before
but now they were pursuing independence
   and hoped to gain their freedom as reward.

Then Francis Eaton stepped out of the crowd,
   the company's ingenious carpenter,
and smoothing out the splinters said aloud,
   "I have a way to make this beam secure."

He said he had a tool that he had packed
   and with some men went to the hold below,
then carried up a stout cast-iron jack
   and set it underneath the beam that broke.

Then cranking up the grooves of the jack's screw,
   they lifted the thick beam back into place,
then so their dauntless journey could resume
   they wedged a post for the supporting brace.

Chapter 5

Man Overboard
October 1620

The storms continued testing the group's mettle
   as they were pressed together desperately,
the ship was but a tender flower's petal
   upon the vast convulsions of the sea.

They all depended on the ship and crew
   as they were merely passengers on board
and there was little more for them to do
   but hold together while the tempest roared.

They chose to chart a course for unknown lands
   to find an open place to build their lives
but at the mercy of their circumstance
   they had to hope and wait they would arrive.

But as they sat in perilous extremes,
   they could not help but pause and realize,
that from the hardships they were suffering,
   their ordeals from before were paradise.

And even if they reached the other shore,
   they would be stranded desperately alone
without assistance or assured support
   and left to fend completely on their own.

Below the deck there were a few small cabins
   that offered a few people privacy
but mostly they were huddled in the open
   sprawled in the hold with thin partitioning.

And it was easy to be irritated
  as everyone was rubbing up together
and flaring with the bothersome frustration
  as nothing could be done about the weather.

The time they made at sail the month before
  was wasted as their progress was erased
and with the buffeting of the fierce storms,
  – heaved to – they were blown back the other way.

And then one night a man sought some relief
  and chose to walk into the storm outside,
the nauseating air they had to breathe
  was stifling in the cram they were confined.

John Howland was a capable young man,
  a servant of the Governor John Carver.
He had agreed to venture with the band
  and work to settle terms he was indentured.

And in the night he climbed up through the hatch
  to breathe the freshness of the open air
and waved up at the sailor on the watch
  who looked out with a salty, squinting glare.

Then Howland staggered to maintain his balance
  by waves that pitched the boat as they rolled on
and even though below was cramped and crowded
  at least they had each other to hold on.

So carefully he walked across the deck
  above the grating where he grabbed the rail
and in the disengaging openness
  the air refreshed with the force of a gale.

He looked out in the stormy mystery.
  The mist was everywhere yet out of reach.
The storm was pressing them relentlessly
  and then went far beyond what could be seen.

The pitching boat was nodding in agreement.
  It couldn't argue with the sea and sky.
Of nature's reasons through the turning seasons
  — the only answer is to live or die.

Then a cross current sent a sudden surge
  that lifted the ship's side on a steep swell
then smartly rolling with the wave's round turn
  John Howland flipped and flew over the rail.

He flailed his arms as he was tumbling down
  and wildly groped and grabbed to find a hold
as in the sea he certainly would drown
  beneath the surface of the salty cold.

Then flopping on the water he was seized
  with the extent of the emergency,
there was no means for his recovery
  while lost in open sea's immensity.

Then bobbing in oblivion's pale wake
  he felt something that slid along his side,
there was one final chance that still remained,
  the halyard ropes the ship dragged out behind.

But grabbing on the line was no sure hope,
  the current pulled him several fathoms deep
but he would not release his clenching hold
  and he would not surrender easily.

And dragged behind the ship beneath the sea,
  one thread of hope was in his hands again
and then another cause for his relief
  — he felt the heaves of the rope hauling in.

Then at the surface gasping for some air
  he clenched the rope held firmly from above
and from the depths of desolate despair
  — John Howland fell but never would give up.

With the ship's hook, they snatched him from the storm
  and as the boat dipped with another wave,
they all together dragged him back on board
  and cheered because a precious life was saved.

They helped him back where he would be secure
  and drying from his bath in the cold sea,
he climbed back in his place inside the berth.
  He'd had enough refreshment and relief.

With grit and fortitude they braved the storms
  while holding to the hope of a new life
and through their labors they all heard one morn
  the rapture of a new born baby's cry.

Then born into extreme adversity
  and yet received in warmth and love and fondness,
a child of Stephen Hopkins' family
  whom they decided to name Oceanus.

Chapter 6

Land Ho!
November 1620

The ship had weathered many weary storms
  yet they were buoyed — hopeful for success.
The tempest cleared with the new baby born
  and they continued making slow progress.

Yet the enjoyment of the brightest days
  must alternate with frightful chills of night
as William Button was in sickness laid
  with surgeon Samuel Fuller at his side.

The youthful Button was receding fast
  and desperately the surgeon tried to save
the boy with all the remedies they had
  but helplessly they watched him slip away.

Nov.
6

They gathered for a ceremony next
  and Brewster was consoling as he prayed
and somberly they all stood on the deck
  as they released the body to the waves.

Their rally rescued Howland from the sea
  but in return had watched another go,
then after night from their unsettled sleep
  they were awakened with the shout, "Land Ho!"

Nov.
9

The happy news was hollered through the hold.
  In unison they jumped up to their feet
and as they quickly wrapped up in their coats
  they lined up at the hatch so each could see.

The hatch door overhead was opened wide
  and patiently they climbed up one by one
and saw the sky was glowing with the light
  and touched their lives with warmth of the new dawn.

And over sloshing jostles of the waves
  and rolling over swells in endless turns,
they'd been at sea for sixty-seven days
  and finally saw something that was firm.

Yet with the destination within reach
  and all the urgency that's held in store,
one lesson that experience will teach
  — the greatest danger is in sight of shore.

And then the Captain told the company
  according to the charts they were off course.
They were far from where they wanted to be,
  the fitful storms had blown them to the north.

They turned to sail in the direction south
  to make a harbor at the Hudson Bay
but while they sailed alongside of Cape Cod
  they started having trouble by midday.

There was dissension and ire argument
  amongst the company's contentious folks.
The ship had turned into a stiff headwind
  with roaring waves breaking on shallow shoals.

"We see the land! Why don't we go on shore?"
  "Why are they taunting us by sailing on?"
"Please stop! We cannot take this anymore!"
  "Once we make land, I'll go off on my own!"

And even though the deacons tried to calm
  discordant squalls erupting from the group
by reasoning with the complaints and qualms,
  the chaos was impossible to sooth.

And from the bitterness of argument
  in all the spats Chris Martin seemed to start,
with his accomplice – snide John Billington –
  they seemed to want to tear the group apart.

And then the crew began resetting sails.
  The Captain turned the ship on a new course.
The wheel was turning round upon the helm
  and spun the ship to sail back to the north.

While Billington and Martin were embroiled
  and busy stirring others' shrill discord,
the Governor stepped back from the peeved foil
  to figure out why the ship had changed course.

He waved to Brewster and the other deacons
  and they requested time with Captain Jones
so they could make inquiry of the reason
  for changes in direction of the boat.

The Captain brought the deacons to his quarters
  and then explained their dire predicament,
"The ship and everyone is in grave danger
  and we are sailing into counter winds.

"The breakers from the shoals are all around.
  We cannot set our sails straight on this course
and if we try to tack we'll run aground.
  I will not risk the ship this close to shore.

"We saw an inlet earlier today.
    We're sailing to the lee side of the Cape.
The winter's nearly here and time is late.
    We need to find a harbor that is safe.

"The season is too late for our return.
    We won't set sail for England till next year.
The ship will stay through winter for support
    and lend you all assistance while we're here.

"Your group must get ashore to scout the land
    and find a place to build your settlement
and quickly get a foothold while you can
    before the ice and snow's impediment."

The Governor and deacons walked back out
    and strolled onto the open of the deck
and then approached the rancor of the crowd
    to call attention for the group's assent.

The turmoil had arose from aggravation
    that stirred and clouded with uncertainty
and Deacon Carver offered explanation
    to re-establish peace with clarity.

And as they understood the plan's design
    then everyone was calmed with a relief,
no longer feeling that they were denied
    from landing on the shore they all could see.

And Martin's efforts to tear them in twain
    and pit the merchant hires against the Pilgrims
were mended when the Governor explained
    the nautical decision of the Captain.

Then Carver and the deacons gave instructions
   to get prepared to haul up on the beach.
In retrospect it was a pert deduction
   — folks work together on what they agree.

Chapter 7

The Mayflower Compact
November 11, 1620

They spent the night out in the open sea
    and planned to harbor the ship the next day
and all the group was working eagerly
    and focused on the safety of the bay.

Then after everyone retired to sleep
    the leaders of the group met through the night.
They knew they had to plan this carefully.
    This was a time for crucial oversight.

Throughout the trip there had been rank dissent
    and they would often struggle for agreement.
They all had different aims and interest
    in the bold venture for their independence.

On board the group was forced to stay together.
    No one could choose when no one had a choice.
But on the shore would be a different matter
    and if they strayed their hope would be destroyed.

^{Nov.} In lofty light of the next early morn
¹¹   the sailors diligently worked the rigs
and as the ship began to cruise to shore
    the hopeful prospects of the day were big.

As every word they spoke sounded like song,
    they shared their joy and meal where they all gathered
and after breakfast cheered the new day's dawn
    as they assembled in the common cabin.

The leaders stood beside the center table,
    the milling group collected all around
and after everyone had calmly settled,
    they waited to see what this was about.

The Elder Brewster sat behind the table
    beside him set a plume and well of ink
and then he stood when everyone assembled
    and joined the others gathered in a ring.

Then Mr. Carver stood before them all
    and easily within each person's reach,
a modest man who answered duty's call,
    he cleared his throat as he prepared to speak,

"Elected as the Governor at sea
    I've held this grave responsibility
yet more than how I humbly hope to lead
    I'm one amongst you in this company.

"Some say we are divided in two groups
    — the merchants and the members of the church,
and we must choose one or the other view
    as interests of each group always diverge.

"I am one of the deacons in the church,
    however, I have been a merchant too
and through my trade and commerce that I earned
    I purchased portions of our tools and food.

"And from diverse devotions of our lives
    no matter what a person may believe,
there are essentials no one can deny
    such as for practical necessity.

"No one will doubt that our vitality
    depends on whether we can stay together
so the most critical necessity
    is our reliance trusted in each other.

"For anyone to hope to reach their aim,
    one must ensure that one can stay alive
and at the edge of a remote domain,
    together is our best hope to survive.

"We have been bold to set ourselves apart
    but now we must make sure we can maintain.
As boldness is required in every start.
    It's prudence that is needed to sustain.

"We are beyond the rules and bounds of law
    that set the standards to instruct our lives
but now we must rely on our resolve
    and follow our discretion as our guide.

"Our courage and our reach have seized our freedom
    but it must be preserved responsibly.
Now we may live our lives by our own reason
    that is conserved through our competency.

"Each one has talents and developed skills
    and we must balance our abilities.
And complementing we may all fulfill
    to make a harmony with unity.

"We each make contributions to demands
    through our belief in equanimity
and with our diligence of craft in hand
    we build assurance for community.

"We seek a world as we envision it
 and we are at the threshold of our home
but if we want to build it as we wish
 then we will have to build it on our own.

"We are far from the world that we had left.
 There is a sea between what we have known.
And now arriving at a wilderness
 we must rely upon ourselves alone.

"And as we gathered all together here
 in preparation of soon making land
as we begin to work it will be clear
 our unity is our best tool at hand.

"We set in ink the terms which we agree
 will be the Compact we elect to make
and with our honor and integrity
 we make our pledge as we each sign our names.

"If anyone object, let it be heard
 before this gathering of all involved
so there will never be a doubtful word
 of our commitment and of our resolve."

Here Deacon Carver paused his weighty speech
 and slowly looked at each one in the room
and seeing they all solemnly agreed
 he took another step as he resumed.

"And from the rank you all entrusted me
 I'll be the first to sign upon this page."
Then dipping the plume in the well of ink
 he scratched the vellum as he signed his name.

Then all the company stood on their feet
and organized themselves into a line
and for the service of community
confirmed the honored Compact as they signed.

Chapter 8

First Expedition
November 13 – 17, 1620

After they all agreed on the Compact
   and pledged by name scripted in each one's hand
they all decided that they would elect
   John Carver as the Governor again.

But when they all climbed back onto the deck
   they were not greeted with applause or cheers.
The ship's crew treated them with no respect
   as they were targets of the sailors' jeers.

The sailors taunted them with baiting doubt,
   "You Puritans will never be safe here!
You all escaped the royal lion's mouth
   and ran into the jaws of a wild bear!"

Besides the taunts there were the constant threats
   that they must quickly find a place to land.
They had to start to build their settlement
   or they would have their things dumped on the sand.

Of course the Pilgrims wanted to begin
   to build their settlement upon the shore
but needed to unpack their shallop then
   so they could start to scout and to explore.

From down below where their boat had been stored
   they brought it up into the open air
but found it had been shattered in the storms
   and would take several days to be repaired.

Nov.
13

41

Instead of waiting for the carpenter
    as they could feel the press of winter winds
they organized a small discovery tour
    with Captain Standish and the younger men.

Nov. The crew took them out on the ship's long boat
15   but dragging shallows kept them from the shore
so some men waded through the chilly foam
    to stand upon the land they would explore.

They walked for miles along the sandy beach
    until they saw some aborigines
but when the group approached in hopes to meet
    the Native people quickly turned to flee.

The group then followed them into the woods
    but with their gear they couldn't keep the pace
then pausing in the thickets where they stood
    they thought they'd wait to meet another day.

Nov. Then deep inside the forest parched with thirst
16   they hoped to find some water safe to drink
but drinking water had been a concern
    — they'd only known what washed from fields and streets.

But all their throats were parched and sorely dry
    and down a cove they found a bubbling spring
and cheered in the refreshment and surprise
    — the water that they drank was pure and sweet.

Then as the men continued to explore
    they found a clearing in the wooden stands
and rising from the open forest floor
    they noticed mounds that had been made by hand.

Then finding bows and arrows set inside
    they dug to find what more the mounds contained
but then were mortified once they realized
    that they were desecrating someone's grave.

Then carefully recovering the grave,
    respecting memory and sanctity,
they thoughtfully set things back into place
    for precious life of all nativity.

After the group had walked a little farther
    close by they found something more puzzling
— a set of boards that must have been a shelter
    and a ship's kettle that was European.

Nearby they found there were more earthen mounds
    but these appeared to have been made of late.
They saw the prints of hands that packed them down
    and each mound was too small to be a grave.

Then many in the group were overjoyed
    to find what these small mounds were covering.
They dug up baskets that all overflowed
    with kernels of a corn they'd never seen.

They all were hungry, they all needed food,
    but this presented moral quandaries.
The planters then debated what to do
    to handle matters most responsibly.

As he was Elder Brewster's prodégé
    the Goodman William Bradford spoke up first,
"Good men, we must conduct with some restraint.
    We must refrain from careless, ravished urge.

"We are not pirates robbing on the sea.
    We are a decent and a civil group
respecting others as we hope to be,
    keeping account for what we choose to do."

Attending the discussion Bradford led
    there was a lull affording thoughtful pause,
then someone in the group abruptly said,
    "Would it be right to let your family starve?"

For this the Goodman William Bradford answered,
    "There is abundance here without a doubt
but that does not give us free leave to plunder
    and then in turn leave someone else without.

"Although we are confronting desperate need
    we can't allow ourselves to lose restraint.
We hold ourselves accountable for deeds
    and are not driven by what impulse craves.

"We must consider our predicament
    and we cannot deny necessity.
We must remember we are godly men
    and all this corn is other's property."

The rectitude of William Bradford's stand
    was not approved by the whole company
and there were smearing mutters – "Puritans!"
    and rumbling grumbles goading mutiny.

Then someone blurted into the debate,
    "But what about the kettle someone stole
and left outside to rust and waste away?
    It's not from here and evidently poached!"

"We can't assume the kettle has been poached"
    retorted Bradford who went on to say:
"We can't condemn on what we do not know.
    It may have been obtained through honest trade."

Here Edward Winslow stood to interject
    and find a way to solve the argument.
Both sides had drawn a line of interest
    and he proposed to make a settlement.

"This does appear to be the Native's corn.
    We don't know how the kettle was obtained.
We'll make no friends by robbing others' store
    and we will need their friendship to make trade.

"However we are desperately in need
    and are responsible for families.
We are not satisfying wanton greed.
    We have a whole community to feed.

"And then from all we know and we believe
    when we hold surplus of what we have made
we do not stand aside while others grieve,
    we generously offer others aid.

"We do not plan to act rapaciously.
    We do not want to pillage and make waste.
This store will be next season's planting seed.
    We'll pay our debt with what we cultivate."

With this all of the group came to agree
    and filled the kettle with the grains of corn
and when they could they would repay indeed
    to satisfy what they took from the store.

Nov.
17
Then through the day they hiked back to the bay
and fired a musket volley from the shore
to notify the need to send away
the long boat that would bring them back onboard.

Chapter 9

Second Expedition
November 27 – 30, 1620

After the shallop had been tightly fitted
   a group was formed for a courageous band
preparing for a second expedition
   to venture further to explore the land.

They needed a place for their settlement
   with fertile soil and sources of fresh water.
They needed lumber for development
   and a deep harbor where a ship could anchor.

Returning to the place they were before
   they found the bay too shallow for a ship
and since the men were wading to the shore
   many of them were starting to get sick.

The snow was falling with a sudden freeze
   and half the party opted to return
and those remaining pressed intrepidly
   refusing to give up the urgent search.

Then after hiking many miles inland
   they stumbled on another earthen mound
that was more massive and far larger than
   all of the mounds they had already found.

Inside they found some arrows and a bow
   and decorations carefully arranged
but lifting planks that were buried below
   they recognized this was another grave.

But on the corpse they were surprised to find
    the canvas cassock of a mariner
and covered with embalming dust ground fine
    the head retained some clumps of yellow hair.

They kept some ornaments to show the others
    and then reset the wood planks carefully
and cautiously rebuilt the mound that honored
    what they had found a curiosity.

Nov. 30 On the next day they found some Native homes
    but the inhabitants all ran away.
Each time they saw some people to approach,
    the people quickly fled in fearful haste.

And then one of the men openly made
    a blurted statement of perplexity,
"Will we be able to establish trade?
    Whenever we approach, these people flee."

Then Captain Standish gave some clarity,
    "You need to take this in consideration
— we're practically a marching armory.
    Most people would find us intimidating."

Then Edward Winslow walked up to a house
    to see the aboriginal abode
and noted the exotic things throughout
    yet recognizably another's home.

Then stepping out he watched the other men
    begin to rummage through the Natives' homes.
They only sought what they could take from them
    with no compunction for what others owned.

Someone brought out a European pail
    and others carried types of pottery
as if by curiosity compelled
    more than by any real necessity.

Then Edward Winslow pulled Bradford aside
    and said, "If we continue doing this
we'll only outrage and antagonize.
    This isn't how we ever will make friends.

"The deacons and the Governor would not
    approve of us ransacking through these homes.
One does not choose in fear of being caught.
    One only chooses left out on one's own."

The two men were pressed with a quandary
    as they were only members of the group,
they did not have any authority
    and little means to sway what others do.

Yet leaders do not blindly follow crowds.
    They are not made by drifting leisurely.
They are the ones with courage to step out
    and be the first to face adversity.

Bradford and Winslow both knew what to do
    and they stood forward to address the men
and gaining the attention of the group
    the stalwart William Bradford said to them:

"Good men, take heed of our integrity.
    We are not pirates here to loot and spoil.
We cannot lose our honest dignity.
    We are not here to rob another's toil."

Then instantly the group all stood and stared
   and in the pause one man was heard to say,
"I do not think these people seem to care.
   This was abandoned when they ran away."

Then Edward Winslow stood forth with his speech,
   "Don't make excuses for your own protection.
These are not spoils of war. We're here in peace.
   There is no blindness worse than self-deception."

Then William Bradford added in support,
   "We're here in peace and seeking to make trade.
We certainly aren't searching for a war.
   No one of us wants a dishonest wage.

"The strength we have is for our own defense.
   We do not seek to cause another harm.
We will not be disposed to make offense
   except to face a threatening alarm.

"Be mindful men, we came here to be free
   so we may live and worship as we choose
but if we waver irresponsibly
   the gains we've won, we will in turn then lose."

Then from the group another voice announced,
   "How will we ever be able to trade
when here and now we're clearly all without
   a common language to communicate?"

Then Winslow took a step out to explain,
   "There is another way to look at this.
There is a language that we know the same
   that's spoken with our lives as we exist.

"Each one of us knows hunger, love and pain.
    Although we call them by some other names,
we all essentially feel them the same
    in every different circumstance and way.

"If we take something from one of these homes
    there is no need to translate what we said
in any language and in any tongue
    the statement that is made is 'wanton theft'.

"Yet if we leave something of ours instead,
    something of use desired that's put in place
then with equivalence of difference
    we will declare that we are seeking trade."

Then walking from the woods back to the bay
    they found the shallop and the sailing crew
but saw the boat was carrying new freight
    and wondered what the crew had been up to.

The sailors told them that along the wait
    they found some Native houses in the woods
and in the huts they found some things to take
    and loaded up on the deserted goods.

Winslow and Bradford then said they must wait.
    This made them all appear as ruthless thieves.
But then the sailors said they'd done the same,
    reminding when they took the corn and beans.

The light was dim, the boat must ferry back.
    If they got off, they would be left behind.
The choice was theirs, they could help set the tack
    or they could stay and would be left to die.

Then Bradford stood before the other men
and said, "Right now we must be on our way
but mark my words we will return again."
And in eight months repayment had been made.

Chapter 10

Interval
December 1620

The next day after the group had returned
    they all assembled in the common cabin
for a discussion of what they had learned
    the previous exploring expedition.

Bradford described where they'd explored on shore,
    the bay and shallow harbor that they found.
It was where they uncovered beans and corn
    and was a spot where they could settle down.

As everyone was eager to begin,
    they wanted off the ship with land in view.
They needed a site for the settlement
    and the majority favored the move.

The bunching crowd began to lean one way,
    eager for the first opportunity,
then Stephen Hopkins stood to have a say
    to offer other possibilities.

"Before we move to the first site we find,
    although the place is close and within reach,
there are some things that we must keep in mind,
    dire problems often rise from hasty ease."

Then Stephen Hopkins went on to describe
    some circumstances they had overlooked.
None of the others had lived in the wild
    and there were things that they misunderstood.

The harbor was too shallow for a ship.
   Fresh water was too difficult to reach.
The Cape was but a narrow little neck
   that's pinched between the bay and open sea.

There has to be a place they could sustain.
   They couldn't build a town on shifting sand.
They needed to explore across the bay
   to search for a good site on the headland.

Congested coughs were rasping as he spoke
   as everyone onboard had become sick.
They all were aching, wheezing, wet and cold
   and urgently they wanted off the ship.

Then Governor John Carver led up front
   and stood before the weary company
and as their ailing bodies sagged and slumped
   he lifted up their spirits with his speech.

"We all are desperate to find a home.
   This journey has worn everybody thin
but even as our bodies weigh us down
   we liberate our spirits to transcend.

"Our Goodman Hopkins has experience
   in wild frontiers where we have never gone
and his advice may be deliverance
   from circumstances we have never known.

"He was amongst some castaways at sea
   after a ship they sailed wrecked in a storm
and then upon a desert island beach
   they built a ship to finish up their voyage.

.

"He settled at the Jamestown colony
    and had lived in Virginia six years,
  then back in London some years following
    he and his family now joined us here.

"We all are eager to get off this boat
    but we should listen to what he advised.
There will be troubles anywhere we go.
    We must make sure we choose the finest site."

Then as another voyage was proposed
    one of the pilots, Robert Coppin said
"One comment please, before this meeting's close,
    there is something that I have to suggest.

"Before this trip I had explored this bay
    and coasted with a crew along the side.
There is a harbor not too far away
    that's deep enough for a large ship to lie."

The harbor Coppin mentioned was received
    as something worthy to investigate
and everyone assembled all agreed
    and then decided they should see the place.

Then they selected the principal men
    to join the Governor along the voyage
but they were suddenly surprised again
    with an outburst from John Billington's boy.

Although John Billington had gained attention,
    he seemed to be resentful of the group,
incessant with his insolent contention
    by criticizing everything they do.

Yet countering with an offset rebellion,
  it seemed the rebel's son defied his father,
Francis, John Billington's twelve year old son,
  wanted to join the company endeavor.

The Governor attended this surprise
  and diplomatically addressed the scene
applauding the boy's noble sense of pride
  without offending the rude father's spleen.

So Carver credited his loyalty
  and praised young Francis with encouragement
— they needed him with his stout bravery
  to stay on board to guard their harbored ship.

And planning for another voyage soon
  the council closed as everyone agreed
and hoped to find the other harbor proved
  a better site to build their colony.

And as they drew the meeting to an end
  they heard rejoicing from the lower deck,
another child was born named Peregrine,
  conceived in one world — born into the next.

Chapter 11

Keg of Powder
December 5, 1620

The day they planned to send the venture out
    they were delayed with a disturbing storm
but sheltered from the squall outside the boat
    they faced more chaos while they stayed aboard.

There was the sudden shock of an alarm
    when through the wind they heard a blasting crack.
What had to be a discharge of an arm
    exploded somewhere underneath the deck.

They saw the smoke that poured out of a room
    and then they busted through the oaken door
and saw a sight that could have been their doom
    when suddenly another musket roared.

Before the window where he fired the musket
    Francis was playing like he manned a cannon
without realizing that the pan's combustion
    would spark the powder barrel in the cabin.

One man ran in securing the wild boy
    another cleared the powder from the flames.
The guns they had were not a childish toy
    and now they wonder where his father's been.

The ship's crew soon were standing at the door
    then stepped aside to clear for Captain Jones
whose boots stomped in across the cabin floor
    and he looked like the keg fused to explode.

The Governor and deacons went with Jones
    topside into the quarters for a talk
but judging from the Captain's angry tone
    there was concern that they would all be flogged.

Then Carver did his best to clarify
    the cloudy muddle of the situation
and tried resolving the disparity
    and offered the most forward explanation.

Before they left the Billingtons appeared
    and somehow slipped into the company.
There's no association that is clear
    and no one seems to know their family.

Then Carver offered a subdued solution
    he hoped that Captain Jones would understand
that when the ship sailed back across the ocean
    they take the Billingtons back to England.

The Governor's suggestion was sincere
    but he could see it was not well received.
He did not mean to make a flippant jeer
    but Captain Jones began to fume and seethe.

With this the Governor and all the elders
    explained they planned another expedition
across the bay to see one other harbor
    the pilot Robert Coppin had suggested.

From this they will be able to decide
    the site where they will build their settlement.
They're grateful for the Captain and his time
    and told him they would soon be off his ship.

Chapter 12

Third Expedition
December 6-11, 1620

In icy early morning they prepared
   to venture out on the discovery
and breathing in the chill of winter air
   they lowered their small boat into the sea.

Dec.
6

One pilot Coppin stood upon the bow,
   the other John Clarke gripped the rudder's helve
and with the oars they turned the boat around
   and heaved together opening the sail.

The families stood on the deck above
   and watched the shallop slowly glide away
and through the falling snow their hope and love
   receded deep into the hazy grey.

And as the men were pulling at the oars
   they fixed their eyes upon their families
and when they could not see them anymore
   they held their faith and love devotedly.

But with the tender warmth of love they guard,
   the lifting light they raise before their lives,
the blast of blustery wind pressed on them hard
   and splashed the sea encasing them in ice.

And as they pushed across the misty sea
   the ice built up and weighed the shallop down
and one of them was chipping frantically
   to keep the boat afloat less they would drown.

Later that day they pulled up to the main
   and chose to split the company in two.
The shallop would explore along the bank.
   The other group would hike beside in view.

For days they trekked and plodded on this line.
   Each night they made encampments as they went.
They knew there was no turning back this time
   without a place to make their settlement.

They gathered driftwood in the evening light
   and built around them sturdy barricades
then set the sentries to keep watch at night
   and tried to rest to ready for the day.

Then through one night there was a howling snarl
   and several times the sentries called alarm
but they saw nothing stirring in the dark
   when they were called to stand up with their arms.

Dec. The next day some were hauling down their gear
8   to load the shallop for the day's advance
and suddenly one of the men appeared
   and yelled for them to buckle in defense.

The arrows stuck in wood with the attack.
   The missiles whizzed and showered all around,
serrated stones on points of feathered shafts
   that stabbed the air filled with the hostile shouts.

Then as some of them stooped behind the screen
   one man asked, "Why are they attacking us?"
"Perhaps because we took their corn and beans."
   another man responded in the rough.

Some men retrieved gear from the boat again
    as arrows flew around them in a flurry
and Captain Standish stood commanding them
    and firmly said, "Well, well — be of good courage."

One of the men ran straight into the fray
    to get a firebrand of a burning log
and lighting matches of the muskets raised
    two blasted a fierce volley from their stocks.

Then Standish organized the men in line
    but on the flank a Brave approached nearby
with prowess any warrior would admire
    and let three arrows in succession fly.

And with the arrows hissing from the distance
    the Captain turned to face the closing fight
and as his musket charged with shot was lifted
    he steadied it along his focused sight.

When the approaching Brave looked down the barrel
    he jumped behind an oak defensively
and when the musket thundered in the quarrel
    it blasted chunks of bark off of the tree.

The clap of the explosion roused the men
    and sent the Natives headlong in retreat
and then the Pilgrims ran pursuing them
    to show they would not be cowed in defeat.

The threat dispersed, the men marched back to camp
    where they had barricaded for the night
and saw their coats they left out from the damp
    were shot with arrows on the bulwark side.

There was a restless and traumatic shock
    and from this skirmish they had proved the victors
but there was more they had to take in stock
    from what they called from thence the First Encounter.

They prayed in grateful thanks no one was hurt
    and finished loading gear into the boat
and broke their camp continuing their search
    to find a site where they could build their homes.

As they continued coasting down the shore
    they could not find another harbor near
and then the heavy snow of a brunt storm
    obscured the land so that it disappeared.

The shallop drove into the surging sea
    and icy water splashed into the boat
and snow was blocking all that they could see
    as all the men were gnawed with bitter cold.

Then Robert Coppin bolstered their resolve
    and said the harbor of which he had spoke
was close and all their troubles would be solved
    — just then the shallop's rudder snapped and broke.

Then shoved with waves and buffeted with winds
    and lashed with icy chills from blasting snow
upon the deep of an indifferent sea
    the little boat was tossed out of control.

Then with two oars they wedged upon the stern
    and grappled with the storm to set them right
defying humors of misfortune's turns
    to hold their course with their determined lives.

And through the haze of snow and slamming waves
   the pilot Coppin spotted up ahead
the inlet opening where they'd be safe
   exactly at the place where he had said.

As day was dimming safety was in sight
   and cruising with their full sail holding fast
they were assured they'd be secure by night
   then suddenly the gale shattered the mast.

The flapping, slapping sail fell overboard
   and tangled tackle dragged them like a net.
They scrambled to release the tied up oars
   and ruthless nature would never relent.

The shallop rocked upon the splashing foam
   as they all spun and tossed unsteadily.
They had to pull the sail back in the boat
   or they would be dragged down into the sea.

Then extricating themselves from the rope
   they freed their oars and dipped them in the sea,
then Robert Coppin signaled them to row
   to pull themselves into the harbor's reach.

But in the chaos they had spun off course
   and turned toward north before they'd reached the bay
and bearing toward the breaker's loudening roar
   the pilot swore he'd never seen the place.

As Coppin tried to orient himself
   the other pilot Clarke called to the men.
He recognized the bluff at Manomet
   and ordered them to turn the boat again.

Then with the bow aimed at the inlet way
  John Clarke gave orders for all them to heave,
"Row men! Row! or we are all cast away!"
  until they reached the bay in sweet relief.

Although by then it was too dark to see
  they knew they reached the inlet from the calm
and found a break from wind behind a lee
  and shivered in the boat until the dawn.

Dec. After a long and agonizing night
9   most of the men could not move in the morn.
Their soggy clothes were all encased in ice
  yet some managed to struggle to the shore.

And after camp was made along the bay
  they brought the others to warm at the fire.
After all they endured the previous day
  it was a miracle they had survived.

They dried their clothes and mended up their gear
  and found they landed on a harbor island
and honoring the one who steered them there,
  they named it after Clarke, one of the pilots.

Dec. Then following was sacred Sabbath day,
10   they honored in devotion through their prayer
and through humiliation and their praise
  they meditated on the Gospel shared.

Dec. Then next they sounded the depth of the bay
11   and through the clearing of the storm and fog
they rowed together on that famous day
  and set their firm first steps on Plymouth Rock.

1621

Chapter 13

Building the Town / Billington's Sea
December 1620 – January 1621

When the exploratory group returned
   there was relief that all the men survived
but joyful news was saddened when they learned
   that in their absence many settlers died.

The Reverend Brewster had led funeral rites
   and held the services consoling others
but most disheartening was Bradford's wife
   who slipped and drown and could not be recovered.

Yet they could not surrender to their loss
   and labored on through weariness and pain.
The greater gains are paid with greater costs
   to build with scattered pieces that remain.

By January the construction crew
   was busy building the new settlement
and organizing into working groups,
   they strove together for their betterment.

Dividing labor by ability,
   one felled the lumber and another sawed,
then riving pieces into planks from trees
   they carried lumber to specific lots.

The leaders outlined a specific plan
   and then explained so everyone could see
and meeting where they all could understand
   they then commenced to work as they agreed.

The Governor John Carver gauged the span
   and steered the crew into their earnest tasks
and then engaging every skillful hand
   he joined right in to pick up any slack.

And with an idea of how they would build
   and then prioritizing for each site
they labored for all the material
   substantiating their careful design.

A storage house was the first on the list
   to give them a place for utility,
a rendezvous for their shared interest
   devoted to the whole community.

The other was a platform on the hill,
   an overlook securing the abodes,
a posting promontory to reveal
   the distance to forewarn of an approach.

And then they planned out individual lots
   all closely organized in tabular
and carefully arranged the family plots
   so no one would be left out unsecure.

They worked in common for community
   but needed motivation on their own
and everyone responsibly agreed
   that every family should build their own home.

However well people are organized
   with a precisely calculated plan
wild nature always will antagonize
   with complications no one understands.

And as the crews were busy cutting logs
   young Francis Billington was climbing trees
and interfering with the workers' jobs
   and jeopardizing everyone's safety.

The women and the children stayed on board
   the *Mayflower* till houses had been built
but Captain Jones made Francis stay on shore
   after the musket powder incident.

Since Francis was too young for heavy work
   his father let him do just as he pleased
and he would spend the days running berserk
   while wildly swinging from the tops of trees.

This caused disruptions with the building crew
   to look out so the boy would not be hurt
as if they didn't have enough to do
   attending to the labors of their work.

And Francis said he'd hold on like John Howland
   and compensating for his dad's indifference,
he swung upon the trees while wildly howling,
   contending to gain all the group's attention.

Eventually the Governor stepped in
   and told the boy to climb a nearby hill
away from the crews of the working men
   in a safe distance while they tend to build.

Then on the hill while climbing up a tree
   he clambered up to reach an eagle's nest
and then began to shout he saw the sea
   farther inland directly to the west.

Jan.
8

The first reaction was of disbelief.
  The boy was vying for regard again.
The sea was definitely to the east
  but they had set upon unchartered land.

Although improbable they were intrigued.
  They knew they needed to investigate.
Another inlet to the west could lead
  to shorter passages around the cape.

Although it was not the time to explore
  – they needed to complete the common house –
with the permission of the Governor
  one of the men said he would check it out.

The man picked up his musket to be armed
  and guard the boy when they walked out of view
and then young Francis caused the men alarm
  by saying he would need a musket too.

Then all the men watched Carver carefully
  after the volatile request was made.
They didn't know if he would laugh or scream
  but the wise deacon thoughtfully explained,

"Young man you should recall the time before
  your recklessness almost blew up the ship."
But what he said surprised them even more
  — the boy claimed he was fighting pirates then.

Then Francis and the man walked in the woods
  to scout out further for investigation.
They all hoped that the sea he overlooked
  was not a figment of imagination.

When hours had passed the two of them returned
  and all the crew paused watching them draw near.
The man's expression on his face confirmed
  that definitely something had been there.

The body was a large fresh water lake
  with game and flocks of fowl and filled with fish.
They also found some huts around the place
  that were abandoned and mysterious.

Intensely focused on their residence
  and driven by the dire necessity
they hadn't paused to note their settlement
  was haunted by an eerie vacancy.

The area was previously cleared.
  They saw the places corn and beans had grown.
There seemed to have been people living there
  but they had no idea where they had gone.

Then Deacon Carver looked out on the bay
  and saw the anchored ship ride on the tide,
then looking at the men he had to say
  they had to work if they hoped to survive.

Chapter 14

The Rendezvous
January 14, 1621

The weather had been an impediment
   and almost everyone had become sick
but the first building of the settlement
   was walled and roofed and finally finished.

Inside the men still slept upon the dirt
   and packed inside a twenty square foot room
but they were covered and could rest for work
   inside the shelter of their Rendezvous.

Some days and weeks passed since the First Encounter
   and they had yet to meet the local tribes
and even though they had not seen a person,
   at night on distant hills they saw bonfires.

They sent envoys in hopes that they could find
   the people setting fires upon the hills.
Mistakes they made before started a fight
   and they desired expressing their goodwill.

Yet with the ventures of their delegations
   they could not find the tribes who lived around.
The scattered huts they saw had been vacated
   and they continued working on their town.

Most of the company was now on shore
   and as they built they moved supplies off ship
but numbers were depleting more and more
   as they were dying with the dread sickness.

And as they starkly stood upon their own
  and tried their best to keep each other safe,
still some complained, "Why bother building homes
  when we are spending more time digging graves?"

And for the members who remained on board
  there was the growing tension with the crew
withholding the provisions that were stored
  and threatening to weigh their anchor soon.

They said the passengers must dump their stuff
  and die together on the settlement.
They said that it was giving them bad luck
  if settlers kept dying on their ship.

The boatswain was particularly cruel
  when he came to inspect the hull each day
and they all dreaded each time he came too,
  discouragements were all he had to say.

One day he stumbled on a horn and drum
  the passengers had packed in with their things
and he amused himself by making fun,
  "This is a circus not a colony!"

But while the planters worked hard on the town
  the ship was riding light upon the bay
and leisurely the sailors were allowed
  to hunt for fowl and fish through every day.

And as the sailors dawdled in their dally
  they put the *Mayflower* in jeopardy
because the crew forgot to fill the ballasts
  and storms could blow the ship into the beach.

The settlers were all resolved to move.
  They were committed to make a new home.
They sought communion with their God above
  and tried to live just as the scriptures showed.

And then they had a reason for elation
  as swelling hope and faith felt to redound
with plans of going as a congregation
  for Sabbath worship at their budding town.

Of course their town was just a single building
  but they had designated lots for homes
and work along their planning was revealing
  the sprouting of design their prayers had sown.

Throughout their lives they lived within convention
  in towns and buildings that were built before
adjusting to a predisposed intention
  demanding that their ways of life conform.

But they had felt there was another way
  that they could live their lives and worship God
and were committed to build their own place
  with families and skills and tools they brought.

Although their building was a Rendezvous,
  a simple structure for utility,
it was the first firm step they made into
  the setting of their new community.

Inside the group could rest and keep their tools
  and build a place they all could share together
and Sunday service at the Rendezvous
  would concentrate their work for something better.

But on the morning of that holy day
    the first watch of the ship sounded alert
and on the deck they saw the smoky flames
    and helplessly they watched their building burn.

They feared the fire was lit in an attack
    and rushed to launch the boat to reach the beach
as families were weeping on the deck
    as all their hopes turned into tragedy.

They launched the long boat for support and aid
    but could not reach the shore — the tide was out,
so they jumped from the boat so they could wade
    but then were stuck in mud from the waist down.

They saw the smoke beyond their trudging slog
    and hoped the group on shore was now awake
most of the men and tools were in the lodge
    and the whole enterprise was then at stake.

Arriving finally they were relieved,
    the Rendezvous was standing and intact.
The group on shore was working as a team
    and told the others they were not attacked.

A spark had flown into the building's thatch
    that quickly burned but did not harm the roof.
The worst concern about the blazing flash
    — another keg of powder almost blew.

The fearful incident they had before
    caused them to take additional safeguards
so they had kept the keg close to the door
    to keep it clear in case there was alarm.

Jan.
14

The accidental fire commanded change
  so they held services upon the ship.
The Sabbath day was holy all the same.
  They rendezvoused wherever they worshipped.

So they adjusted their foregoing plan
  and faithfully they waited one more week
before they held their services on land.
  The key was they maintained their unity.

Chapter 15

The Great Sickness
Winter 1621

Although the planters often felt distressed
   of an encounter of attack again
the greatest danger and the fiercest threat
   was from the sickness that inflicted them.

There was no place for anyone to hide
   and everyone was suffering from loss.
Infections grew perniciously inside.
   More deadly than the cannon was the cough.

Some of the children lost both of their parents
   — becoming orphans through the tragedy,
and parents suffered the loss of their children
   and the whole group lost entire families.

The former Governor Chris Martin died.
   And Isaac Allerton lost his dear wife.
Then almost all the Mullins sadly died,
   by grace Priscilla mercifully survived.

And with the deaths of many hired men
   the colony was weakened at great cost
– as Moses Fletcher, the group's metal smith –
   and with their lives, their crafts and skills were lost.

And even Samuel Fuller, the group's surgeon,
   was helpless in attending those infirmed
and watched the lives of others being smothered
   with gasped consumption and the scurvy's scourge.

And with the sickness in the settlement
   the sailors callously pushed them away
and said they wanted them all off the ship
   whether in camp or in their scattered graves.

They were unwilling to share the stored beer
   kept in the loaded barrels on the ship
and forced the others to drink the brook water
   that many planters feared had made them sick.

Yet even with the aches and pains they felt
   each planter who retained the strength to stand
would rise and work so that they would prevail
   and build their little town upon the land.

And as the population of the group
   seemed to diminish every single day
there was the grace and kindness of a few
   that carried others with their selfless aid.

And as the sick laid in dour misery
   some were too weak to even lift their heads,
these selfless few would wash their laundry
   and then refresh their soiled and sodden beds.

This wasn't something they were forced to do,
   all have to struggle to sustain their lives
but how could they continue living too
   ignoring others who suffered and died.

And as they worked for common benefit
   and offered all to comfort and to mend,
they cradled flames that flickered on the wicks
   with tender hands that blocked the blast of winds.

Two merciful men of this gracious group
  were prominent within the settlement
— Myles Standish who would bravely lead the troops
  and Reverend Brewster, their light of guidance.

They didn't do this to perform a lesson.
  It desperately needed to be done.
This simply was their life's chosen direction
  to help preserve the life of everyone.

Some were surprised to see the kind compassion
  from Captain Standish and his martial might
but thoughtfully he gave an explanation,
  "The cause I fight is in defense of life."

And comforting and aiding the infirmed
  the women offered salves and remedies,
the herbs of purgatives and berry syrups
  with curatives to aid recovery.

And Elder Brewster's dedicated help
  to sooth the misery of people sickened
and offered comforting encouragement
  to lift the spirits of those sore inflicted.

They even had to build a separate house
  to try containing the contagious cough
and the compassion of this selfless group
  kept helping till the sickness could be stopped.

One night that followed a hard day of work
  the Elder Brewster sat by Bradford's side
and Brewster's mentee was sore sick and hurt
  after the loss of Dorothy, his wife.

But Bradford did not wallow in the loss
    insisting Brewster should attend the others,
he would endure the sickness of his lot,
    he hurt more for his sisters and his brothers.

He also thought that Brewster should take care.
    His life was too important to be risked.
He didn't need to breathe infectious air
    while he attended the infirmed and sick.

At this the Reverend Elder Brewster paused
    and felt the sadness hearing Bradford speak
and Brewster knew the goodness of his thoughts
    but sickness had made Bradford very weak.

And in this pause there was tranquility
    and even in the rank and stifling air
the Elder Brewster shined a clarity
    with gentle kindness of a solemn prayer.

Then after pausing for a calm reflection
    where their soft words were not just shared but felt
the Reverend Brewster offered an impression
    and through his contemplative kindness said:

"Dear brother Bradford I'm touched by your thought
    that in the circumstances of your health
and with the sickness you're severely fraught
    your sole concern is others needing help.

"And if my life has gained in prominence
    it only could be built on what we share
and without serving other's benefit
    all we may build will have no base to bear.

"The issue now is trouble on the ship
 as sickness has descended on the crew
and when we try to aid and to assist
 the help we offer is fiercely refused.

"As you well know while we were on the voyage
 we bore the brunt of mocking and abuse
now when we go on board to load our storage
 the crew has worsened and become more cruel.

"As badly as they all had treated us
 they're dealing with each other even worse.
When one is sick they shun him like a crud
 and scold his misery with brutal scourge.

"I told my wife and others on the ship
 we hope to be together soon on land
and as we work to build the settlement
 the others help the crew the best they can.

"Yet brother Bradford I have been concerned
 you hold so much inside with modesty,
still I can sense how sadly you are hurt
 with the loss of your dear wife Dorothy."

With these soft words Brewster saw something rise
 as if a whale had surfaced on the sea
and lonely loss misted on Bradford's eyes,
 a pain far worse than the sick misery.

And Bradford coughed, perhaps to shunt a sob,
 and with a rasping voice he meekly said,
"She'd still be living if I hadn't gone.
 I should have been protecting her instead."

Then Elder Brewster thoughtfully replied,
  "Dear brother Bradford, do not blame your absence,
the mournful passing of your dear wife's life
  had been an accident and sadly tragic.

"You had to go and help explore the bay.
  What we withhold only disintegrates.
Potential unapplied fritters away.
  Only through ventures may we be sustained.

"As we rely upon community,
  our small community relies on us,
yielding stability in unity
  for independent aims through faith and trust.

"Dear Bradford your loss was all of our grief,
  so do not feel this has left you alone,
your wife, your love, was also our dear friend,
  your loss and love is shared with everyone."

Then with a sudden change of circumstance
  some members of the sailing crew arrived
and since they tended to stay clear of camp
  the planters were astounded and surprised.

They said the Reverend was needed on board
  and Elder Brewster somberly agreed
and everyone knew what he was called for
  and the whole camp was hushed respectfully.

Then on the ship they went below the deck
  where sailors of the crew crowded their cots
and led the Reverend to one of the beds
  where a young man expired with sickened coughs.

Then Elder Brewster was profoundly sad
    when he had recognized the ship's boatswain.
The young man's eyes that had been fierce and mad
    were dimming underneath the sickened bane.

And as the Elder carefully approached
    the boatswain's eyes began to fill with light
and then before those who were on the boat
    he lisped these words as tender as a sigh.

"Reverend Brewster I must apologize
    for the abuse I gave your gracious group.
My heated anger and my wicked lies
    were not from anything that you all do.

"While I was cruel, all of your group was kind.
    Then when the sailors turned their backs on me
you all kept helping me time after time
    and tried to sooth my dreadful misery.

"On board, we let each other die like dogs
    yet you were truly Christians faithfully
and are devoted to a higher law
    and now I hope that you will pray for me."

As Brewster held his hand he warmly spoke,
    "The peace I feel I hope that you will find.
My dear son, please be comforted to know
    I have been praying for you the whole time."

And Elder Brewster felt the tremble rest
    as if a weight arose from the man's life
then set the young man's hand upon his chest
    and gently closed the boatswain's tranquil eyes.

Chapter 16

Military Orders
Winter 1621

Then Captain Jones released his firm restraints
   and shared the beer in barrels in the hold
and if they finished what little remained
   the crew would drink the water sailing home.

Feb. He even gave the planters five fat geese
9   after he had a bountiful day's hunt
and all the members of the company
   kept working through the frigid winter months.

Feb. And then one day about a mile from camp
16   a planter saw a group of men pass by,
a surreptitious movement of a band,
   a group of warriors from a local tribe.

And then Myles Standish worked with Francis Cooke
   to gather lumber in the woods alone.
They left their tools to take a break at noon
   and then returning found their tools were gone.

Besides bonfires on the surrounding hills,
   they hadn't seen a person for two months,
now all the company began to feel
   that they may need to put defenses up.

Feb. They held a meeting for their town's protection,
17   the matters of their safety were at hand
and then unanimously they selected
   Myles Standish for the defensive command.

Then with the trust and honor they bestowed,
   they asked for him to stand and give a speech.
They all had known the courage he had shown
   but also wanted to know what he thinks.

Then Captain Standish stood before them all
   and with his discipline and dignity
he answered to the loyal service call
   and spoke his mind with stern sincerity.

"The soldier's work is a necessity
   for any labor of development
and cultivations of communities
   must be protected with a sound defense.

"Just as a roof must stand upon support,
   just as a baby needs protective care,
the straight and solid posts of strong report
   must hold the shelter for the rare and fair.

"The grain is husked with a thick armored shield,
   the tender berries ripen in the briars,
without protection they may never yield
   what their maturity may sweetly share.

"As we have come here seeking liberty,
   we do not fight except in our defense.
We dedicate to the community
   the strength that can preserve the tenderness.

"And in considerations of conviction
   in willingness to make a sacrifice
there is no greater proof of dedication
   as soldiers bravely choose to stake their lives."

Just then the Captain noticed a slight stir
　　as those to whom he spoke looked in surprise
and heedfully he then alertly turned
　　to trace the line of sight of others' eyes.

Upon a hill a quarter mile away
　　two Wampanoag men waved to the group
and gestured in a universal way
　　for them to come up where the two men stood.

The planters answered them reflectively
　　and tried to wave the men down to the camp
and both sides stood away protectively
　　as both suspected it may be a trap.

And then confirming the words of his speech
　　and matching what he said with his true deeds
the Captain's loyal duty was to lead
　　and he would venture up to intervene.

Then Stephen Hopkins also volunteered
　　and grabbed his musket that he had at hand
and Standish chose to go up without arms
　　— the Captain's strength was in his stout command.

And as the planters stood behind prepared,
　　the two brave men maintained a strict conduct.
They threaded a tense line with steady care.
　　A flinch could blow the whole arrangement up.

Then careful and alert for an ambush
　　the men approached the Wampanoag Braves
but nudging onward Standish felt a push
　　by sensing the men start to turn away.

Then Standish subtly signaled Hopkins stop.
   They needed a way to show their intent,
so he instructed, speaking clear and soft,
   to set the musket down without offense.

And Hopkins understood what Standish meant
   and showing there was nothing they concealed
he set the musket down beside of them
   with slow and careful movements of goodwill.

And with the musket lying on the ground
   and holding out to show their open hands
they tried communicating without sound
   in actions universally human.

Then carefully and slowly they approached
   but Hopkins' dry throat made him turn to cough
and without knowing what had caused the broach,
   the Wampanoags suddenly ran off.

Then Standish stood with Hopkins on the hill
   and then from out the woods and all around
they heard the sound of war cries howling shrill
   from unseen numbers all around the town.

Perplexed and disappointed they walked down,
   they tried to show the planters' aims were good
but from the yells they heard from all around
   it's obvious they were misunderstood.

Returning to the camp they can't explain
   what they had done to cause any offense
but hearing war cries made it clear and plain
   there was the need to build a strong defense.

The company continued with their tasks
    as the small town began to come to shape
and piece by piece as tapping nails held fast
    the family homes were lining up in place.

Mar. A month had passed since they appointed Standish
16   to oversee the town's security
and there were matters to address and manage
    requiring an assembly be convened.

So once again outside they met together
    just as they had been holding Sunday service
but in this case discussing civic matters
    to find the way to handle common burdens.

The Governor directed the proceeding
    and Captain Standish stood to speak in place
and carefully explained with forward reason
    the ways to keep their town and families safe.

Then Standish saw an unexpected sight
    — a solitary man walked up their street.
He passed in front the houses in a line
    and strode with an assured nobility.

The Captain told the other men to hold.
    They didn't need to move erratically
and Standish walked to where the man approached
    to meet his course directly in the street.

The Captain sensed this man was not a threat.
    He walked alone defenseless and exposed.
He had no fear or spite in his aspect
    and only wore a loin cloth in the cold.

He had a bow he carried on his shoulder,
  his quiver had two arrows in the hold.
He certainly had not been armed for battle
  and carried himself peacefully composed.

An eagle feather dressed his long dark hair.
  His face was open as the starry sky
and shaped with graceful and majestic features
  he stood aplomb at an impressive height.

His airs were of a tranquil dignity.
  He stood with balanced strength in perfect posture
and some of them believed that he might be
  an emissary who was sent by God.

And then commanding everyone's attention
  there was a moment of astonishment
and looking at each one in the convention
  the man said clearly "Welcome Englishmen."

Chapter 17

Samoset
March 16 – 17, 1621

The group of planters tried to meet the Natives
　　to create ties for friendship and for trade
but previous attempts had been frustrated,
　　they were not able to communicate.

But in the middle of their civic meeting
　　right in the center of their settlement,
a noble man had offered a warm greeting
　　and everyone sat in astonishment.

Commanding all the planters rapt attention
　　he stood with poise and posture statuesque
and then the Governor asked him a question
　　so they could find out who the brave man was.

Mar.
16 And he replied, "My name is Samoset,
　　a Sagamore of the tribe Abenaki.
I'm from the north where all my people live
　　and often visit here to trade and fish."

The man explained he knew the fishermen
　　from whom he learned to speak a little English.
His tribe had profited in trade with them
　　at where he was from on Monhegan Island.

He told them of the trade along the coast
　　and of the local Wampanoag Nation
— the people who were currently his host,
　　and tried explaining different tribes' relations.

And Standish asked about the stolen tools
   and Samoset said he could be assured
that he would find who took them in the woods
   to make for certain they would be returned.

Then he described the horror of the sickness
   that years before had stricken countless tribes
and where they settled had been called Patuxet
   and all the people in the village died.

And as he spoke there was a chilly wind
   as spring had not arrived and it was cold
and hoping to give comfort for their friend
   they offered Samoset one of their coats.

Then with the coat draped on his square, broad shoulders
   they asked the Sagamore if he was hungry
and fixed some food that they could share together
   then offered him an English meal for supper.

They all were pleased with their new visitor
   who ventured in to meet the company.
Then Samoset described the times before
   he had partaken food of Englishmen.

And then the Governor asked Samoset
   of the encounter when they were attacked
and why the people in the area
   would always run away upon contact.

Then Samoset told them of the Nauset,
   who had attacked them before on the beach.
The Nausets thought the English were a threat
   because of the abuse they had received.

He told them about Captain Thomas Hunt
　　who lured a group of them onto his ship
then threatening their lives with swords and guns
　　he held them captive and then kidnapped them.

The Captains whom the Sagamore had known
　　had heard of Hunt and the things he had done
and they all felt from what they had been told
　　he was a diabolical villain.

The planters talked with Samoset all day
　　but as the dusky evening approached,
they wondered how long he had planned to stay
　　and if he was expecting them as hosts.

The planters had a reason for concern,
　　their numbers had decreased since they arrived.
The winter months and sickness were severe
　　and half the planters had already died.

They didn't want to put themselves in danger,
　　emboldening the others to attack
and although Samoset appeared sincere
　　they struggled as a group to stay intact.

They tried to let him stay out on the ship
　　but could not launch the boat in the low tide
and they were sensing Samoset's intent
　　to stay inside their settlement the night.

But something that the planters did not know,
　　the Sagamore had reason for his stay,
there was something that he wanted to show
　　as Wampanoags watched from far away.

He then described the Narragansett threat
   that was attacking Wampanoag tribes
and he was serving to offer his help
   as he knew Englishmen were good allies.

So he had volunteered to walk in town,
   the truest coup of noble bravery,
and then arrived with his defenses down
   on an endeavor of diplomacy.

Then Samoset stayed for the night with Hopkins,
   one of the first to have his home complete,
and Samoset was welcomed in the hospice
   where he could comfortably and safely sleep.

The next day Samoset was wide awake
   — for what he had believed he risked his life.
Although defenseless, he was unafraid
   and no harm had befallen him that night.

Mar.
17

Then Samoset said he could meet that night
   the Sachem of the Wampanoag Sachems
presiding from the town Sowams nearby
   — the noble Massasoit Ousamequin.

He said within two days he would return
   and bring some Wampanoags they could meet
and Samoset concluded his sojourn
   and said he'd bring back trade for them to see.

Before he left the planters offered gifts
   — a metal knife, a bracelet and a ring
as hopeful tokens taken in friendship
   then he was off as if on eagle's wings.

Chapter 18

Samoset Returns
March 18, 1621

Mar.
18 Then Samoset returned on Sabbath day
    attended by five Wampanoag men,
and clearly they approached from far away
    to demonstrate they had no sly intent.

The families remaining on the ship
    had come on shore for this bright, pleasant day
so all together they could have worship
    and Brewster led the service as they prayed.

And to the side and at a proper distance
    the Sagamore and Pnieses calmly waited.
They carefully observed and deeply listened
    of what they could observe as something sacred.

And while the congregation bowed in prayer
    the Governor then nudged some of the men
and whispered to them with a solemn care
    so they would not disturb the reverence.

Then quietly the group walked through the field
    where Samoset considerately stood
and they could see the other men all held
    the tools that had been taken in the woods.

And talking for a moment they agreed
    to leave their bows and arrows on the ground
and then with Governor John Carver's lead
    they all were welcomed in the humble town.

The men wore leggings and plush pelts of fur
   and all were suitably dressed to stay warm
that proved the Sagamore the time before
   arrived unclad to show he meant no harm.

Then gathered in a circle they sat down
   and Samoset began to mediate
and as all of the Pilgrims gathered round
   they worked on ways they hoped they could relate.

And Governor John Carver asked for food
   so something could be carefully prepared
and cordially they offered what they could
   so taste and warmth and nourishment was shared.

Then they thought of the ways to entertain
   and then the Governor had an idea
and asked the others to bring out their games
   to find some ways to build their repartee.

They pitched the bar and played stoolball and quoit
   and then someone brought out a shovel board
and universally they all enjoyed
   the different ways their lives could find accord.

Then Brewster heard the colorful birds sing
   that perched on limbs in the surrounding trees
and gathered the group in assembly
   to sing their psalms in happy harmony.

And as the group stood in ascending rows
   and Brewster waved his hand to set the time,
they lifted up their spirits with their voice
   and spanned the range of notes from low to high.

And then with Samoset's encouragement
   the Pnieses gave performance of their own
and livened up the Pilgrims' settlement
   with ceremony of their dance and song.

And as the Pilgrims stood in noted lines
   and sacred hymns inspired their hearts and minds,
the Wampanoags circled chanting rhythms
   exulting ritual with their whole lives.

And then when everyone had settled down
   the Wampanoag asked about the trade.
They brought four beaver pelts into the town
   and offered them for something in exchange.

As Samoset served as interpreter
   the planters carefully tried to explain
that although they wanted to build rapport
   they would not trade on holy Sabbath day.

And listening while Samoset translates
   they watched the Wampanoag men react
who nodded heads as they heard what was said
   and in a pause offered some comments back.

The Pnieses then discussed amongst themselves
   and gathered up some items they had brought
and gestured with their open arms to tell
   conveyance of intent in what they thought.

Then Samoset attentively explained
   to make a bridge that spanned across the rift,
they understood, they too had sacred days,
   but hoped the planters would accept some gifts.

Then Samoset relayed the gifts to them
— an ornate case to hold a warrior's bow,
and then two pouches with distinct contents
— the grounds of native corn and tobacco.

Accepting the kind Pnieses' offering
the settlers offered their own gifts in kind
and speaking through warm generosity
a language of exchange to share their lives.

Then wanting solemn reverence that day
the planters tried politely to dismiss
the Sagamore and Pnieses on their way
so they could observe Sabbath in worship.

The Wampanoag men planned to return
within a couple days to make some trade
but everyone was shocked when they all heard
that Samoset felt sick and had to stay.

Some Pnieses were about to run away,
they had good reason to fear for their lives,
but one of them insisted that they wait
then they politely parted for the night.

This also struck the planters with bleak fear
they knew the horrors of the sickness too,
and when the hope of friendship had been near,
another tragedy appeared in view.

Then helping Samoset so he could rest,
he stayed in Stephen Hopkins' finished house.
They hoped that he would soon recover health
and convalesce and wholesomely rebound.

Chapter 19

Spring
March 18 – 21, 1621

Then Samuel Fuller diagnosed their friend
  but could not see that Samoset was sick.
He had no symptoms which was a relief
  yet this was a cause for bewilderment.

On the warm day the fresh spring had arrived
  and they still had a lot of work to do,
so trusting their friend, they let him revive
  and after Sabbath, their work week resumed.

The songs of birds were sweetening the air
  and life began to nudge with sprouts about
and in the early hours of daylight fair
  the settlers busily worked on their town.

The ordnance had been mounted on the hill.
  They had a Common House where they could meet
and nearly finished on the lots were built
  the private homes raised by the families.

The little street that teemed with diligence
  was lined with plots of every family house
and to ensure each person's sustenance
  each household dug and sowed a garden ground.

And drawing from each individual home
  that every family labored for themselves
they privately developed from their own
  to congregate and share the Commonwealth.

And gathering on little Leyden Street,
   an avenue to circulate their lives,
they all coordinated thoughtfully
   and traded commerce for prosperity.

And on these days with blossoms of the spring
   they loosened soil and worked to turn the earth
and sowed their seeds in earnest offering
   to nurture cultivation of their work.

On Wednesday morning, Samoset felt well
   and would return to speak with Ousemequin
but first there were some things he had to tell
   to an assembly of the Plymouth leaders.

Mar.
21

After the elders had expressed relief
   that Samoset fully recovered health,
they asked why the group of the noble Pniese
   had not returned for trade as they had said.

Before the Pnieses left the other day
   they said they would return immediately
with beaver pelts and other things to trade
   but then they had been gone for half a week.

Then Samoset explained to reassure
   the deacons of the church and merchant men,
he understood their reasons for concern
   and tried disclosing more of his intent.

He needed them to meet another man,
   a Wampanoag who was named Tisquantum,
who spoke English more fluently than him
   and was originally from Patuxet.

He then explained the Narragansett threat
    and their attacks upon the Wampanoags
and hoped to show the settlers could be friends
    but he would need to bring the Massasoit.

The noble Massasoit Ousamequin
    was cautiously preparing to meet them.
The Wampanoag lost a lot of people
    and would agree to a pact for defense.

Then Samoset said he would soon return
    and introduce them to the man Tisquantum
and then more free and clear they could converse
    like sparkling streams refreshing from the mountains.

The settlers then gave Samoset more gifts
    — a cloth that he could tie around his waist,
a hat and shoes, some stockings and a shirt
    and said they would see him on the next day.

Then after they had parted with their friend,
    they gathered for assembly once again
so they could give assignments and amend
    the issues and the tasks they had at hand.

This was the third time they had held this meeting
    establishing their orders and their laws
but every time they sat for the proceedings
    the visitors demanded that they pause.

Now several private homes had been complete
    and they were working for a fellowship
to have a place of safe stability
    to bring their families off of the ship.

They needed to establish the clear means
   to live together as community
and finding ways upon which they agree
   they could pursue their interest privately.

But as they worked together making plans,
   discussing and debating what they need,
two Wampanoag men appeared again
   and oddly seemed to taunt the company.

They could not understand what the men said
   while standing at a distance on the hill
but from the tone and gestures forwarded
   the men were clearly not hospitable.

So Captain Standish and some other men
   picked up their arms and carefully approached,
responding to see what the signals meant
   but they would not be foolishly provoked.

From meeting with the noble Samoset
   they were surprised by the hostility.
They hoped to gain mutual benefit
   and wanted to avoid calamities.

The Wampanoags taunted with their arms
   and yelled provocatively as to bait
but Captain Standish would not be alarmed
   and ordered they advance with firm restraint.

They hoped their cautious progress would reveal
   exactly what the Wampanoags said
but as they were ascending up the hill
   the taunting men then turned and swiftly fled.

They had to leave the meeting incomplete.
   There was another task for them that day.
Before the night in the cool evening
   they sent the shallop out upon the bay.

And for the final passage that was sent
   they had made sure the shallop was refit
and then completing the new settlement
   they fetched remaining settlers from the ship.

And as the shallop safely pulled to shore
   with the remaining families and stock
an orphan, Mary Chilton, stepped off board
   and set her tender foot on Plymouth Rock.

Chapter 20

Massasoit Ousamequin
March 22, 1621

On the next day the company convened
  to gather in assembly for a meeting
assigning their responsibilities
  and then enacting laws for their agreement.

This was the fourth attempt to hold this council.
  They needed to agree for confirmation.
All of the families had moved to town.
  They needed common order for relations.

Soon after the town meeting had commenced,
  the noble Samoset appeared again,
just as the day before he promised them,
  this time with four more Wampanoag men.

Three of the men appeared to be Pnieses
  with faces painted, standing proud and tall.
They carried beaver pelts and sundry pieces
  intent on peaceful trading for withal.

Yet Samoset had brought another forth
  to introduce him to the company.
Then after Samoset had prompted him
  the man expressed in English fluently,

"Greetings Englishmen. My name is Tisquantum.
  This place where you are building your new town
had been my home, the village of Patuxet,
  but from the sickness, everyone is gone.

"I had been kidnapped by a Captain Hunt
    who tried to sell me as a slave in Spain
but thankfully was rescued by some monks
    and then lived with a merchant in England.

"While I had been a resident in London
    — the strangest place that I have ever been,
I learned the tongue and followed English custom
    until I could return to home again.

"Eventually I shipped with Captain Dermer
    and crossed the sea that spanned for days beyond
but then when I was able to return,
    I found my people and my home were gone."

With this Tisquantum stopped in somber pause
    and they all quietly stood to reflect
and felt a sadness that had touched them all
    and then respectfully John Carver said,

"Tisquantum we are sorry for your pain
    and we have heard what Captain Hunt had done.
For certain not all English are the same.
    We know how sad it feels to have no home.

"We see you have brought beaver pelts to trade
    and we have meat and drink to share a feast.
We come in search of friendship to be made
    and build communities prosperously."

Then Samoset, Tisquantum and the men
    were helped to settle down in restful seats
and then the planters brought some food to them
    and all together they ate heartily.

And then the keen sight of the Pnieses' eyes
   kept watching while partaking of the meal
and noticing the others had arrived
   directed their attention to the hill.

And then a group of Pilgrims from the town
   all walked together to the trilling brook
and up above upon the rocky mound
   the Wampanoag warriors proudly stood.

There numbers were at least of sixty men,
   some wore the fur of lions, deer and bear
with bobcat tails and fox tails blended in
   and eagle feathers braided in their hair.

The soaring eagle feathers touched the sky
   and standing strong with faces dressed in paint
in vibrant red and yellow, black and white,
   they crowned the hill in glorious array.

The settlers sent Tisquantum up to meet
   the group with Ousamequin on the hill
and he inquired how they all should proceed
   and peacefully discuss each other's will.

They learned that Ousamequin wanted them
   to send a representative to speak
and then negotiations would begin
   when they could more approximately meet.

And so each side took incremental steps
   and slowly gained a feel for the unknown,
not fearfully obstructing to protect
   nor foolishly outstretching to expose.

Then Edward Winslow said he'd volunteer
  and gathered up the gifts they planned to give
and with Tisquantum as interpreter
  the two approached the party on the hill.

And with Tisquantum, Winslow marched ahead
  and climbing heard each rasp of breath he drew.
His heart was drumming on his corselet
  as the spectacular group came in view.

And spanning broadly off to either side,
  each statuesquely stood up in the sky,
unflinching — not even blinking their eyes,
  the Pnieses made a perfectly straight line.

Slowly and cautiously the two approached
  where at the center stood the Massasoit.
While most kept watch upon the town below
  some of the Pnieses stood around Winslow.

The noble Massasoit Ousamequin
  stood with his Sachem brother Quadiquina,
imposing figures with majestic features
  dressed in their ceremonial regalia.

The Massasoit's face was painted red
  and rising with the swell of every breath,
he wore a mass of Wampum on his chest
  that held a fearsome knife just like a sheath.

Then as the Pnieses crowded all around
  and standing at the Massasoit's brace
Tisquantum turned to Winslow fixed profound
  and simply asked, "What do you have to say?"

106

With strong, clear words delivered in respect
   while Edward Winslow held his upward gaze,
he carefully, articulately said,
   "I come with greetings from England's King James.

"As neighbors and as friends we come in peace
   in hopes that we may jointly realize
agreement to live in prosperity
   and strengthen one another as allies."

After Tisquantum translated these words
   the Massasoit with resounding voice
spoke with a volume all his Pnieses heard
   and the sound echoed on the town below.

Then all as one the Wampanoags yelled
   and all the settlers shuddered with concern
as Winslow and the others couldn't tell
   if they rejected or approved the terms.

But Samoset could hear what had transpired
   and then told Standish that Winslow was safe
and then Tisquantum motioned Winslow's eye
   and nodded to confirm what he had said.

Then Winslow gave Tisquantum the good gifts
   as offering of friendship that they sought.
To Ousamequin he gave the presents
   — a bracelet and two knives of metal wrought.

And then for Ousamequin's Sachem brother
   they gave an earring and another knife,
hard water and their biscuits and their butter
   for them to share with others in their tribe.

Then Ousamequin offered with a trade
   for Winslow's metal corselet and sword
but he had to refuse the offer made
   and could not part with armor that he wore.

And while they shared the food that he had brought
   to Ousamequin, Edward Winslow said,
the settler's Governor John Carver sought
   to meet and then negotiate their trade.

Then they agreed to leave their bows behind
   and Edward Winslow stayed as the ransom
and with Tisquantum serving as the guide
   the Massasoit left with twenty men.

Then at the brook within each side's clear view
   the Captain and six of the musketeers
along with one of the Mayflower crew
   met Ousamequin and his warriors.

The groups were able to meet face to face,
   the tiny brook was running in between,
the little trill of water set the place
   to serve as a distinguished way to meet.

The brook could be traversed with just a step,
   yet it allowed the two groups to approach
and was something they both knew to respect
   — a tacit agreement as they drew close.

Then Captain Standish offered a salute,
   not raising weapons but an open hand,
and Massasoit Ousamequin too
   responded with a gesture of his hand.

Then Standish opened with the greeting words,
    "We welcome you to our new town of Plymouth.
We welcome you in peace as friendly neighbors
    and seek to meet so we may find agreement.

"Our Governor wants to discuss some trade
    and how our people can become allies
and with the understanding that we make,
    protect the interests of our people's lives."

After Tisquantum made a translation
    the Massasoit nodded and agreed
and all together they walked into town
    along the line of houses on the street.

Then they arrived at an unfinished house
    to gather for the meeting to take place.
They hoped that no suspicion would be roused
    because the openness would feel more safe.

The structure was a simple unroofed frame,
    a simple sketch of plans and an outline,
yet it provided an important stage
    for the security of all their lives.

A large green rug served as the flooring mat,
    four cushions were all set around as seats
and Massasoit Ousamequin sat
    upon the place of honor handsomely.

As everyone was set in place inside
    then Standish said to the assembly
that Plymouth's Governor would soon arrive
    then stepped outside to signal down the street.

After he had returned inside the house
   off in the distance something had begun,
a sound their guests found to be curious
   — the rapid tapping of a rolling drum.

Then down the street there was a small parade
   approaching slowly with the Governor
and then a horn began to toot and play
   — the strangest bird the guests had ever heard.

And with the instruments' delightful din
   they played a concert out upon the street
performing for their audience within
   until they finished their sweet symphony.

Then after they had played the final note
   and as the two musicians took a bow
the settlers all began to clap and shout
   and hollered how they had made a great show.

The Massasoit clearly was amazed.
   The Pnieses watched the settlers clap their hands.
They certainly found the behavior strange
   but were delighted with the marching band.

And then the Governor stepped in the house
   and Ousamequin stood responsively.
Then they saluted and gave cordial bows
   and kissed each other's hands respectfully.

And then they brought in hard water to drink,
   and hardy plates of meat for them to eat
and finding tastes upon which they agree
   they joined together to partake the feast.

As they all ate, the company could tell
   that something unexpected was astir.
They saw the Pnieses talk amongst themselves
   and whisper in the Massasoit's ear.

So Carver asked Tisquantum to inquire
   if there was something that the other's need
to see if there was some rude oversight
   that compromised their hospitality.

Then after hearing Ousamequin's say,
   Tisquantum happily turned to report
the Pnieses were impressed with the parade
   and wanted to try playing on the horn.

The settlers gladly gave the guests the horn
   so they could handle the brass instrument
and they admired the strange tubular form
   that cast reflections in the brassy glint.

And then one of the Pnieses raised the horn
   to see if he could play the instrument
but was soon disappointed and forlorn
   when the brass horn would not sound out for him.

Then the musician tried to demonstrate
   the proper position of embouchure.
The Pniese then did his best to imitate
   and slowly took the steps so he could learn.

Then they all saw the sign of sheer delight
   when music lets the spirit soar unbound
and light was shining in the Pniese's eyes
   the moment that the horn began to sound.

And then expending his capacious breath
    that lifted them in a rhapsodic thrill,
they pooled into the note's impressive depth
    and heard the sound resounding through the hills.

The Pnieses then began to pass around
    and taking turns they tried to play the horn,
each demonstrating for the other how
    the embouchure was made so notes were formed.

Then one began to play a scale of notes
    ascending and descending in a balance
and everyone could hear what had been spoke
    — the clear expression of a natural talent.

Then the musician made a melody,
    a string of notes of the engaging tones,
to test the Pniese to play a mimicry
    then make a tune entirely his own.

So as they shared to sate their appetites
    with food they gathered and together ate,
they found the different ways their lives entwine
    in the accordant harmonies they made.

Then soon negotiations had been reached
    as they enjoyed the ways they could be friends
and terms were settled as they all agreed
    and strength was bolstered in their joint defense.

And with the Compact that they had conceived
    and through commitment that they had consigned
to live as neighbors in protected peace
    and strengthen through the trust and trials of time.

Then Ousamequin lit the Calumet
   and then he passed it round ritually,
an ember from one person to the next
   to verify the Compact made in peace.

Chapter 21

Tisquantum Teaches
March 1621

The next day Ousamequin and his men
   left for Sowams, a two-day hike away,
but said that they would soon return again
   and set a summer camp in eight more days.

They planned to set their corn across the brook
   and keep a camp nearby for several months.
Tisquantum would stay in a settler's house
   and Samoset returned up to the north.

As winter passed the days turned warm and bright
   yet there was still the sadness of their loss.
One could not bask beneath the clearing skies
   without considering the mortal cost.

The flowers that were blooming on the lawn
   were sprouting from the winter's unmarked graves.
The cheery birds that filled the air with songs
   reminded them of those who passed away.

But even as their numbers had been weakened
   they persevered in loving memory.
They had been damaged but were not defeated.
   They honored their lost love with industry.

And as the air began to clear in spring
   they recognized the progress they had made
and working all together dutifully
   they saw their little village taking shape.

But greater than the structures that were raised
   were careful contacts and relationships
in understanding and agreements made
   with Wampanoag tribes with whom they met.

In everything laboriously built
   and delicacies carefully arranged
of all the matters structured and instilled
   one must have understanding to sustain.

Then after Samoset had returned home,
   Tisquantum had been welcomed in their village
and although sadly he had been alone
   he relished the new status he was privileged.

Tisquantum was more than an honored guest
   amongst the members of the settlement
he was an original resident
   from Patuxet, London and new Plymouth.

And through the pleasure of the free exchange
   they prospered in collective benefit
and strengthened one another through their trade,
   developing through their relationship.

He taught them how to sow the native crops
   and different ways to fertilize the ground
and how they cultivated managed plots
   by planting corn and beans in a round mound.

In turn the planters showed Tisquantum tools,
   the cast of metal in a furnace made,
alike in shape of what the others used
   but far more durable than stones that break.

Then one day after they were working late
   and they had labored after dinner time
Tisquantum then astonished and amazed
   and offered yet another new surprise.

He took them to one of the nearby streams
   and waded in the water to his knees
then told them something no one could believe
   — he said he could catch eels with his bare feet.

They knew quite well the streams were filled with eels.
   They waded in the streams and splashed and grabbed
but lunging, plunging in the water's chill
   none of the eels they groped for could be nabbed.

They even tried to use the fishing nets
   but eels swam through the spacing of the knots
and every different trap they tried to set
   the eels always evaded being caught.

Then what they heard Tisquantum boldly claim
   was something none of them could understand.
Although they tried in several different ways
   the slippery eels would wiggle from their hands.

Mar. Then as the planters carefully observed
23   Tisquantum dug his feet into the sand
then as he trod up to the shallow shore
   the eels jumped from the water onto land.

Chapter 22

The Mayflower's Departure
March – April 1621

As spring arrived with warming of bright days
　　there was the hope of a new growing year.
The grip of sickness had begun to wain
　　yet still their prospects weren't completely clear.

The sailors had been busy chopping wood
　　and filling water barrels from the spring
and it was evident they would leave soon
　　embarking to return across the sea.

The winter had been hard for everyone
　　and only half the planters had survived.
The chill of death had brushed or touched each one.
　　On some days two or three died at a time.

The sickness had reduced all of their numbers
　　and on the ship they were inflicted too
from when they had set sail on the *Mayflower*
　　they had already lost half of their crew.

And through the challenges they all had faced
　　and the contentions that put them at odds
the sailors and the planters both could say
　　they shared the sadness of departure's loss.

And as the *Mayflower* prepared to sail
　　then Captain Jones called all the company
for parting words that he needed to tell
　　to everyone in the community.

And with the somber losses they had suffered
    the Captain looked upon those who remained,
the prospects for success were dour and doubtful
    for anyone stubborn enough to stay.

He figured when the next ship sailed the bay
    in the uncertainty of months ahead,
although the Captain wouldn't dare to say,
    he feared they'd find all of the settlers dead.

Mar. So as they gathered at the Common House
29   in the rough timbers of the settlement
the Captain of the *Mayflower* announced
    that anyone could sail back on the ship.

This caused a stir amongst the company
    as everyone confirmed what they all knew
and by acknowledging their unity
    each one assured they all were resolute.

Then of the company of common folk
    an undistinguished member of the group
stood from and of them all and kindly spoke
    what nods from everyone affirmed as true.

"I beg the pardon of our Captain Jones
    and if the elder and the deacons please,
I ask to share of what I feel and know
    articulated in a public speech.

"It is the practice of our pious church
    that everyone has an important voice
and as we each may thoughtfully discern
    each may decide to join and to rejoice.

"We all have known the perils of our lives
    and suffered sacrifices to be free
and have endured the trials time after time
    and are committed to what we believe.

"Now gathered in our little settlement
    we know our hardships have only begun
and standing upon each accomplishment
    a greater challenge demands to be done.

"I claim to speak for no one but myself
    and thankful for a chance to have my say,
assured through what I've known and what I've felt
    — I am committed and resolved to stay."

And at the end of this personal speech
    not just in what they said but in their deeds
in unison each one stood on their feet
    and all together everyone agreed.

Within a week the ship was set to sail
    and all the settlers gathered at the bay
and with their modest means waited to hail
    to see the steady *Mayflower* away.

Apr.
5

And in the amber light of early morn
    and on the pull of anchor chain she rides
the *Mayflower* was beautifully born
    to glide upon the smooth departing tide.

Then as the anchor heavily was weighed
    the sailors climbed the rigging of the masts
and to the sea the ship then turned away
    and then saluted with a cannon blast.

As beautiful as the sight had appeared
  the company then knew they were alone
the ship was sailing out into the clear
  and they had work that needed to be done.

Chapter 23

John Carver
April 1621

In early hours the sky was bright up high
  but light had not yet touched to dry the dew,
the Governor was calling all to rise
  to rouse the families and working crews.

Each night he scarcely had the time to rest
  as people ceaselessly knocked at his door
and as they came in anger and distress
  his guidance left them peacefully restored.

The night before John Carver was up late,
  he always was the last to savor sleep
and late at night he planned to coordinate
  the village needs with their collective means.

Then in the early moments of the day
  he cherished his soft stroll along the street
to see the progress all of them had made
  and feel the village settled peacefully.

Indoors the families began to stir
  and sprouts of life stemmed from the garden rows
and waking voices from inside were heard
  as the horizon brightened with day's glow.

Although each house was basically the same,
  a simple place for each to call their own,
there were the signs in how each had been made
  in little hints that subtly were shown.

As every family built their homes themselves
    their places showed their personalities,
of course they offered one another help
    while managing responsibilities.

And as the homes were built with family labors,
    they coordinated efforts earnestly
and all the individual endeavors
    combined to strengthen the community.

And as the family garden plots were made
    so each could live more self-sufficiently,
there was a joint task for them all that day
    for their employment in the colony.

For weeks they worked together in the field
    to turn the ground and loosen the packed soil.
They had no plow or cattle for the till.
    They did the work by hand with grueling toil.

What was acquired always comes with a fee
    and the investors would have to be paid.
All they had gained in order to be free
    was put to work so it could be sustained.

So as the people walked out in the street
    John Carver organized them into crews
and as all the assignments were received
    each person knew exactly what to do.

The men were hauling bags of seed in hand
    and passing out the tools of iron cast
then organized in the appointed bands
    they focused on their designated tasks.

The women worked as hard as all the men
   and were the inspiration through the days
renewing all their vigor without end
   and made their contributions just the same.

And as each one was working busily
   and cultivated talents were employed
John Carver grabbed a heavy bag of seed
   and with the others sowed along the rows.

Through morning hours John Carver pushed himself
   just as the Governor tended to do.
His foresight and his judgement earned respect
   but through his work he truly led the group.

And as he led the planters on the rows
   keeping a pace of steady thorough work,
he set the standards in his labor shown
   by filling expectations of his worth.

And driving forward to the zenith peak
   with sunlight shining bright from overhead
they turned to work through afternoon's steep heat
   and crossed the fields from end to end again.

And as they watched while Carver worked ahead,
   the only shade from brims of their felt hats,
they trudged and toiled while following his lead
   and worked to raise the crops from grounded flats.

But as he pulled the others as a team
   he pushed himself beyond what could be borne
and others shuddered watching as he seemed
   to totter on his feet while planting corn.

Lifting his hat he mopped his sweaty brow
   and staggered as he dropped the bag of seed.
He told the others, "Keep your courage now."
   then stumbled from the field holding his head.

Brewster and Standish rushed to give him aid
   and helped him to the shade of a near tree
and tending next to where John Carver laid
   they hoped for his robust recovery.

While Brewster knelt along John Carver's side
   he waved his hat to fan a cooling breeze
although the Governor would not revive
   despite the ways they tried to give relief.

And as the others worked across the fields
   they looked in hope for any sign of change
with Standish standing with his stalwart will
   but Brewster shook his head in dour dismay.

The surgeon Fuller then was called upon
   in hopes to lend some of his expertise
but Carver was not able to respond
   and seemed to be receding from their reach.

Then everyone felt like their hearts had dropped
   and even standing in the springtime sun
they felt their bodies shiver as they watched
   as their good Governor was carried home.

Chapter 24

Memorial
April 1621

Lamenting sounds were winding from the horn
    as everyone stood in the street outside
and sang sad psalms respectfully to mourn
    after John Carver peacefully had died.

Then with the opening of the front door
    there was a sudden hush amongst the crowd
as waves of grief were lapping at the shore
    and all the Pilgrims' heads were sadly bowed.

And then the deacons of the church emerged
    and carried Carver's body carefully
and with the Reverend Brewster's tender word
    they raised him to their shoulders on the street.

Before they stood in vigil through the night
    and cradled tapers flickering soft flames
and then they walked into the brilliant light
    beneath the bright sun of a clear spring day.

And bearing heaviness of the sad pall
    the deacons transported the shrouded corpse
and led the grieved procession of them all
    through quiet vacancies of the forlorn.

And following the simple shouldered bier
    the members walked behind in rows of three
and silently without a single word
    in reverence of hopes and memories.

But more than a sad train that filed through town,
   in unity they came to pay respect
and then assembled in the Common House
   to recognize and solemnly reflect.

Then Brewster led the group bereaved and somber
   to stand inside the open common space
and their esteemed past Governor John Carver
   was softly set where they all congregate.

And as the members slowly gathered round,
   encircling the body with bowed heads
then Brewster's voice soothed with a touching sound
   and led the group in tender, gracious prayer.

And with their loss they all confirmed their faith
   and piously affirmed life's sanctity
as they released John Carver into grace
   to lift the spirit of his memory.

And with the closing of devoted prayer
   the Reverend Brewster gave a eulogy
commemorating times of life they shared
   of one now passed into eternity.

"Brothers and Sisters we are gathered here
   in memory of one we love and know
and on our Pilgrimage upon this earth
   we know John Carver is finally home.

"And as he now may rest in sweetest peace
   from labors of his dedicated life,
just as before and even more he leads
   in all his life continues to provide.

"Our Governor John Carver was a man
  who did not elevate himself up high.
His greatness was not from a scepter grand
  but how his earnest work touched all our lives.

"The greatness of his life was not achieved
  because he towered above anyone.
His greatness was a magnanimity
  with breadth and strength that could reach everyone.

"He did not lead because he stood before.
  He led because he lived and worked among,
instructing us to manage fulsome store
  and in our dearth he helped to carry us.

"Yet the assistance that he offered us
  was not elixirs of a charity.
He led in ways to help develop us
  and opened doors of opportunities.

"A pious deacon of our simple church,
  devoted to the whole community,
austerely seeking unembellished truth
  with hopes aspiring for the heavenly.

"A man accomplished and with ample means,
  he lifted us – withholding nothing down.
His large estate helped fund our common dream.
  He wholly gave himself to church and town.

"The food we ate upon the *Mayflower*,
  the tools we use to build the settlement,
were largely given by the Governor
  who gave in sum and in significance.

"And all he seemed expecting in return
    is we succeed as a community
and worship God together in our church
    and live with purpose independently.

"Perhaps John Carver's worldly work is done
    and he has moved onto a greater role
as he has led the ways to carry on
    the living river pouring from our souls."

The elder and the deacons then arranged
    themselves around where Carver had been laid
and lifted him before the reverent train
    to carry him back out into the day.

They set him in a gentle place prepared
    and closing with a reverent sanctity
they blessed the somber place with sacred prayer
    then muskets fired salutes across the sea.

And with each one's dear love and stout respect
    they left the woe and kept warm memories
so Governor John Carver then could rest
    between the solid rock and branching trees.

Chapter 25

The Town's Election
April 1621

After the Governor John Carver passed
 the planters gathered in the Common House
and they assembled for the day to ask
 who would be capable to lead the town.

While they discussed who they would nominate
 before deciding whom they would elect
they weighed abilities of candidates
 and pondered who to trust with their respect.

And from discussions they seemed to agree
 that Reverend Brewster was most fit to lead.
With vision, wisdom and integrity
 he proved his judgement and capacity.

Yet feeling certain of their candidate
 they suddenly were puzzled and confused
as when the nomination had been made,
 the nomination flatly was refused.

Then as the Reverend Brewster always did
 he openly and lucidly explained.
He knew that he had disappointed them
 but there were reasons for the choice he made.

The Elder Brewster had not been ordained,
 Pastor John Robinson appointed him
to serve as godly council in the main
 until their Pastor could rejoin with them.

Then Brewster stood before the gathered town
   so everyone attended what he'd say
and as a hush calmed all the people down
   their honored elder carefully explained:

"Sometimes the breadth and depth of contemplation
   can blur the focus of direct decision.
A minister is made through inspiration
   but Governors are chosen by election.

"And we must keep apart the two positions
   — the Civil and the Ecumenical,
and separately they can provide assistance
   between the practical and spiritual."

While Reverend Brewster held the group's attention
   in making his pellucid explanation
he humbly offered his own nomination
   of William Bradford for the lead position.

With this there was a stir within the room
   and many looked in Edward Winslow's place,
that after William Brewster had refused
   they thought Winslow the next best candidate.

Winslow was always first to volunteer,
   accepting every daunting challenge met,
what could be asked more of a Governor
   than his capacity and selflessness?

And although Bradford was held in esteem,
   a humble man with sure abilities,
for months he had been sick and rarely seen
   and had been absent from their company.

He did his best to pitch in with the work
 but every time he wearily had tried
his sickness would become severely worse
 and several times they thought that he might die.

John Carver held him with assured respect.
 He proved his merit in the expeditions.
But on this meeting day he was absent
 and was not present during the elections.

After the meeting rankled in debate,
 a sudden hush was poured across the floor,
an opening let in the light of day
 and they saw Bradford standing at the door.

While Bradford hoped that he could be discrete,
 he was arriving at the meeting late
and everyone was froze in disbelief
 as if they saw someone back from the grave.

He pushed himself from his ill misery
 despite how bad he felt when he awoke.
He still had his responsibilities.
 It was his duty to be there to vote.

Then Bradford blushed in humble rectitude
 from stumbling in the center of attention
but while he held the focus of the group
 he steered them in beneficent directions.

And as they stared he felt his strength and health
 returning with a new invigoration
and then from the renewal of himself
 he felt obliged to give an explanation.

"I beg the pardon of the company
    that I'm arriving at the meeting late
and offer my sincere apology
    for being burdensome for lengthy days.

"While all of you have labored on the town
    and half our numbers are now lost and dead,
I feel I have let everybody down
    and been a dead weight lying sick in bed.

"I've been no help to the community
    and haven't even carried my own load.
I hardly feel a legitimacy
    to make a contribution in the vote.

"And now I feel I am regaining health
    and join you all again as we may serve
to work together for our Commonwealth
    in godly guidance of the holy word.

"And from this point I feel I will return
    and labor hard to earn my worthiness
and prove my value so I may deserve
    to be a part of this establishment.

"And hoping I will be allowed to sit
    and cast my vote as others may report
I feel for certain Edward Winslow is
    the best of us to serve as Governor."

Then William Bradford with no more ado,
    with modest quiet and unconscious grace
walked in to join the others in the group.
    Then Edward Winslow stood up and he said:

"We choose our leaders in respect and trust
    as someone everyone can look up to,
who's dedicated to preserving us
    through courage, wisdom and strong fortitude.

"We must have someone who commands attention
    to guide our efforts into excellence
but not promoting selfish elevation,
    authenticates a firm establishment.

"Someone who holds the helm in the tempest
    and never will abandon ship or boat
and keeps the course for common interest
    no matter which direction winds may blow.

"With understanding for each one of us,
    protecting values individually
and building everyone from valued trust
    by strengthening our commonality.

"Not someone with desire to seize control
    and domineer with blind complacency.
Someone who can be strong yet is not cold
    and still can feel with sensibility.

"Someone who can inspire the best of times
    for personal and common benefit
and through the desperate and direful trials
    becomes the model of resilience.

"I'm honored by all the recommendations
    but for promotion I choose to defer
and second Reverend Brewster's nomination
    of William Bradford for the Governor."

Then William Bradford walked across the floor
    and stood to face the gathered company
and then electing him as Governor
    the planters all in unison agreed.

Chapter 26

First Pilgrim Marriage at Plymouth
May 12, 1621

In May the days were filled with warm sunshine
  and in the town the world felt fresh and new.
The fields were sprouting neatly in sown lines
  and each home's garden had begun to bloom.

The forests filled with teams of vibrant life
  with weaving nests of sweetly singing birds.
The gnarly branches of the winter ice
  were warmed with leaves the gentle breezes stirred.

The planters had good reason to be proud
  for what they had accomplished commonly.
The progress they achieved with their new town
  was made with everyone collectively.

But each accomplishment that has been made
  would fall apart with lax complacency.
What is achieved can only be sustained
  with full commitment and fidelity.

And as they built their lives reliantly
  and coordinated honest business,
they cherished the soft warmth of family
  — the nurturing of love and happiness.

And branching like the forest's stands of trees
  and lifting up the ground into the sky
and flourishing with crowns of verdant leaves
  they nurtured life in their community.

There was a need for an assured defense,
  the guiding laws of fair authority
with trade and commerce for development,
  but Plymouth was made by the families.

Then reservations for one day were made
  and everyone was welcome to attend
so they could merrily all celebrate
  another monumental town event.

The town of Plymouth had the first marriage
  between two of the planters who had lost
each of their spouses in the sickness days
  and after mourning they became betrothed.

Susanna White's husband died earlier
  and cared for all her family alone
and Edward Winslow was a widower
  and finding love they chose to share their homes.

And having made agreements for the day,
  a single day for all the rest of time,
the vows and the commitments were both made
  for dedication to each other's lives.

Although they had no Pastor to preside
  the ceremony's proven sanctity
was the devotion of their faithful lives
  professed to God and the community.

The ceremony is to celebrate
  the lacy beauty of the wedding ties
but holiness is not one formal day
  but every day for their entire lives.

And through the difficulties they endure
    and through temptations of the good times too,
in every way and moment they confirm
    to prove together that their love is true.

Chapter 27

Envoy to Massasoit Ousamequin
July 4 – 7, 1621

In summer time the Pilgrims chose to send
    their own ambassadorial envoy
confirming their goodwill as a close friend
    with the good Wampanoag Massasoit.

The Compact they had all agreed to make
    could not be left to carry on its own,
it needed to be carefully maintained
    as only epitaphs are set in stone.

The Compact was a means for good relations,
    a guide to manage their development,
and they had to maintain negotiations
    to make sure that it kept its relevance.

They needed laws to organize their lives
    and drew for guidance from the living word
and with the grit of practice they applied
    they worked to reach a spirit that was pure.

Then William Bradford as the Governor
    and Isaac Allerton as the assistant
proposed they send the best ambassadors
    to meet with Massasoit Ousamequin.

Tisquantum would be guide for the envoy
    and Hopkins would accompany Winslow
and they would make a journey to consort
    where Wampanoag people made their home.

Both Hopkins' and Winslow's wives were concerned
   but duty called for the community
and they assured them they would soon return
   in their devotion to their families.

The whole town stood and watched the party leave
   and walk beyond the planted fields that day
and as they disappeared into the trees
   the planters bowed their heads while Brewster prayed.

Jul.
3

And as the party walked into the shade
   the distant thickness of the forest seemed
to clear before them in an open way
   as they were following Tisquantum's lead.

They were surprised no brush or bramble snags
   were clumped about and later on they learned
the Wampanoags cut the bushes back
   by managing the woods with controlled burns.

And as they walked along the dented path
   that game and people tramped out in a line
they noted all the different, mingled tracks
   to witness how the forest life entwined.

And Edward Winslow always looked around
   to feed his endless curiosity
and made a mental map of covered ground
   and tried to understand all he could see.

One of the tasks they needed to complete
   was learn the route to Ousamequin's home
so if there was an urgency to meet
   they would know the most direct route to go.

But more than finding the most direct route
   his mind inquired so he could understand
to learn of the identities and rules
   for local culture, language and the land.

And then developing his comprehension
   they could exchange more openly and free
and gaining from more fluent interaction
   they'd find more ways for them all to agree.

Along the winding path Tisquantum led
   encountering kind people on the way
they often stopped to partake of the bread
   made with ground kernels of the native maize.

Some people shared the shad they caught that day
   and in return the party shared the food
they brought with them and made a warm exchange
   along with gifts of beads they had brought too.

And as they journeyed, they found warm welcome
   while making good relations with each stay
and with each friendship mutually won
   they opened paths for ways they could relate.

The local tribes had all been generous
   but Winslow noted sparsity and dearth.
The soil was rich and could yield fruitfulness
   but they lacked tools to help them with the work.

And then Tisquantum told them of the past
   and countless numbers of the people gone
and from the sickness people died in masse
   and showed them places sadly strewn with bones.

Then staying for a night at Nemasket,
   they rose together in the early morning
and left with six of the inhabitants
   to guide them through the local territory.

Jul.
4

Later that day they came to Pokanoket
   the area where Ousamequin lived
and hoped to find the mighty Massasoit
   so they could strengthen bonds with their new friend.

But Ousamequin had been gone that day
   and was out hunting the surrounding grounds.
So Winslow, Hopkins and Tisquantum stayed
   and waited till their friend came back around.

The village stirred as all the women worked.
   They picked the weeds from the round garden beds
and trained the beans to grow on stalks of corn
   just as Tisquantum earlier had said.

Then they would sit in circles as they mend
   the clothes and tools for all the people's needs
and helping one another as they tend
   the conversations flowed refreshing streams.

Winslow and Hopkins were both curious
   of the conduct of Wampanoag ways
but were polite, careful and courteous
   and did not stare with an intrusive gaze.

Then to the side and at a careful distance
   the diplomatic envoy kept away
and properly respected for their visit
   the village where they stayed in civil grace.

Tisquantum then suggested that the men
  pull out their matchlocks and to ready them.
When Ousamequin was in sight of them,
  they'd fire their pieces in saluting him.

But when they pulled their heavy iron guns
  with the suggestion of their guide and friend
the women screamed and all began to run
  thinking the planters were attacking them.

Winslow and Hopkins knew the danger here
  and put the guns back where they had been stowed,
if carelessness ignites with sparks of fear
  all they had built could tragically explode.

Then Winslow told Tisquantum he must tell
  the Wampanoags there was not a threat,
they all were safe, the planters meant them well,
  and sadly their intentions were misread.

After Tisquantum carefully explained
  with reassurance that soon soothed the squall
the envoys remained carefully contained
  and all the people of the village calmed.

They knew this was a delicate endeavor
  to venture in the Wampanoag town
and carefully maintained their friendly favor
  at Massasoit Ousamequin's home.

And when they saw the great Sachem approach
  they fired their muskets up into the sky,
a salutation they felt rather bold
  but as their guide Tisquantum had advised.

And when their muskets safely were discharged
   the planters waved enthusiastically
to make sure their intentions and regard
   were clear and well received hospitably.

Then Ousamequin with stern countenance
   approached with Pnieses as his entourage
and greeting with their peaceful open hands
   the planters showed the gifts that they had brought.

They brought a dapper suit of woven cloth,
   a copper bracelet with a gem inset
and best of all a handsome riding coat
   with fabric dyed in vibrant English red.

And then when Ousamequin tried them on
   he filled the clothing with his dignity
and both the planters and the Pnieses saw
   the Massasoit in noble esteem.

And then the group was courteously led
   inside the home where Ousamequin stayed
and Edward Winslow openly then said
   the business of their visit for the day.

"We thank the Massasoit and our friend
   for welcoming our envoy in his home
and from our Governor we have been sent
   in confirmation of our neighbor's love.

"With gracious offers from the gifts we brought
   we hope to find ways to communicate
and then amend our grievances we caused
   and strengthen one another through our trade."

And with Tisquantum as interpreter
   they said to bring the new bracelet to them
when Ousamequin sent his messengers
   and they would know the message was from him.

And with the sundry messages relayed
   Winslow spoke of the seed they dug from mounds.
There was a debt they were obliged to pay
   and he asked where the owners could be found.

They found the mounds soon after they arrived
   and took some baskets of both corn and beans
and without finding anyone nearby
   they couldn't pay for what they took in need.

If Ousamequin was able to find
   the people at the place they called Corn Hill,
then satisfaction would be made in time
   with their commodities and English meal.

Then Edward Winslow went on to explain
   about the richness of the soil they'd seen
and they would show them how the tools they made
   would boost their harvest's productivity.

He also mentioned Wampanoag visits
   and how the planters welcomed them to town
but they could not continue giving victuals
   until the harvest season came around.

And with these matters and then sundry more
   Winslow explained the planters situation
and made the effort to disclose before
   the issues irritated with frustration.

And trying to avoid the tedious
   Winslow provided the communication
to touch upon the points without a fuss
   for the diplomacy of good relations.

The Massasoit listened to each statement
   that was relayed through the interpreter
and with alert attention indicated
   that he acknowledged what had been conferred.

Then finally Winslow made one request
   if Ousamequin could provide some seed
and then the planters could experiment
   with cultivating native corn and beans.

When Edward Winslow had finished his speech
   the Massasoit answered the same way
addressing every point from memory
   in the exact sequence they had been made.

And in respect of the formality
   and the esteem of the held company
through honesty and rationality
   they found the ways where everyone agreed.

Then Massasoit Ousamequin stood
   so gathered Sachems could together see
and spoke to everyone inside the room
   with the strong music of his noble speech.

Some interjected from the statements made
   then Ousamequin would inflect in turn,
commanding emphasis in what he said
   and led each one till they had all confirmed.

Then with a statement bent into a question
  the Massasoit Ousamequin paused
and waited to hear from the group's reaction
  and then the Sachems answered with applause.

Then Ousamequin began to sound out
  to prompt each individual response
so every single Sachem said out loud
  what seemed a confirmation from each one.

And then the hallowed Calumet was lit
  and passed to each one who was circled round
and through the ceremonial event
  they peacefully confirmed the terms then bound.

And then the groups informally conversed.
  The planters asked of Wampanoag ways
and Ousamequin was quite curious
  and wanted to know more about King James.

Jul. The party stayed with them for two more nights
7   and Ousamequin promised to retrieve
the corn and beans for them so they could try
  to see how well they did with native seeds.

Then Ousamequin sent Tisquantum out
  to circulate a message for exchange,
encouraging the villages around
  to take their pelts to Plymouth and make trade.

And even though they were beseeched to stay
  the planters wanted to return to town
and make it back on time for Sabbath day
  and worship with their families at home.

146

So rising early in the morning dew
  the Massasoit sorely let them go
with Tokamahamon, a man they knew,
  who then escorted them back to their home.

Chapter 28

Journey to Nauset
July 1621

Shortly thereafter in the summer months,
   the folks at Plymouth had another scare,
there were distraught reports the Billingtons
   had lost a son who'd wandered off somewhere.

They searched around the town without success
   and through the passing days their panic grew
and everyone in the town was upset
   although this lamb had been a rascal too.

They sent a message to the Massasoit
   in hopes to contact all the nearby tribes
and spreading word throughout the Wampanoags
   they asked for help in finding the lost child.

They waited for no more than a few days
   then Tokamahamon returned with news,
the boy was in a town across the bay,
   so they assembled a recovery group.

They learned the place they needed to set sail
   was nearby where they first had visited
and where they found the corn and English pail,
   a place where they fear they had made offense.

The boy was safe and with the Nauset tribe
   and this was a good opportunity
to find a way that they could reconcile
   the First Encounter's rife hostility.

But every opportunity has risk
   and every hope can turn into dismay
and even minor details that are missed
   can cause a loss of everything at stake.

The planters gathered ten of their brave men,
   Tisquantum, Tokamahamon were guides
and all together in the shallop went,
   the fairness of the day seemed a good sign.

But after they had sailed out of the bay
   and could no longer see the Plymouth port,
foreboding clouds rolled in later that day
   and tossed the shallop in a daunting storm.

There was no cover on the open sea.
   The lightning flashed and rolling thunder broke,
the wind was rushing in a howling scream
   and in the rain they all were drenched and soaked.

And then nearby they saw a water spout,
   a whirling column linking sea and sky
and then there was a parting of the clouds
   and the fresh air was shimmering with light.

Recovering, they set back to their work
   and bailed the boat with buckets of the rain
and with the canvas from the mast unfurled,
   as the storm passed they set the sail again.

They pressed the sail for the rest of the day
   but could not reach the shore before the night
and reaching Cummaquid off of the bay
   they rowed to harbor in the faint moonlight.

In morning they arose from their beach camp
  and others in the distance could be seen
searching for lobsters as the tide drew back
  and so their guides walked off to talk with them.

Then Tokamahamon and Tisquantum
  returned to tell the planters what was said
— the boy was safe from harm and in good health
  and he was definitely at Nauset.

Shortly thereafter the group was approached
  and greeted by the Sachem Iyanough
and with Tisquantum he graciously spoke
  and told them more about the boy they lost.

He said he'd take them to Nauset that day
  but first invited them into his village,
being the custom for the guests to stay
  with entertainment for a friendly visit.

Four men agreed to stay and watch the boat
  and then the others went to Cummaquid
and Iyanough proved a most noble host
  assuring that his guest would be content.

And as the conversation was exchanged
  through laughter and enjoyment that they shared,
there was a sudden wailing sound of pain
  from an aggrieved grandmother who appeared.

They turned to look and see the lady sob
  and they sat stunned while bafflement set in.
The lady seemed to have a sudden shock
  that poured remorse at the mere sight of them.

The Sachem stood and went to speak with her
and then Tisquantum stood to listen too
and they could see the lady speak through tears
as they all sat bewildered and confused.

After she spoke they saw Tisquantum speak
to Iyanough as if to make request
and then before her set down on his knee
to speak directly and not overhead.

Although the planters could not understand
the cause of sadness of what she had said,
they watched the gestures of Tisquantum's hands
and saw the solemn bowing of his head.

There was no doubt the lady was aggrieved
and somehow thought the planters were to blame
and she stood crying while Tisquantum seemed
to take the delicate time to explain.

Tisquantum pointed where the planters sat
and then the Sachem's and the lady's eyes
looked with an anguished stare mournful and sad
and then he waved his arms as to deny.

Then focusing their eyes to him again,
he pointed to himself as if to plead,
explaining that the planters weren't to blame
and that he too had reason to be grieved.

Then calming from her sobbing they could see
the overwhelming sadness she had felt,
begin to sooth and settle tenderly
while looking at Tisquantum as he knelt.

And then Tisquantum stood up on his feet
   and led them back to where the planters sat
and then explained so they could clearly see
   the reason that the lady was so sad.

With just the name of Captain Thomas Hunt
   the planters all let out remorseful groans.
They had been hearing of his monstrous stunts.
   He was a man whose heart was cold as stone.

Tisquantum said the lady had three sons.
   Hunt lured them on the ship and kidnapped them
and he had suffered the same transgression,
   recalling they were on the ship with him.

The planters then denounced what Hunt had done
   and offered their consoling sympathy
for the appalling loss of her three sons
   and gave her gifts to help appease her grief.

Then later in the evening they set sail
   with Iyanough and two more of his men
and hoped they could arrive before night fall
   to harbor near the village of Nauset.

The planters knew the grief the lady felt
   was also felt by many nearby tribes
and visiting the village of Nauset,
   their greeting could be fearsomely hostile.

When they arrived it was already dark,
   the tide was out, they could not pass the shoals,
so in the distance they stayed in the barque
   and people began lining on the shore.

Then Iyanough said he would go to speak
    with Aspinet, the Sachem of the tribe,
and let him know that they had come in peace
    and they were here reclaiming the lost child.

And Iyanough then waded to the shore
    and spoke to people standing on the beach,
a brief announcement that he made before
    then walked inland beyond where they could see.

Then after Iyanough had disappeared
    the men began to wade out toward the boat
and as they all began to close in near
    the air was taut as a string of a bow.

And then the planters had Tisquantum say
    they wanted to be friends and came in peace
and asked if anyone was from the place
    where they had found the stash of corn and beans.

A man from Manamoyick made a sign
    to indicate that he was from the place
and they waved him up to the shallop side
    and with Tisquantum's help tried to explain.

They told him they had settled at Patuxet
    and that they wanted to repay their debt
and if he visited, he would be welcome
    or they could soon return to repay him.

The Manamoyick man said he would visit
    and when he did their debt was satisfied
and on this night nearby the Nauset village
    they gave him gifts from what they had that time.

Then shortly after Aspinet arrived
   and with him were at least a hundred men
and they all lined up on the water side
   and they had Billington's lost boy with them.

With fifty men then Aspinet approached
   and in their little boat the planters stood
and with respect and dignity they spoke,
   discussing matters for mutual good.

There were admissions of the First Contact
   — the fearsome battle from the months before.
The planters said that they had been attacked
   when they had camped one night along the shore.

They also mentioned corn and beans they found
   and the arrangements for repayment made
for all the owners of the corn filled mounds.
   The aim was that they all prosper in trade.

They then described their neighborly friendship
   with Ousamequin and the Wampanoags
and the agreement for their joint defense
   against the hostile threat of Narragansetts.

They then extended out to Aspinet
   the hope that they may live in peace and trade
and offered gifts in token of friendship,
   the proven substance of proposed exchange.

With this the Sachem of the Nauset turned
   and with his stalwart voice he loudly spoke
and then a Pniese lifted the boy on shore
   and on his shoulders brought him to the boat.

And carried so his feet weren't even wet
   inside the boat the boy was gently set
with Wampum bracelets hung around his head
   to show that he was treated with respect.

The planters then prepared to journey back
   and lastly Aspinet forewarning said,
the Narragansetts recently attacked
   the Wampanoags and many were dead.

And then the planters knew they must make haste.
   They needed to return immediately.
They had to sail and could not wait for day.
   Their town and friends needed them urgently.

But as they tried to sail across the bay,
   they fought the counter winds all through the night
and as they wrestled with their oars all day
   they found their course was blown wide to the side.

Then on the beach they spotted Iyanough
   who had been walking back to Cummaquid
and picked him up to carry him back home
   and fill their cask with water for the trip.

And after they had brought their boat to shore,
   they tried to find fresh water at a spring
and they were welcomed as they were before
   with gifts and kindness all were offering.

But there was urgency for them to leave
   and they were grateful for the friendship shown
and all together walking to the sea
   the women sang and danced to bless the boat.

They gave more gifts before they voyaged out
   and Ivanough placed Wampum on their heads
and quickly sailing back to Plymouth town,
   the winds blew favors with their new found friends.

Chapter 29

The Shadow of Sachem Corbitant
August 1621

Returning from the journey to Nauset
   with Billington's young son, they were relieved,
despite the talk of threats from Narragansetts
   they found their town in peace and quite serene.

They rowed the shallop into Plymouth harbor
   and others took a break to welcome them
to hear the news of their fulfilled endeavor
   rejoicing that the boy was home again.

They sent Tisquantum to a nearby village
   to hear if there had been any assaults
and he returned with one of the tribe's Pnieses,
   a noble man who's name was Hobomock.

Tisquantum then explained the Massasoit
   appointed Hobomock to live nearby.
He was a Pniese of local Wampanoags
   and he would be a close and firm ally.

A Sachem by the name of Corbitant
   opposed the Massasoit's peace agreement
and many of the Wampanoags said
   he was conspiring with the Narragansetts.

Then Hobomock made a close settlement
   and all his family were daily guests
and welcomed as new Plymouth residents
   and proved to be the Pilgrims' trusted friends.

Tisquantum had profound respect for him
  and Tokamahamon revered him too,
one of the Wampanoag's bravest men
  of keen intelligence and vision too.

And with Tisquantum, Hobomock soon learned
  more English words and manners of their speech
and taught the eager planters in return
  more of the local language and beliefs.

But through the summer they heard Corbitant
  was furious with the Compact's allies
and that he planned to kidnap both of them
  and cut the planters off from local tribes.

They thought that Corbitant might soon attack
  so Hobomock accompanied Tisquantum
and travelled to the village Nemasket
  to meet with Massasoit Ousamequin.

But soon thereafter Hobomock returned
  sweating profusely, breathless and alone.
Tisquantum had been forcefully captured
  and Hobomock escaped upon his own.

Then Hobomock said he met Corbitant
  at Nemasket where they had stayed the night
and with his men he threatened stabbing them
  and Hobomock feared that Tisquantum died.

By then all of the town had slowly gathered
  to hear what Hobomock tried to explain.
There was confusion in the stressful matter
  as neither language or motive was plain.

But as the Pniese carefully made his statements,
   the planters comprehended what he said
— they'd been attacked the night at Nemasket
   and their dear friend Tisquantum might be dead.

Then they began to stir into a clamor
   and heated up into a fuming rage
but then as if upon a soaring banner
   the voice of Bradford's rational was raised.

"Please hold my brethren, we must think this through,
   this is no time for us to lose our heads.
We must take care in what we choose to do
   to handle the abuse suffered our friends."

The Governor then settled down the crowd
   after they heard the speech of Hobomock
and stood to lead the members of the town
   instead of stoking frenzies of a mob.

Then gaining their attention with his statements
   all of the people paused to hear him speak.
The Governor explained the weights of judgement
   articulated with his clarity.

"We cannot rush off seething for revenge
   and run off in a rampage to destroy.
We must find out what happened to our friend
   and then decide what means we will employ.

"The Sachem Corbitant is Wampanoag
   with whom we have agreed to live in peace
but he has disobeyed the Massasoit
   if he is acting in hostility.

"With Ousamequin we have made agreement
    to stand up for our mutual defense
and Corbitant may have committed treason.
    His unprovoked attack is an offense.

"We must find out what happened to Tisquantum.
    We do not know for certain if he's dead.
If proven Corbitant committed murder.
    We will exact the judgement on his head.

"It seems that Corbitant has forced our hand.
    We cannot let our friends be so abused.
If we allow his offenses to stand,
    the trust we've built, we are at risk to lose.

"Now Corbitant has made an act of war
    and threatened to destroy what we achieved.
He is attacking our friendly neighbors
    and we must show our strength to keep the peace.

"But keep in mind our strength is not for harm,
    our strength is in alliances held true.
The Sachem Corbitant has brought alarm
    and our response is for our friend's rescue.

"We must assemble a group of our men
    and Captain Standish will serve in the lead
and travel to the town of Nemasket
    to aid our friend Tisquantum for relief.

"We hope our friend Tisquantum is ok
    and we can bring him back to town safely
but if he's harmed then Corbitant must pay
    and we'll uphold our defensive treaty."

So they assembled fourteen volunteers
  and Hobomock agreed to be the guide
and with instructions from the Governor
  got ready to dispatch in a short time.

They left for Nemasket in early morning
  and had to march more than a dozen miles
and laden with the arms that they were bearing
  they trudged all day through rain in single file.

Aug.
14

And then within a few miles of the village
  they set off of the trail for a short rest
and planned how to conduct the apprehension
  and waited there until the sun had set.

Then in the cover of the pitch of night,
  their muskets charged with powder and with shot,
they tried to sneak up to the village site
  but oddly Hobomock kept getting lost.

Although their guide had seemed to lose the way
  Winslow was able to recall the path
as him and Hopkins had been that same way
  to visit Ousamequin in the past.

The fact that Hobomock may have been lost
  was something that no one seemed to believe
and some had thought they were able to spot
  suspicion of a trap and treachery.

But Captain Standish noticed something more
  and he pulled Hobomock aside to speak.
Perhaps it was a sense of warriors
  but what the Captain saw was loyalty.

The Captain sensed the guide had been concerned
　of leading the armed group into the village.
He was afraid there'd be a massacre.
　But Standish proved they had no mind to ravage.

Then quietly along the trail's blind bend
　the Captain took a moment to make clear,
the Wampanoag people were their friends
　and only Corbitant had need to fear.

The women and the children would be safe.
　They hoped to save their friend Tisquantum's life.
They've no intent attacking in a rage
　but in defense they were prepared to fight.

And with this reassurance Hobomock
　led them into the village at midnight
and pointed out the house where he had thought
　that Corbitant and his group were inside.

The Captain posted men around the house
　to capture anyone who tried to flee
and with their matchlocks burning like a fuse
　they rushed with Captain Standish in the lead.

There was commotion and sharp startled screams
　but Standish led the men in discipline
and strong and steady in the stormy scene
　maintained their self-control and confidence.

They saw that Corbitant was not inside
　and told the people they would not be hurt
and asked them if Tisquantum was alive
　but no one in the house would say a word.

Then after everyone began to calm
   some quickly scrambled out a secret door
then with a tussle they were quickly caught
   and then again there was a loud uproar.

So two men fired their muskets through the roof
   and sent a shock of fear throughout the house
and as the rancor was at last subdued
   then Hobomock began to shout out loud.

And then Tisquantum suddenly appeared
   with Tokamahamon and a large group
and all the planters were relieved from fear
   to see their friends were safe and not abused.

To see if Corbitant came back about
   the planters stayed through the remaining night
but first released the people from the house
   so they would not be caught up in a fight.

By morning Corbitant had not returned
   and they had breakfast at Tisquantum's house.
All those aligned with Corbitant dispersed
   and friendly villagers remained in town.

Aug.
15

Then as the villagers had gathered round
   and with Tisquantum as interpreter
the planters took a moment to announce
   and spoke directly to make themselves clear.

Their friends had tried to meet the Massasoit
   and Ousamequin was their close ally
and they were friends with all the Wampanoags
   but Corbitant tried cutting friendly ties.

They knew the Narragansett had attacked
  and killed their people many times before
and with their people they made a Compact
  that Corbitant was trying to destroy.

He had been threatening their closest friends
  so they had come to speak with Ousamequin
but Corbitant ambushed and kidnapped them
  and there was fear he had murdered Tisquantum.

They'd done nothing to Sachem Corbitant.
  They didn't have a sinister intent.
They wished to trade and not to make offense
  but they will arm defending peace and friends.

If Corbitant continued to harass
  and chose to kidnap and attack their friends
they will not suffer the abuse to pass
  and they will come in force direct to him.

The night before three people were injured
  and they were sorry for the accident
and they would help them with a mending cure
  with surgeon Fuller at their settlement.

The planters travelled back later that day,
  two of the injured villagers came too
and they recovered quickly with the aid
  of Samuel Fuller mending their sore wounds.

Chapter 30

Envoy to the Massachusetts
September 18 – 21, 1621

After they calmed the qualms with Corbitant
   the planters settled back into their work
and tended to their tasks with diligence
   — they weren't disturbing nor were they disturbed.

And in the summer warmth of brilliant days
   there was a sense of joy and modest pride
to see how steadily the fields were raised
   to be sustained in cultivated lines.

Their hopes were set upon the harvesting
   but carelessness is how hope can be lost
so as the fields were slowly ripening
   they carefully kept tending to their crops.

They also fished the bay for bass and cod
   and through the summer lived contentedly
and with Tisquantum and with Hobomock
   enjoyed the friendship of those neighboring.

In fact they had been gaining more respect
   from all the Sachems of the local tribes.
Their recent management of Corbitant
   had proved they were a strong and firm ally.

The messengers arrived and offered gifts
   on days the planters humbly tended crops
and they were offered statements of friendship
   as far as from the isle of Capawack.

Even the Sachem Corbitant sent word
    that he was satisfied to live in peace
although through Ousamequin's messenger
    as he did not want to directly meet.

They still had not heard from the Massachusetts,
    a nation that lived further to the north
and people said that they did not approve of
    the planter's Compact with the Massasoit.

The planters then decided they would send
    another envoy of ambassadors
to prove that they sought peace and trade as friends
    with a sincere and neighborly gesture.

Sept. Then with Tisquantum, ten men set to sail
18   September eighteenth at around midnight.
They'd ride the tide to navigate the swells
    and they could travel through the cool moonlight.

The journey proved much farther than they thought.
    They sailed a distance nearly forty miles
and on the steady course that they had plod
    by the next night they finally arrived.

On the south shore of Massachusetts Bay
    they set the anchor and rode through the night
and tried their best to rest for the next day
    in bilge on boards in the open moonlight.

Sept. On the next day they made it to the shore
20   and met a local lady fetching lobster
and as Tisquantum gently spoke with her
    she looked to be fearful in the encounter.

The planters in the distance kept away
   and did not press to make a hint of threat.
They knew they looked imposing in array
   with all the gear and armor that they kept.

Tisquantum spoke at length with the lady
   then walked to where the planters stood in wait
and said that they should make the boat ready
   to take the shallop where her people stay.

Then they were led into a wooded camp
   to meet the Sachem Obbatinewat
and cautiously the locals met the band
   who offered friendly gifts from things they brought.

The Sachem offered many explanations
   that although at the Bay of Massachusetts,
they were not in the Massachusett Nation
   and were under the rule of Ousamequin.

He also told about the Tarrantines,
   a hostile tribe residing to the west
and they'd been pillaging relentlessly,
   killing his kin and stealing their harvest.

They dare not live in any settlement
   and render themselves helpless from attacks.
Their numbers did not give a strong defense
   and they were forced to live in roving camps.

The planters then explained that they were friends
   with noble Massasoit Ousamequin
and they agreed for mutual defense
   with all the people of the Wampanoag.

And then the planters offered a Compact
  to help defend the Sachem and his tribe
so they could better fend off the attacks
  and prosper through the trade that they could find.

So then the planters made another friend
  and were committed to the peace agreement
and as they built they promised to defend
  the practical and mutual achievements.

They also asked about the Massachusetts
  and they had hoped to visit and make trade
but heard the Massachusetts would refuse them
  and there was word that some threats had been made.

They hoped to meet the leader of the nation
  and prove to them that they had good intent
and wanted to arrange negotiations
  and hoped acquaintance could be made with them.

Then Sachem Obbatinewat explained
  that the Squa–Sachem was an enemy.
Yet still, a meeting with them may be made,
  they too were threatened by the Tarrantines.

He then agreed that he would be a guide
  and help them with a meeting to make peace
and through this he may also reconcile
  his friendship with the Massachusetts' Queen.

Then Obbatinewat joined the envoy
  and in the boat they sailed across the bay
and through the epic archipelago
  the tiny shallop cruised through the bright day.

And piloting, the Sachem was escort
   and pointed at the mouths of two large rivers
where fleets of ships could harbor at a port
   far larger than their tiny Plymouth harbor.

And even though this was a better place,
   they'd never build if they kept moving round.
The settlement decision had been made.
   They were resolved to stay in Plymouth town.

Through afternoon and to the early night
   they sailed the boat through the expansive bay
and then arrived in the glow of moonlight
   where people of the Massachusetts stayed.

They slept off shore inside their open boat
   and at first light they landed at the beach
but as the tide ebbed with the ocean flow
   none of the Massachusetts could be seen.

Sept.
21

So Obbatinewat led them inland
   to where he knew there was a local town
and they saw signs of the inhabitants
   but not a single person could be found.

There was a field where crops of corn had grown
   and recently a harvest had been made
and there were traces where they set their homes
   but everything seemed to be cleared in haste.

Then Obbatinewat showed them a home
   that stood unoccupied a mile away
set on a hill and standing all alone
   with a commanding and impressive state.

Built up to tower upon massive poles
    with elevated planks upon them set,
it had been one of multiple abodes
    of former Sachem Nanapeshamet.

Then Obbatinewat led past the hill
    where they arrived at an impressive site
and saw a massive fortress had been built
    and learned the Sachem was entombed inside.

And further on for no more than a mile
    there was another house upon the hill
that was another royal domicile
    where Sachem Nanapeshamet was killed.

Then Sachem Obbatinewat explained
    that after Nanapeshamet had died
the Massachusetts' Queen assumed his place
    and as a Squa–Sachem governed the tribe.

But as the group continued to explore
    they didn't see the people anywhere.
They saw fire pits that had been used that morn
    but all the villages in haste were cleared.

And then they found some women in a group
    who looked exhausted lugging corn in heaps
and as the planters came within their view
    they huddled up together fearfully.

Then as the planters stood away they sent
    Tisquantum and then Obbatinewat
to let the women know they came as friends
    and they were seeking trade with things they brought.

Then as the women were assured and calmed
   they cautiously tried to relax and rest
and then the planters showed they meant no harm
   just as their gentle attitudes expressed.

The men brought forth some victuals from their packs
   and then the women began boiling cod
and everyone was able to relax
   while they were sharing comforts of their food.

One of the Massachusetts men then showed
   and though at first he had been hesitant
he soon relaxed and felt at ease to join
   the casual and neighborly event.

The planters said they hoped to make fair trade
   and interact through goods commercially
and building on the true relations made
   they hoped to meet the Massachusetts' Queen.

The man told them the Queen had been away
   but he would bring some beaver pelts for trade
then shortly he returned to make exchange
   and on that day a partnership was made.

And as they shared a meal at the campfire,
   enjoying one another's company,
Tisquantum pulled some planters to the side
   to make conspiring comments secretly.

He slandered all the Massachusetts people
   and claimed that they were all both bad and foul.
He said they had been planning something evil
   and threatened to attack the planters' town.

The planters felt it odd to hear these words
  while gazing at their pleasant company
and something sinister inflamed and burned
  in what Tisquantum was disparaging.

And after making these dire accusations
  he said that they should steal their pelts and corn.
The Massachusetts had the worst intentions
  and they deserved nothing but hurt and scorn.

These statements caught the planters by surprise
  as they were happy with the friendships made
and then the planters thoughtfully denied
  insinuations that Tisquantum bade.

They said the Massachusetts did no wrong
  and had received them well without offense
and in like manner they chose to respond.
  Their aim was friendship and good business.

And even if some others slandered them,
  they did not fear others insulting words.
Let others scream and cry disparagements
  but solid, structured deeds are undisturbed.

And if the Massachusett tribes were ill
  and had been lost in darkness and are evil
the planters would shed light from their goodwill
  through the good deeds they have done for their people.

All that they knew was those they met that day
  had all been courteous and warm and kind
and meeting with the others, let them say
  this day they found the planters of like mind.

Then later when returning to their boat
 the group of Massachusetts followed them
and waiting with them till the tide had rose
 they offered gifts with sundry pleasant things.

Then after sunset in the soft moonlight
 the women sold their pelts they wore as clothes
and modestly in the warm dusky night
 they covered themselves with the leafy boughs.

And then Tisquantum made a leering glance
 and all the planters sternly shook their heads,
retaining honor in the circumstance,
 they virtuously sailed to their homestead.

Chapter 31

The First Thanksgiving
Autumn Harvest 1621

With standing fields the harvest season came
　　and acres of the ground were ripe with food
and they set off on cool and joyous days
　　to gather what their labors had produced.

The native corn had flourished on the fields
　　and sturdy stalks stood over twenty acres
and husky ears were snapping as they filled
　　the baskets carried by the happy planters.

They also had six acres of their barley
　　but peas they brought had not faired quite as well,
the summer heat had parched all of the blossoms
　　that were more suitable for English fields.

And when they gathered everything together
　　with loads of baskets everyone had filled
they estimated portions for each settler
　　to have each week eight quarts of their own meal.

Then after they reserved some meal for trade
　　and more was kept aside for next year's seed
from all the produce that would still remain
　　they all would be sustained sufficiently.

And they set busily to fix their homes
　　to daub the clapboards for the winter storms,
repairing and preparing for the cold
　　while autumn days were relatively warm.

And as the harvest had enriched the town
   from toils of summer with the fruits of labor
the main of Leyden Street had been laid down
   extending to the shore of Plymouth Harbor.

And on the main were seven residents
   built on the North and South sides of the street
that started from the rock of settlement
   and then climbed up the hill above the trees.

They also raised four buildings for the place
   intended for the whole community
and more were planned and the foundations laid
   to service everyone's utility.

Then with the bounty of their first harvest
   the Governor decreed they celebrate
and they broke bread together for a feast
   with gifts they shared to bless and consecrate.

They had endured the winter's tragedy
   and worked through hardships of the desolation
as they had lost half of their company
   through winter's pestilence and devastation.

Then through the year the ones who had survived
   and graciously the chill of death passed by
they earnestly devoted all their lives
   to build their town through hardships they defied.

And with persistence night turns into day.
   The freezes thaw into soft summer blooms.
The only sure fortuitous pathway
   is through endurance and one's fortitude.

And although sweet success can be enjoyed,
  it starts to spoil when overly indulged.
If one is disengaged and unemployed
  the blunt of softness makes one's edge turn dull.

But for the season's thankful festival
  the hands all joined confirming unity
and lifted praise devoutly worshipful
  to cherish gifts of their community.

So William Bradford as the Governor
  sent four men to hunt turkey, ducks and geese,
then shortly after the four men returned
  with birds enough to feed them for a week.

And in the celebrations that they made
  they reveled with the loud, bombastic blasts
and with their ordnance and their muskets blazed
  announcements with the powder's smoke and flash.

Soon after, they realized the message sent
  had definitely been misunderstood
as they soon saw their Wampanoag friends
  had gathered on the hills and near the woods.

They saw the Massasoit Ousamequin
  was standing with no less than ninety men
and then the Governor went out to meet them
  along with several from the settlement.

And with warm salutations they approached
  and with Tisquantum as interpreter
then William Bradford courteously spoke
  the formal greetings of the Governor.

They learned the Massasoit was alarmed
    and thought the planters were under attack
and called his Pnieses to take up their arms
    to honor their agreement and Compact.

And then the Governor felt a relief
    and all the other planters felt the same.
Their friend had brought an army to their feast.
    They feared they had offended him some way.

The Governor then carefully explained
    that they had gathered for a celebration
and Ousamequin with this noble train
    were all extended a warm invitation.

The Wampanoags then laid down their bows.
    The planters put their muskets all away.
And they all sat together to compose
    the Celebrations of Thanksgiving Day.

They set the tables out on Leyden Street
    between the facing rows of the town's homes
so everyone could find a place to eat
    within the peaceful setting of abodes.

The tables were no more than wooden boards.
    They set in line upon some sturdy stands
and turned the street into a banquet floor
    with seats they made with thick logs set on end.

So they made sure each person had a seat
    and all together they could celebrate
the fact that they had plenty food to eat
    enjoyed together through the friendships made.

And of the chairs the planters had in store,
    the Massasoit had an honored seat
and next to him sat the interpreter
    so they could talk while they sat down to eat.

And Ousamequin sat in Brewster's chair,
    the elder graciously had offered him
to match the Massasoit's royal air
    with dignity of them receiving him.

And next to him sat Plymouth's Governor,
    then Captain Standish and the church deacons
and down the length of the long table's board
    sat Wampanoag Pnieses joining them.

The planters then removed their tall, felt hats
    exposing sweaty brows of bowing heads
and Elder Brewster stood from where he sat
    and leading them in prayer, the meal was blessed.

The busy planters served their honored guests
    and food was set on shiny pewter plates
and the long tables were thoughtfully dressed
    with flowers to adorn and decorate.

The Massasoit was the first to eat
    and as he carefully chewed the first bite
all of the planters watched him eagerly
    in hopes he found the meal to his delight.

They had prepared the bird the English way
    and spiced it with their own home recipes
and hoped that it appealed to their friend's tastes
    compared to how his people cooked turkey.

And after some suspense there was relief,
  Tisquantum was not needed to translate,
in language spoken universally,
  they saw the smile arise upon his face.

Then eagerly they asked about the corn
  Tisquantum had instructed them to make
and let them know how well they had performed
  the preparations in the local ways.

Then as their friend ate portions of the food,
  they had a cheer when they saw he was pleased
and they said they were glad they had made good
  from growing crops from his own gift of seeds.

They told him that the Nausets were repaid.
  They gave them twice as much corn in exchange.
And thanking him for the corn seed he gave,
  he would be paid handsomely in the trade.

As one together they enjoyed the meal
  and at the tables they politely dined
and tastefully felt something that was real
  — the satisfaction of their appetites.

Then after everyone had ate their fill
  they found some other ways to entertain,
continuing the happy festival
  with music and the friendly sport of games.

Later the Massasoit gathered men,
  his greatest Pnieses, then sent them away
and soon they had returned with venison
  they bagged with bows and arrows on that day.

And from the five fresh deer the Pnieses brought
   they offered two to the town's Governor
and the three others that their arrows shot
   they gave to Standish and his good neighbors.

And then accepting Ousamequin's gifts
   the skillful Pnieses had expertly won,
the planters then expressed their gratefulness
   then shared the venison with everyone.

The festival continued for three days
   with meals they blessed with thankful sanctuary
and celebrated with the friendships made
   the meal has proven to be legendary.

Chapter 32

Fortune
November 1621

After the celebrations had been made
    the planters turned back to their earnest work.
Those mirthful moments sour to the profane
    without the labors that give them their worth.

With careful cultivation of their fields
    they made a modest mountain of supplies
but on the moment that they ceased to build
    they knew that they would then start to decline.

For each accomplishment that can be made,
    there never is assurance it will last.
Success is a foundation that is laid
    to set upon an ever greater task.

And even with the failures of dour loss
    when careful plans of forethought fall apart
those are the lessons that are not forgot
    and linger with the burning sting that smarts.

Then with the strength and wisdom that is gained
    and courage in persistence is applied
an even greater earning may be made
    than could have been expected the first try.

There are always restrictions set to bound
    and nature weighs with countless balances
and whether lifting up or boring down
    the greater tasks have greater challenges.

Encountering the obstacles that block
   applying patience, skill and balanced strength,
as when confronted with a solid rock
   a master sculptor makes a masterpiece.

Then tending to the gains of the harvest
   they organized their yield of grain and corn
ensuring they sustained the populace
   through winter's scarcity with what was stored.

They also needed some to save as seed
   sustaining cycles for necessity
and stay prepared for next year's early spring
   through ebbs and flows of tides each season brings.

They also had to work and turn the soil
   of all the ground of their harvested fields,
returning nutrients with sweat and toil,
   preserving the rich dirt's fertility.

They sent the shallop out to fish the sea,
   continuing to build upon their gain.
Abundance was not time for laxity
   but opportunities to be sustained.

And with the surplus they could set aside
   this served as an emergency reserve
but also for the trade with local tribes
   to build upon relations they had earned.

Then all together through their friendly trade
   their profits could supply each other's needs
and honoring the payments that were made
   reciprocate the valued specialties.

And as the planters struggled to survive
    there were finance conditions to be made
and although circumstances had been dire
    they still had debts to London to be paid.

And as the planters busied with their work
    and kept their focus fixed upon their jobs
they greeted an arriving messenger
    who had been sent by Nausets on Cape Cod.

Nov.
9

The messenger said they had seen a ship
    that had been slowly searching off the coast.
They did not know the visitors' intent
    or if the people were their friends or foes.

The planters thanked him for the message sent
    and paid him kindly with some gifts and food
along with gifts for Sachem Aspinet,
    their friend and neighbor living on Cape Cod.

Then all the leaders of the settlement
    gathered together in the Common House
and there discussed the new development
    that unexpectedly had come about.

No one expected any ship this soon.
    The *Mayflower* left earlier that year.
The settlement's investors in London
    could not have fitted a new ship with gear.

Then they considered how long it had taken
    for all the chaos to be organized
so they were able to embark from England.
    It couldn't be a ship with fresh supplies.

So they thought it may be a fishing ship
   like one that Samoset said he had rode
but sounded more like menacing pirates
   in how they had been prowling on the coast.

So they agreed on how they would react
   and diligently went back to their work.
They wouldn't wait and fret of an attack
   but vigilantly readied for the worst.

Nov.
11 But later the watch sounded an alarm
   and fired a cannon from the hill's platform
and called the planters into town to arm
   because the ship approached the town's harbor.

Then everyone retrieved their charged matchlocks
   positioning with Standish at the shore
and then defensively on the hilltop
   others manned cannons aimed from the platform.

They didn't know from where the ship had hailed
   nor what the aim the captain had in sight
but if the ship had come to cause travail
   the planters were fully prepared to fight.

Then anchored down the vessel slowly turned
   to ride the rising tide as it flowed back.
They saw the name of *Fortune* on the stern
   and then the crew raised up the English flag.

Chapter 33

Weston's Letter / Bradford's Speech
November 1621

The planters stood along the harbor's edge
   and watched the longboat lower from the ship
and then a group of men climbed from the deck
   and shoved the boat off from the open slip.

The boat spun round as sailors turned her to,
   then dipping oars, pulled the boat toward the town
and as the group came closer into view
   the water's calm stirred with the splashing sound.

The Governor was standing on the Rock
   and waved his hat to guide the boat to land.
The tide was in, the boat could come to dock.
   They wouldn't touch their boots on the wet sand.

Then as the boat continued to draw near
   the mist of distance cleared and they could see
familiar faces begin to appear
   that glowed with warmth of friends and family.

The Deacon Robert Cushman sat up front
   and Elder Brewster recognized his son
with Prence and Adams and a friend from France
   and Edward Winslow saw his brother John.

The planters offered welcoming rapport,
   the others appeared weary from the trip
and as the new-comers approached the shore
   they saw the planters with astonishment.

The planters' clothes were clearly rough for wear
   but there was fire alight within their eyes.
They had endured a rough and tumble year
   but through this they were vibrantly alive.

As Cushman stepped upon the rock on shore
   he warmly greeted everyone on land
and as the others quickly climbed off board
   they gathered as they shook each other's hands.

Then Robert Cushman asked where Carver was
   surprised the Governor had not been there
and the arrivals felt a sense of loss
   while calling names for whom no one answered.

Then William Bradford somberly described
   the winter sickness that afflicted them
and how so many of them sadly died
   — whole families were lost along with friends.

Then Bradford told how their dear Carver fell
   while working hard upon the field one day.
He set a standard that had served them well
   and they kept working honoring his way.

Then all together along Leyden Street
   they took a tour of the new settlement
and there were Wampanoags visiting
   and the new-comers met the planter's friends.

And then they saw each private residence
   and were relieved to see the food in store
and then the new-comers made some comments
   how stingy the ship's crew had been on board.

Then on the platform they built on the hill
    they noticed that the new comers were cold
and wondered why out in the autumn chill
    that many of them were not wearing coats.

Then walking down into the Common House,
    the planters quickly started a warm fire
and asked the new-comers about their clothes,
    then learned they hadn't brought proper attire.

With this the planters began to inquire
    of the provisions they had on the ship
and the new-comers honestly replied
    they didn't even have one sea biscuit.

They said the crew could not spare any food.
    They needed it for the trip back to England.
Investors gave them a few penny suits
    but hadn't time to furnish them equipment.

Some grumbles of contention could be heard
    but all the planters exercised restraint.
No doubt the situation caused a stir
    but they accomplished nothing with complaint.

Yet still there were some practical concerns.
    They used the season's surplus to make trade
and then divided what they had reserved
    and there was nothing extra they had saved.

The freeze of winter was upon them now
    and the next harvest was a year away.
Soon they would all be buried in the snow
    and buildings were already cramped for space.

They didn't bring a single bite to eat
  nor any kettle they could cook it in.
They hadn't brought a single tool they need
  nor nothing more than what they wore right then.

They had been told to find the settlement
  but if they found all of the planters dead,
they were told to continue down the coast
  and find another settlement instead.

The group soon settled in a sense distraught.
  Some felt a pain as if they had been burned.
Then Cushman showed a letter he had brought
  and handed it to the new Governor.

The letter was to former Governor
  John Carver without knowing he had passed
and had been written by an investor
  and William Bradford broke the seal of wax.

Then as he read the group calmed from their stir
  and watching Bradford closely while he read
they hoped expressions from the Governor
  would show them some of what the letter said.

The lines of irritation and distress
  were clearly seen on William Bradford's face
and everyone could see he was upset
  in what the London letter had to say.

The Governor then brought them all to order.
  The letter was from Mr. Thomas Weston
who was one of the venture's chief investors
  and was composed with a tone of contention.

Then William Bradford read the letter out
    disclosing openly the note's content
then each one in the meeting would not doubt
    of the complaints that Thomas Weston sent.

He was irate the ship was gone so long,
    a year had passed before restored to port
and from the length of time that it was gone
    the ship returned with no cargo of worth.

He said this was due to the planters' weakness
    but not because they lacked hands for the work.
He blamed them for a weakness in their judgement
    and did not care what the planters endured.

Apparently he thought they spent their days
    debating and discussing their religion
and tediously arguing away
    instead of getting any labors done.

There was a list of numerous complaints
    and Bradford read each one to the whole group
that often grumbled with Weston's disdain
    and then the Governor gave a reproof.

"My brethren, do not let this irritate.
    We have become accustomed to abuse
and all the criticism that was said
    we know is certainly not of our due.

"We gather in the Common House we built
    and notched the lumber set with our own hands
from timber we had lugged across the fields
    and we are living where our town now stands.

"The street outside is lined with private homes.
    We reaped a harvest of a growing year
and although the investors may not know
    there is no question what we have done here.

"Then with our neighbors who reside nearby
    we have confirmed agreements that were made
and as relations strengthen over time
    this will continue to produce more trade.

"We scratched this town from frozen ground this year.
    We suffered through the winter's pestilence
and stood upright with burdens that we bear
    when death appeared to be our only friend.

"And through the hardships that we have endured
    and facing every challenge that we found
there is no question of our honest work.
    That question has been settled with our town.

"All the investors in the distance know
    is that an empty ship returned to port
and this first ship is not able to show
    all we have done upon the distant shore.

"Then setting doubts aside for the firm truth
    and persevering through our own travails
we have laid down the fundamental proof
    — the proof that we have given to ourselves.

"This proof is not in idle minded statements
    or arguments contesting some intent
but in what we are tangibly creating
    — fulfilling foresight with our labors spent.

"With every victory that we have won
    and every contest we have lived up to
we are confirmed with all that we have done
    and from this we see what more we can do.

"The burden of the proof that we have born
    we answer with the labors that we do
and from our work of this year's trade and store
    this ship will take to England solid proof.

"The *Fortune* will return with laden stowed
    with clapboards and with hogsheads of soft fur
that value no less than five hundred Pounds
    and future shipments will send even more.

"We all have heard what Weston's letter said
    and of the weakness we have been accused
but we will show that he has been misled
    and more than words we send our weighty proof."

Then grumbles of disruption had now ceased
    as everyone agreed with focused purpose
and then the Governor resumed his speech
    to get beneath another common burden.

"Another matter that I must address
    regards the new arrivals we received
and of their seeing ill-preparedness,
    it does appear that they had been deceived.

"Although they had been sent to us in haste
    and hadn't been supplied with tools or food,
they certainly are not the ones to blame
    and we will share the burden for the good.

"They all seem to be standing in good health
    which is much better than how we arrived.
  Their youthful numbers will add to our strength.
    The added weight will soon revitalize.

"Our friends and family are not a burden
    as every single person contributes
  and complementing one another's service
    the body of us all is strengthened too.

"The rations of the harvest that we have
    of which we had divided into doles
  will have to be divided into half
    ensuring that we can sustain the whole.

"The first ship to our harbor is named *Fortune*,
    a gift arriving unexpectedly,
  as every gain can also be a burden,
    requiring more responsibility.

"We did not come to shirk away from challenge.
    We did not come to find an easy way.
  The difficulties managed with our balance
    will keep our course along the narrow way.

"And all together we will bear this weight
    as old and new will lock into a link
  and as resolve and fortitude will stay
    the weight will turn into increase of strength."

Of thirty-five new people who had come
    one person was a pregnant Widow Ford
  and after she was led into a home
    another Pilgrim on that night was born.

Chapter 34

The Governor's House
November 1621

The visit of the *Fortune* would be brief
  and Cushman was instructed to return.
He had been sent to make an inquiry
  and to report to London what he learned.

And Cushman was a deacon of the church,
  had worked with Carver to procure the funds
and lived in London where he could confer
  and manage the investor's liaisons.

The Pilgrims proudly showed him their new town.
  There was no question of the work they'd done
and now that they had firmly settled down,
  they'd send some lading back on the *Fortune.*

If the investors doubted what was done
  because the work was far beyond their view
the Pilgrims would dismiss any questions
  and answer with the goods their works produce.

Then in the Governor's house on one night,
  the leaders met with Cushman privately
and hoped to bring some issues into light
  — the practical facts of reality.

They would have hoped the ship brought more supplies,
  equipment to address more of their needs.
Instead they were sent people unsupplied
  with only hungry mouths that they must feed.

If they had been some castaways at sea
   and treading water on the deep alone
all the investors had been offering
   for help was tossing them a heavy stone.

They had received the others with their love
   but their supply of food could hardly last
and this endangered every single one
   and what they've built could topple and collapse.

And William Bradford made response in full,
   he was not making whimsical complaints,
as Governor he was responsible
   for all the people at the settlement.

The people had been working hard all year
   and diligently pulled on their own oars.
Elected, they had chosen him to steer
   and make sure that their vessel stayed on course.

The furs they had, they gained through honest trade
   and now they had no more commodities
and even with relations they had made
   — any exchange requires an offering.

The surplus food was used for trade and debt.
   The Massasoit was repaid the seed,
they had made sure to repay the Nausets
   as they upheld the Compact with their deeds.

And afterwards the food that had remained
   they had proportioned equally exact
so through the winter they could be sustained
   but now those rations had been cut in half.

With harvest done they all were comfortable
  and for the time they had all that they need
but winter's freeze would not be merciful
  if suddenly they had no food to eat.

With William Bradford's perspicacity
  he saw a problem looming up ahead
and to protect them from emergency
  he worked to steer them safely clear instead.

They had endured the winter time before,
  they would endure the winter time again,
and resolutely with the Governor
  they would all live to see the spring again.

They had ideas in how they would adjust,
  dividing rations to feed everyone,
and with more people who could fish and hunt
  make supplements with cod and venison.

Then furthermore the Governor explained
  that Weston's criticism was undue,
another shipment should be sent again
  with more supplies that they can put to use.

If there was doubt about their industry
  then Cushman could report what he had seen
in their first year their productivity
  was evident in their established seat.

They have a harbor where they built their town
  and were prepared to ship what they could trade
and there was commerce that would soon abound
  through the alliances that they had made.

Although the shipment they sent back that time
    was only worth about five hundred Pounds
the value of the shipments would soon climb
    as they kept building where they settled down.

They had been able to live peacefully
    and the alliances that they had made
had helped to sooth surrounding rivalries
    and through their friendships they were making trade.

They had been cultivating fertile fields.
    They feel they could supply themselves with food.
The gains they made were tangible and real.
    The prospects of the settlement were good.

Then after Bradford had outlined the whole,
    he ventured with a singular request
that for the Sabbath services they hold
    if Cushman could make the next church address.

As Cushman was a deacon of the church
    the Governor had hoped that he could preach
a layman sermon from the holy word
    of selfless virtue and of unity.

Then on the Sabbath that they held each week,
    the Pilgrims gathered in the Common House
and listened as the deacon Cushman preached
    with lessons for the faithful and devout.

Then parting Cushman left someone his coat
    and promised to send back tools and supplies.
Then after hauling in the ship's long boat
    the *Fortune* left with the outgoing tide.

1622

Chapter 35

The Narragansett Threat
January 1622

Soon after the ship *Fortune* sailed away
  a stranger paid a visit to the town
and though Tisquantum was not home that day
  he came with their friend Tokamahamon.

Without their friend Tisquantum to translate
  there were some challenges in the exchange.
They could not perfectly communicate
  and what the man had brought seemed rather strange.

Through interactions that they had enjoyed
  they had exchanged nice gifts with those they met
and with no common tongue they could employ
  each understood the language of kindness.

But trying to reciprocate the gift
  and match the gesture with one of their own
they found the stranger turned indifferent
  with nervous looks from Tokamahamon.

The Governor and other leaders came
  and looking at the gift tried to make sense
of what appeared peculiar and strange
  — a clutch of arrows bound in a snakeskin.

Was this a ceremonial message?
  An ornament of local, sacred rites?
A thoughtful bundle of a bricolage?
  Or an expression of malicious spite?

The gift was arrows that were tools of war.
  The viper's fangs suggested treachery.
This was something they had not seen before
  and they suspected animosity.

The messenger was treated with respect.
  They tried to find from whom he had been sent.
The Pilgrims offered food and warm kindness
  but wanted to know what the message meant.

Then Tokamahamon tried to explain
  in worried tones that sounded to be urgent
but all they understood from what he said
  was that he kept repeating "Narragansetts!"

Then with some gestures and a simple question
  the Pilgrims asked the man who brought the message
and then the man confirmed with an expression
  that yes, he had come from the Narragansetts.

Of course they understood the situation
  and circumstances suddenly were dire.
The Compact with the Wampanoag Nation
  was for protection from this hostile tribe.

They let the Narragansett messenger
  go after they had learned his origin,
without Tisquantum as interpreter
  they were not able to converse with him.

Now they were grateful for the new members
  as they were strengthened with the people sent
yet Narragansetts had fierce warriors
  attacking everyone that lived near them.

The sickness that had hurt the local tribes
    had left the Narragansetts all unharmed
with hundreds of their towns where they reside
    and several thousand warriors in arms.

They fought the Pokanokets to the east
    and Massachusetts living to the north.
They were attacking Pequots to the west
    and with the Wampanoags were at war.

They used advantage of their sudden strength
    to take control of all the local tribes
and found the little village at Plymouth
    to be a hindrance of their empire.

After Tisquantum had returned to town
    the Pilgrims showed the message that was sent
and then he spoke with Tokamahamon
    and said the message was a hostile threat.

By now most of the town had gathered round
    inquiring with their curiosity
— the clutch of arrows in the snakeskin bound
    the Governor held up for them to see.

The Governor then stood on a tree stump
    to make sure everyone could clearly see
and as they wondered what was to be done
    he took initiative to make a speech:

"It seems we have received a hostile threat
    from bitter Sachems of the Narragansetts
who have been angered with our good friendship
    with Wampanoags and the Massachusetts.

"The Massasoit had informed of them
    and told how they attacked some of his tribes
and how they had harassed and harried them
    and taken many Wampanoag lives.

"We will not cower to their idle threats.
    We will defend our town and our good friends.
And if they make the error to attack
    what they begin we will bring to an end.

"The message that they sent, we will reply
    that if they choose to violate the peace
then let them come into the face of fire.
    We will rebuke their animosity.

"We do not seek nor do we want a war
    but will defend our town at Plymouth Bay
and if they come then we will be prepared
    and they will find they will be entertained."

Then Bradford took a fist of metal shot
    and packed it with some powder in his hand
and with the arrows and snakeskin tied taught
    he sent their threat directly back to them.

Chapter 36

Fortification and Drill
February – March 1622

With the imposing Narragansett threat
    the settlement felt suddenly exposed
and they agreed to build a battlement
    to guard against the threat of the unknown.

After a year there was some discontent
    and the arrivals added to their load
but the hostility that threatened them
    had pressed them to a unifying force.

The discontentment that is often felt
    is simply nature's way to motivate
but an attack upon the settlement
    meant prickly quibbles certainly could wait.

And now the new arrivals who had come
    were thought of differently with the new turn.
No longer seeming to be burdensome,
    they added strength and pitched in with the work.

Then with the foresight of some thoughtful plans,
    they organized their efforts all as one
and with assignments took each task in hand
    and worked to fortify their humble town.

Encompassing the village all around
    they built a barricade of sturdy poles
and standing eight feet up above the ground
    the barrier served a defensive foil.

They also built four bulwarks into place
   with platforms looking out in each direction
and three of them were built with working gates
   that could be locked securely for protection.

Then with the bulwarks and the strong platform
   that stood upon the hill with cannon mounts
they would be able to defend the town
   in every angle compassing around.

And every post was snugged without a hole,
   a single gap could cause a fatal breach.
Together they all bolstered every pole
   to total twenty-seven hundred feet.

But battlements themselves become targets
   if they cannot be properly maintained
and everyone was given assignments
   as they were organized and strictly trained.

The Captain was the chief of the command
   and Standish answered to the Governor
and they prepared to make a fearsome stand
   if they could not avoid a tragic war.

And everyone who was able to fight
   was set into four squads they organized
and every squad was separately assigned
   a leader in direct commanding line.

But more than simply being organized
   they kept prepared with their activity
and coordinated so they coincide
   their force and strength found in their unity.

Each one of them relied upon the other
    to hold the massive weight of a strong line,
the links of iron chain held fast together
    withstanding any strain at any time.

Each held their own assignment and position
    and each was trusted to fulfill their role
and weathering extremes in all conditions
    each task combined to fortify the whole.

They built their strength by raising battlements
    and lifted timbers to secure in place
with pass lines linking their accomplishments
    and rising high upon a solid base.

The sparks may fly into the shifting wind
    but metal cast by tempering of will
is shaped with hammers of stout discipline
    and sharpened on the grinding stone of drill.

So time and time again they all were trained
    to operate in seamless unison
and regularly tested to take pains
    to monitor and maintain formation.

So when they heard the sudden alarm sound
    they knew exactly what they had to do
and as each stood defending Plymouth town
    they could rely on everyone else too.

Each squad would arm and take defensive place
    on bulwarks each of them had been assigned
and uniformly setting a charged flank
    they'd fire their muskets all at the same time.

Another caution that they took in store
    — the possibility of fire attack,
in case the Narragansetts tried to torch
    their houses by igniting roofing thatch.

They would line up to circle round the home
    protecting others while the flames were doused
not leaving their position on their own
    for honor and for duty of their vow.

They understood the leadership's instruction
    that even if their own house had been torched
they never could abandon their position
    or else they risk the whole town be destroyed.

They fortified the town within a month
    and worked together like a fierce machine
and were prepared to withstand any front
    with readiness they made defensively.

The Narragansetts wisely stayed away.
    Perhaps the Pilgrims' booming drills were heard,
perhaps it was the barricades they made
    but thankfully the peace was kept secure.

Chapter 37

Second Envoy to the Massachusetts Delayed
March 1622

Through March there still had not been an attack
  and although everyone stayed on their guard
precautions had been holding them all back
  and they felt pent and stifled in their ward.

They had refrained from venturing to hunt
  and were not gaining supplements of game
and they kept everyone close to Plymouth
  lest some of them be ambushed while away.

They had been carefully rationing food
  but the last harvest they had kept in store
had dwindled and their prospects destitute
  as they had a long wait to harvest more.

They needed to begin to venture out.
  The time had come for them to sow the fields.
They could not move ahead if buckled down.
  They had to address practical details.

Then stirring doldrums of the winter grey
  the birds began to sing beautifully
and with the warming prospects of the day
  the world renewed in blooms of peaceful spring.

They had been busy through the winter time,
  adjusting well to address complications
and felt the town securely fortified
  and with that done, they had more obligations.

They told the Massachusetts they'd return
  in spring time to continue with their trade
and build upon respect that they had earned
  fulfilling obligations they had made.

Then they began preparing an envoy
  to take what few commodities remained
and with a group sail to the bay up north
  to make sure their relations were sustained.

But while Tisquantum was gone on some tasks,
  their good friend Hobomock spoke earnestly
and mentioned things he recently saw pass
  and thought Tisquantum up to treachery.

He said Tisquantum privately would meet
  with people in the woods and slyly speak
and on occasions Hobomock had seen
  him pull others aside to whisper things.

He said he thought the tribes of Massachusetts
  now thought the Pilgrims were their enemy
and they had been aligned with Narragansetts
  and that Tisquantum had joined them in league.

He said that's why Tisquantum had been gone
  as he was planning a conspiracy
to cut the Captain and the others off
  after they sailed away from the town's seat.

He said it's not the Wampanoag way
  to lose their virtue with this treachery.
They honor the Compact that had been made
  and choose to deal with their friends openly.

A council was called by the Governor
　　with Captain Standish, Allerton and others
to see the views from different settlers
　　and take account of factors all together.

Each person said they felt they should go out.
　　They cannot sit and hide inside the town
and they were not afraid to say aloud
　　they needed to step out and look around.

They felt the town was ample and secure.
　　They drilled in preparation to defend.
They cannot look like they all live in fear.
　　That only would invite hostile offense.

If they refused to venture out in spring
　　and didn't push themselves for further growth
then they condemned themselves to withering.
　　There is no harvest if no seeds are sown.

They are not ones to wander and to roam.
　　They're working with a purpose on their own
but if they wanted to stay in their homes
　　they should have stayed in England all along.

The homes they keep are for their families
　　and nurture love of all their closest kin
and through civility and industry
　　they work in building and development.

They told the Massachusetts they'd return
　　and were establishing a partnership
and were determined to stick to their word
　　and build together through confirmed friendship.

For everything developed and obtained
    the ventures come with certainty of risk
but no accomplishment can be sustained
    without accepting careful ownership.

If they remained in stale security
    and did no more than what they needed to,
stuck in diminishing dependency
    they soon would die when they ran out of food.

The chance they took by making the journey
    would prove their courage and their fortitude
and they pursued the opportunity
    by challenging themselves to be renewed.

They made the preparations to be safe
    considering responsibilities
and planned to venture on an April day
    to keep exploring possibilities.

Before they left, Tisquantum would return
    as him and Hobomock would be on board
as their two friends and the interpreters
    to meet the Massachusetts to the north.

Both Winslow and the Captain tried to learn
    to speak the language of the Wampanoags
and made phonetic records of the words
    in hopes to converse with the Massasoit.

Tisquantum had been teaching both of them
    and pointing out the meaning of the words
and as the two developed a pidgin
    they carefully and cautiously observed.

They thoughtfully considered Hobomock
   who had shown honor and respect to them.
His comments of Tisquantum were a shock
   and they were worried for both of their friends.

Chapter 38

Tisquantum's Accusations
April 1622

In April they were ready for the trip
   and Standish chose ten able bodied men
and Hobomock was in attendance with
   Tisquantum their interpreter and friend.

The shallop had been fit when they set out
   and carried victuals and commodities
and everyone in town saw the men off
   with blessings and with prayers for their safety.

The day was calm without a hint of wind
   and patiently the men began to row.
They had a lengthy journey before them
   with forty miles of sea before the bow.

Then everyone in town prepared for work.
   They thought about the brave men who had gone
and hoped the men a quick and safe return
   and they set to attend the fields at home.

The Governor held up a hoe in hand
   and in the other lugged a bag of seed
and he began to toil about the land
   and others followed his example's lead.

And as they all were lined up on the rows
   they plodded on the open fields to tend
while turning earth so seeds were set and sown
   then someone rushed up wailing out to them.

They recognized the person in distress
    from their good friend Tisquantum's family
and the fresh gash across his face professed
    that he had been assaulted recently.

Repeating "Narragansetts!" with a shriek
    the man kept looking back into the hills
as if at any moment he would see
    them furiously charging at his heels.

The Governor then sounded the alarm
    to gather everyone back into town
and all the men then posted with their arms
    and others safely drew into their homes.

He ordered for the cannon to be fired
    to signal back the shallop with the men.
They couldn't have rowed more than a few miles
    and quickly would be back to town again.

With the defenses firmly set in place
    and signals for the shallop to return,
the surgeon checked the wounds on the man's face
    and they assured him that he was secure.

And as the frantic man began to calm
    the Governor asked for more information,
he needed to know more of the assault
    and of the plans the hostile tribe was making.

Without Tisquantum there to intercede
    they struggled so they could communicate.
They recognized some words and what they meant
    but couldn't understand all that he said.

He kept repeating the name, "Narragansetts!"
    who gathered in the village "Nemasket"
and then expressing in a nervous panic
    he kept repeating, "Sachem Corbitant!"

He then said something that they understood
    yet something that they hardly could believe
and all around attentively they stood
    and listened as their hearts filled with sick grief

as he said, "Massasoit Ousamequin!"
    in the same line as all the enemies,
and then knit up his hands and all his fingers
    as if to show a bound conspiracy.

He then began to pantomime defiance
    as if he stood up for the colony
and then made signs that this had been the time
    he had been struck and slashed upon the cheek.

And then he indicated his evasion
    and how he narrowly made an escape
from the hostility and the aggression
    and fled to them in hope to be kept safe.

They slowly pieced together the report
    and then they heard the swinging of a gate
and at the bulwark facing the harbor
    the envoy had returned without delay.

They saw Tisquantum wince with saddened pain
    to see his kin with the gash on his cheek
and surgeon Fuller carefully explained
    they treated him to heal the injury.

Then William Bradford told them of the threat
   and then gave order for the company
to take their posts to guard the settlement
   while keeping Standish for a summary.

And then they asked Tisquantum to translate
   to make sure they had got the message straight
and find out if they really were betrayed
   and Ousamequin was a renegade.

And as Tisquantum conversed with the men
   they noticed Hobomock press to be near
and Standish closely watched his warrior friend
   for his reactions of what he could hear.

Tisquantum then turned to the other men
   and with reluctance mournfully confessed
that Ousamequin had turned against them
   while slyly watching Hobomock's distress.

Tisquantum said that he could prevent war
   and he would shortly visit Nemasket
and meet the parties who were in uproar
   and then dissuade them from any attack.

And then Tisquantum looked at Hobomock
   who shook his head and said this was a lie.
He would not listen to Tisquantum mock
   the honor of the Massasoit's life.

Chapter 39

Tisquantum's Deception Exposed
April 1622

As Hobomock was sent into a rage
   Tisquantum skulked and turned as if to flee
and as the Pilgrims kept them separate
   they kept Tisquantum close where they could see.

Then Hobomock emphatically denied
   the Massasoit would betray the group
and he would not be secretly aligned
   with Narragansetts or the Massachusetts.

Their custom was to hold a large Powwow
   with local Sachems and the Pnieses too.
For Ousamequin to have left him out
   was something Ousamequin would not do.

He was a Pniese and held an honored rank
   and what Tisquantum claimed could not be true.
If everyone at Plymouth was betrayed
   then Hobomock would have been betrayed too.

The Massasoit was a noble man.
   The honor that he held was well deserved.
For him to stoop and join with Corbitant
   would stain the dignity that he had earned.

The reasoning of Hobomock was clear
   and he had proven to be a good friend
and both the Captain and the Governor
   regarded all while they were listening.

The Governor explained they did not seek
    a war with any of the local tribes.
They sought their God and built with friends in peace
    and then he made a point to clarify:

"The thought that caused us all the most despair
    was Ousamequin may become our foe.
And this is not because we are in fear
    but rather that we all love him the most."

That night they all stayed on a careful guard
    but saw no signs nor heard of any threat
and nothing marred the peacefulness of stars
    till dawn poured daylight over their bowed heads.

The next day Hobomock's wife volunteered
    to run some errands to the local towns
and see if Narragansetts gathered near
    or if some threats were anywhere around.

They were concerned when she was gone for days.
    They feared she had been caught and held captive
but Hobomock was sure that she was safe
    and soon she had returned to the Pilgrims.

She said that she went up to Nemasket
    and didn't see a single Narragansett.
She didn't see the group with Corbitant
    or a conspiracy with Massachusetts.

Then as she spoke with people in the town
    she heard suggestions of some treachery
and there were rumors passing all around
    repeating lies of slander and deceit.

So she hiked forty miles out to Sowams
   in hopes that she could clear the foggy air
and see if Ousamequin was at home
   and hear what people were discussing there.

And in the village of the Massasoit
   they all responded every time she asked
— the Narragansetts and the Wampanoags
   had not joined forces for a sneak attack.

She asked to speak with Ousamequin then.
   He was enraged to hear what had been said.
He was an ally to their Pilgrim friends
   and would not violate the Compact made.

The Narragansetts were attacking them
   and proved to be a hostile enemy.
If he abused the trust of his good friends
   then he would put them all in jeopardy.

And then he sent his messengers around
   to find out more of what was going on
and when they had returned from different towns
   they learned Tisquantum had deceived them all.

Tisquantum claimed that he made war and peace
   and lied about the Pilgrims threatening them
and must rely on him for their safety
   and turn away from their local Sachems.

He told the villagers they'd be assailed
   by Pilgrims who had planned attacking them
and the attacks could only be curtailed
   if they gave opulent tribute to him.

He also said the Pilgrims had the plague
    and they could send it anywhere they will
and kept it buried in a secret case
    that they released to murder and to kill.

He told the Sachems that the Massasoit
    was helpless in providing their defense.
Only Tisquantum could provide protection
    from treachery that was a threat to them.

With this the wife of Hobomock returned
    with Ousamequin's message to his friends
— he would stand firm with his compacted words
    and faithfully expects the same from them.

Then Ousamequin held a big Powwow
    to let the Sachems and the Pnieses know
that they confirmed the Compact's loyal vow
    and that Tisquantum's lies had been exposed.

The Pilgrims also sent out messengers
    to clear the slander and the treachery
and let the Wampanoag villagers
    know their commitment to keep friendly peace.

Then after twists and turns of the delay
    they set the shallop for a trade envoy
and sailed off to the Massachusetts Bay
    engaged with every moment to employ.

Chapter 40

Saving Tisquantum / Ousamequin's Demand
May 1622

Returning from the Massachusetts Bay
    the shallop teetered through a blustery storm.
They made the beneficial trip for trade
    but there was no exchange of native corn.

The Massachusetts had no corn to spare
    but had been rich in trade of beaver pelts.
The Pilgrims made the most for travel's fare
    but their supply of food had gravely fell.

They were still learning to raise native corn
    but if their harvest yield could be increased
they could produce provisions to support
    effective trade with this commodity.

They took Tisquantum as interpreter
    although they closely watched how he behaved
and Standish was then able to converse
    with Hobomock in a laconic way.

But when they rowed back into Plymouth Bay
    Tisquantum was struck with a mortal fear.
As they approached the lapping shore that day
    he saw the Massasoit standing there.

The Pilgrims pulled the shallop to the beach
    unloaded pelts that they had gained in trade
and then Tisquantum made a desperate plea
    — they'd kill him if they carried him away.

Tisquantum carefully stayed far away
　　from noble Ousamequin and his men
and pleaded that the others keep him safe
　　and kept the Pilgrims between him and them.

The Massasoit Ousamequin stood
　　with Sachems from the nearby tribes he led
and speechlessly each person understood
　　they would not leave without Tisquantum's head.

Then as they stood together on the shore
　　with trusted Hobomock attending them
the Captain and the Plymouth Governor
　　spoke with the Massasoit and his men.

They all condemned Tisquantum's treachery.
　　He had betrayed his people and his friends
and tried to turn them into enemies
　　to cravenly obtain his selfish ends.

From this he proved that he had been a threat
　　for Wampanoags and the Pilgrims too
but since they found the wicked traps he set
　　the feeble threat he caused had been removed.

They needed him as an interpreter
　　to make sure they could still communicate.
For this he proved to be invaluable
　　ensuring they could neighborly relate.

Then Ousamequin made a quick reply
　　that made a point as sharp as his own knife
and he demanded that Tisquantum die
　　since everything Tisquantum said was lies.

The Governor then said this was not true.
　He had explained the Compact they attained.
Now that they had exposed Tisquantum's ruse
　they were alerted for deceptive taints.

When they considered what he did deserve
　they tried to stay the urge for vengeful spite.
There still was helpful purpose he could serve
　so he was able to redeem his life.

Yet Ousamequin would not hesitate
　and he demanded perfect satisfaction.
This was not time to circle in debate.
　The circumstance demanded direct action.

This forced a choice the Pilgrims had to make.
　They knew that if they let Tisquantum die
they would lose their means to communicate
　so they risked peace to save Tisquantum's life.

They said they willingly would vouch for him
　and if Tisquantum proved to be untrue,
Tisquantum would be turned over to them
　so Ousamequin could give him his due.

The Massasoit Ousamequin staid.
　He knew to take Tisquantum then by force
would cause them all unnecessary pain
　and would be taken as an act of war.

They all could see displeasure in his face
　but Ousamequin was too disciplined
to fly out of control in a hot rage
　and with some bitterness gave his consent.

There was no Calumet they passed around.
  No formal ceremony that was made
and with the Massasoit's heavy frown
    the group of Sachems turned and walked away.

There was an absence settled down on them,
  a lack of understanding and a void,
as then the Pilgrims stood in fogginess
    not knowing if they had made the right choice.

Chapter 41

The Sparrow's Shallop
May 1622

There was a sudden change the Pilgrims felt
    and from the woods they heard the mocking sounds
while they were working to maintain the fields
    and slander seemed to come from all around.

They were relieved that Hobomock had stayed.
    Tisquantum's execution was deferred.
But asking them what other Natives said
    they simply shook their heads without a word.

They could not break from work because of shame.
    They needed to prepare the season's corn.
They could not simply sit and pine away.
    Their victuals were exhausted from their store.

Then soon a local messenger was sent
    who asked to speak with Plymouth's Governor
and on the Massasoit's own behest
    he pressed Tisquantum's direct surrender.

The messenger went further to explain
    Tisquantum had been trying to make war
and turn their friendship into bitter hate
    and from their harmony create discord.

Through conference the Massasoit learned
    Tisquantum wanted both sides to explode
then as the towns and villages were burned
    Tisquantum would take over in control.

With Hobomock, the Governor replied
   the loyal friendship binding them together
withstood Tisquantum's tricks and had survived
   — confronting wickedness, their love proved stronger.

He said the aim was for security.
   The greatest danger was in vengeful rage.
Tisquantum served a purpose for their peace
   providing the means to communicate.

The Pilgrims felt the threat had been removed.
   They had exposed all of his wicked lies.
They felt his honest merit would be proved
   so they decided to preserve his life.

The messenger's frustration could be seen.
   He made a statement that was curt and plain,
that if Tisquantum had betrayed them once
   they should expect him to betray again.

Then in response the Governor explained
   that retribution often conflagrates
in the retaliations that are made
   and causes problems to perpetuate.

They did not seek to feed destructive flames
   nor leap into the fire in senseless rage.
A greater strength may be found in cool grace
   so people have a chance to change their ways.

With both sides putting in their argument
   and then without a resolution made
they firmly stuck with their resolved intent
   and for the time left what had been sustained.

After departure of the messenger
  they had a close and confidential talk.
The Captain, Brewster and the Governor
  asked for insight from noble Hobomock.

Then Hobomock weighed words to try to say
  the problems they were causing Ousamequin.
The Wampanoag Nation was betrayed
  and his authority may be in question.

Tisquantum was evading punishment.
  People could doubt the Massasoit's rule
and make a mockery of his judgement
  and Ousamequin would look like a fool.

They also know the Pilgrims were betrayed
  and that Tisquantum was deceiving them
and by them guarding and keeping him safe,
  it made them look both weak and insolent.

The Governor acknowledged the insight
  and recognized the dire predicament.
They hoped to spare someone the loss of life
  but then they caused another grave offense.

And tied in tangles of the knots cinched tight
  they saw the same trap that Tisquantum used,
provoking each side with offended pride
  and twisting honor to cause self-abuse.

There lies the narrow path to find the means
  between what people feel and think and see
with the projections of convinced belief
  all whirling in concrete reality.

They all looked deep into the mystery
  and the perplexities of the whole world
and all those gathering had to agree
  they had to keep the faith and to endure.

The messenger returned within a day
  and gave a statement from the Massasoit.
He said the Pilgrims made the choice to break
  the peaceful Compact with the Wampanoags.

With this the messenger went on to say
  that in respect of love for his dear friends
the Massasoit offered to exchange
  Tisquantum for a trade of beaver skins.

At this the Pilgrims grievously refused.
  They knew the gesture was made in respect
but couldn't send their friend off to his doom
  and let Tisquantum die for their profit.

The Governor then offered to explain
  Tisquantum should receive his judgement due
but they felt that he had changed in his ways
  and ample time would let him prove this true.

And then the messenger asked where he was,
  he had been hiding where no one could see
and if Tisquantum truly was then just
  then they must see before they would believe.

Tisquantum was then brought from where he hid
  and saw the group that gathered for the talk
and flagrantly denied all that he did
  and then began accusing Hobomock.

As Hobomock began to shake his head
　　the messenger looked very satisfied.
He thought Tisquantum was already dead
　　and then unwrapped the Massasoit's knife.

He said that in accordance to their custom
　　Tisquantum's head and hands would be chopped off
and then he would return to meet the Sachems
　　and show what had been done to right the wrong.

He said they would still pay the beaver skins
　　but as the Pilgrims were getting prepared
to hand Tisquantum over to the men,
　　they would not take the payment for the fare.

Then suddenly they heard someone announce
　　a boat was sailing right before the bay
and everyone was called back into town
　　and Bradford told the messenger to wait.

They can't be foolish killing one another
　　when there may be a risk of an attack.
They needed to see if this ship was trouble
　　and so they chose to hold Tisquantum back.

The messenger and men were boiling hot
　　and left in more frustration than before.
They thought the issue certainly resolved
　　and then had disappointment to report.

Tisquantum was led back into the house.
　　They still were holding him in custody
and armed and ready at their posts' lookouts
　　they watched the boat that sailed in from the sea.

Chapter 42

Thomas Weston's Deception
May 1622

The shallop rested in the small harbor
   and men on board gave English salutations
and asked as several waded to the shore
   if this was Plymouth and the new plantation.

They said they were of Thomas Weston's men
   and sailed the *Sparrow* fishing to the north
and they had letters for the settlement
   to be delivered to the Governor.

John Carver was the letters' addressee
   — they still did not know that John Carver died.
The isolation of the colony
   was just as desperate as their supplies.

The visitors could see the town was built
   with diligence and thoughtful industry
but careful planning could not yet refill
   the store of food they had been rationing.

They had been fair to the new members sent
   and made adjustments to disperse the store
but rations that remained were nearly spent
   and there were months before they'd harvest more.

The Governor then pulled the men aside
   to speak in earnest with them privately
and asked them if they brought any supplies
   as Thomas Weston's letters were received.

But standing round the planters all could see
    as Bradford asked the visiting party,
the visitors all shrugged perplexedly
    as they were unaware of desperate need.

And then the Governor turned to the group
    to let the planters know what he had learned
and as he soberly relayed the news
    he watched reactions as the others heard.

"Our friends who have arrived came in a ship
    that currently is fishing to the north.
The shallop is supplied for just this trip,
    but hopefully the larger ship has more.

"They also brought more people who will stay"
    at this the other's made a grumbling sound,
"and we will warmly welcome them today
    as they will add more strength to our small town.

"The Council now will join me to review
    the letters from investors that arrived
and after we have been informed with news
    we'll send our shallop up for fresh supplies."

The promise of supplies evoked a cheer
    refreshing with the openness of hope
that gave relief from burdens of despair
    — the worried weight of a deflected load.

The Council gathered with the Governor
    but Weston's letters gave them no good news.
He didn't send supplies with his report
    but he was generous with his abuse.

The letters said investors were upset
  and they refused to send supplies and tools
to build and manage the new settlement
  until the Pilgrims proved they could produce.

Then Weston said that he was sending men
  – the men who had arrived that very day –
and said the Pilgrims should provide for them
  and give them any salt that may remain.

He said that he would send another ship
  that would deliver about sixty more
and to receive them at the settlement
  as they would also need providing for.

They hoped by now the *Fortune* had returned
  so the investors saw the gains they made
but reading Weston's harsh and bitter words
  it was like he described a different place.

There was another letter Weston wrote
  also in January of that year
that stated the investors gave up hope
  and were preparing cutting themselves clear.

Then leading them along the twisting turns
  the letter said the settlement should break
from the investors and conditions' terms
  since they were all abandoned anyway.

And then confirming in a separate letter
  all of the statements Thomas Weston claimed
the signatures of eight London investors
  expressed the plans to end agreements made.

Another letter said of what occurred
  in dreadful messages from fishermen
where Natives in Virginia massacred
  hundreds of people in a settlement.

Inside the home of the town's Governor
  the Council read the letters passed around
and even though their solemn hearts were torn
  their ties together would not be unbound.

The Governor then rose upon his feet
  and stood before the other's downcast seats
and lifted tension like a canopy
  that swelled like sails with his delivered speech:

"We have been facing many obstacles
  that are not from our fault or our neglect
yet still we know we are responsible
  in answering conditions where we live.

"Let's hope the *Fortune* has returned by now
  and the investors will see our produce.
We know the work we have put in this town
  and Weston's criticism is undue.

"He may have baited some merchants away
  but dozens more did not endorse that letter
so most of the investors were retained
  and others will return in fairer weather.

"We must tell others of the massacre
  and take precautions everyone is safe
and do whatever we can to deter
  hostilities with our defenses made.

"We should withhold the letters Weston sent
    as they're confused with rancorous abuse
and he is doing what Tisquantum did
    — disrupting with deceitful subterfuge.

"Right now we are in an alarming need
    as all the food we stored is nearly gone.
More people have arrived than we can feed
    and we must take immediate action.

"The men who came today have no supplies
    but at Monhegan where they set to fish,
they said in each direction set nearby
    there are no less than thirty other ships.

"The Captain needs to stay for our defense
    and Edward Winslow will sail to Monhegan
and take our shallop with some other men
    to ask the ships if they can spare provisions.

"We'll have to take the bills on our account
    but spare no cost as famine soon will strike
and honestly agree to asked amounts
    — the greater debt would be the loss of life."

Chapter 43

More Rationing
June 1622

So Winslow and some men wasted no time
   and fit the shallop and set off on course
and through the flux of storms of the spring time
   they had a distant journey to the north.

After a couple weeks, Winslow returned.
   They found the fishing ships of Monhegan
and making sure they went to each in turn
   they sailed and rowed around the whole island.

He said the Captains of the ships were kind.
   They took no bills and gave what they could spare
but all of them were also in a bind
   as none of them had much surplus to share.

But as they visited the scattered ships
   they managed to acquire biscuits and bread
to fill the shallop for the return trip
   in hope that all their numbers could be fed.

The people then were crowding at the boat
   appearing like they had no food for days
and verged upon the loss of all control
   as their restraint was starved and desperate.

The Governor then quickly intervened,
   reminding everyone of decency
and they passed out the portions orderly
   less everything be spoiled rapaciously.

Then as each person had a hardy meal
    the Governor stood up front to explain
that Winslow and the others had done well
    but they must follow a strict rationing.

There were almost a hundred mouths to feed
    and harvest time was half a year away.
They had to make sure everyone could eat
    and all together they would be sustained.

They'd keep the bread secured within a store
    then evenly provide portions each day
so each received the same and nothing more
    or else they would all starve in a few days.

As Bradford spoke to everyone in town
    each person saw that he was looking lean
and no one in the crowd could have a doubt,
    he too was sticking with the rationing.

And following the wisdom of the lead
    of Governor John Carver who had passed,
as Bradford was elected the town head
    he must be satisfied with what was last.

As Captain Standish led them in courage
    and Elder Brewster led them all in faith
so Bradford knew for the town to be saved
    in times of dearth he must lead in restraint.

Chapter 44

The Meetinghouse
June 1622

With Winslow's journey refilling the stores
   they had a sense of some stability.
The meager portions left them wanting more
   but famine was averted thankfully.

But when they had returned to tend the fields,
   they were reminded of the sour relations.
They saved Tisquantum so he wasn't killed
   and Wampanoags were infuriated.

They had been living in security
   of peace that was established and preserved,
their Wampanoag friends were visiting
   and their lives interacted undisturbed.

Before they walked at ease on forest trails
   and visited their neighbors frequently
but then they heard the taunting without fail
   and threats to cut them off because they're weak.

It seemed that the surrounding Wampanoags
   were agitating with intimidation
but they could not contact the Massasoit
   as he had ended all communication.

Tisquantum was in fear to leave the town
   and hearing of the recent massacre
with taunts and threats persisting all around
   the people in the town felt some concern.

The noble Hobomock faithfully stayed
   and proved to be a worthy, steadfast friend
objecting to the choice the Pilgrims made
   yet honoring Tisquantum in defense.

So they decided to strengthen defense
   and built a blockhouse on top of the hill
and sentries would be looking over them
   when they were working in the open fields.

Although it took them the whole month of June
   and the neglected crops were choked with weeds
they worked together lifting heavy booms
   on top the hill above the fields to see.

After the fort was solidly complete
   it served the Pilgrims' whole community
providing strength for their security
   — a larger Common House where they could meet.

And on the morning of the Sabbath day
   the Pilgrims would line up on Leyden Street
and three by three they walked along the way
   devout and silent in solemnity.

With Bradford, Brewster, Standish in the lead
   the long procession of community
strolled in commitment to their unity
   through the devotion of their families.

In ceremony of the sanctity
   they would ascend together Sabbath day
with the completion of another week
   and in their Meetinghouse thankfully pray.

With love and faith to bound integrity
    and courage, patience, fortitude for strength
and guided by obliged humility
    they rose on what they commonly achieved.

And the two buildings that were most revered
    — the Meetinghouse atop the hill was one
and then the other equally held dear
    — the building of each family's warm home.

Chapter 45

Charity
July 1622

That summer two ships Thomas Weston sent
  arrived at Plymouth harbor with the tide.
Informed, the Pilgrims were expecting them
  but were uncertain of what would transpire.

The *Charity* and *Swan* set anchor down
  and boats made shore with a large group of men
that felt like an invasion of the town
  although they thought the men were sent by friends.

Then Weston's brother Andrew asked out loud
  demanding words with the town's Governor
and William Bradford formally stepped out
  to meet the leader of the visitors.

Then Andrew asked where they could sit and speak
  as there were matters that they must discuss.
He needed somewhere to get off his feet
  and privately explain their business.

As the commotion settled in the town
  the Captain stayed to watch the group of men
and Bradford led Andrew into the house
  with Allerton and Brewster joining them.

And in politeness of diplomacy
  the Governor gave Andrew his own chair
and in the Pilgrim's honest courtesy
  they hoped that he would be forthright and clear.

The letters Thomas Weston sent before
   expressed his anger for the settlement
but they could prove the error of reports
   and greeted Andrew with civil respect.

There was no question of the work they'd done.
   The sturdy buildings stood along the street
and with his visit to the plantation
   Andrew could see their productivity.

They were established firmly in their seat,
   they built the basis where they could produce
and soon would fill the cargo of a fleet
   and prove the value of their proper use.

They would not burst with swollen, gloated pride.
   They stay well-grounded in their temperament
but their achievements could not be denied
   with concrete proof of their accomplishments.

Then Andrew Weston spoke severely
   after he squirmed to settle in the chair,
"As chief investor in the company
   my brother wisely quit everyone here!

"The disappointment of this settlement
   has proved to be beyond what can be saved.
With no returns in trust of money lent
   we have decided on another way.

"And of the minor merchants who remain
   they will not send you victuals or supplies
and have no interest to communicate
   until some terms agreed are satisfied.

"In fact you are indebted to my brother
 for shrewdly making these discoveries
and he suggests you break with all the others
 accounting the investor's treachery.

"Before departing, Thomas checked the ship
 and questioned all the passengers on board
to see if any sneaky things were shipped
 and went through all the gear that they had stored.

"He cornered one man whom he held suspect
 and found a letter that the man had hid.
Eventually he cowered and confessed
 and said it was something investors sent.

"He said they told him to buy some new shoes
 and sow the letter in between the seams
that doubtlessly will only go to show
 the lengths of their conniving treachery.

"So Thomas promptly broke the letter's seal
 and read along the script of crooked lines
and quickly learned why it had been concealed
 — the letter was completely filled with lies!

"Accusing him for blocking the supplies
 and any letters they tried sending through
and every statement is a shameful lie
 and for this Thomas wrote an answer too.

"I brought the letters I deliver here
 and you are welcome to read for yourself.
All that I said is written very clear
 and keep them with the books upon your shelf.

"In fact, from all the books that I can see
    I understand why you all do no work
all any of you do is sit and read
    and contemplate the topics of no worth.

"The *Charity* will soon sail further south
    as we deliver several passengers
and then until we sail back to Plymouth
    we'll need you to keep sixty visitors.

"We'll leave the visitors with their own food
    and make demands you leave their stuff alone.
They'll need to work with their supplies and goods.
    We trust that you all have food of your own.

"A number of them have been gravely ill
    so make some space inside your shabby homes.
Some others may be kind and merciful
    and help to tend your fields all overgrown.

"We know your wives have things for you to do,
    with your eyes closed and heads bowed in your church
and you can read and talk until your blue
    but we brought able bodied men to work.

"A group will sail the *Swan* up further north
    and find a place to make a settlement
and then we won't trouble you anymore.
    We'll be too busy with our working then."

When Andrew finished his coarse diatribe
    he tossed the letters at the Governor
and Bradford looked with scrutinizing eyes
    and asked about a member of the church.

"One of our friends worked closely with your brother,
  a deacon, Robert Cushman is his name
and we expected him to send a letter."
  Then Andrew raved he'd never known the man.

Then Andrew Weston returned to the ship
  and tossed off sixty rude men to the side
and then the *Charity* drew up the skiff
  and rode out on the ebbing of the tide.

Chapter 46

Strength in Weakness
July 1622

After the rowdy visitors were housed
   and their goods had been carefully secured
and the commotion had been settled down
   there was a meeting at the Governors.

The Governor was holding civil court
   with leaders of the town's community
on how to best address the new discord
   and reach agreement in assembly.

They had no room inside their private homes.
   The men were kept inside the common space,
then they would have a place set on their own
   to keep their goods and gear secure and safe.

The meeting with Andrew had not gone well.
   They were subjected to abject abuse.
They had a strong sense they had been assailed
   with exploitation and were being used.

They read the letters that Andrew had brought
   but nothing gave any sure clarity.
Apparently all the investors fought
   and rankled in their hot disparity.

First Thomas Weston blamed the other men
   but then the "letter in the shoe" brought in
had the investors blame the same of him
   and then the doubt was left on all of them.

And sadly all that seemed to be confirmed
    was that the shipment they had sent was robbed.
The *Fortune* had been seized before return
    and all the hard earned goods they sent were lost.

Then suddenly a knock upon the door
    evoked another shared perplexity
while wondering what more could be in store
    to trouble further the calamity.

As Winslow stood to answer who arrived
    the council members heedfully all turned
and as a Goodman Pilgrim stepped inside,
    they worthily allowed him to be heard.

The man explained a letter from his wife
    who had remained in England for sometime
had been brought by the ship that had arrived
    and he found something curious inside.

He said the envelope was marked for him
    and had been sent from his dear wife in London
but held a letter for the Council men
    and written by their Deacon Robert Cushman.

They gave the letter to the Governor
    who read the message while arching his brows
and then within the meeting's corridors
    he read the letter for them all out loud.

The deacon had to sneak the letter through
    and said the company has faith in them
but to beware of Thomas Weston's crew
    — he sent them to supplant the settlement.

He sold his interest in invested stock
    and was in conflict with the company
and everything they did he tried to block
    and had been raving with sour jealousy.

Then Cushman said that Weston's men were rude
    and try to keep them out of Plymouth town
and have Tisquantum spread the message too
    and warn about the group to tribes around.

Then earnest Thomas Peirce added a message
    "find strength in weakness through faithful belief"
in an allusion to the Bible's passage
    and from their weakness patiently build strength.

And with the reading of the Governor
    they were relieved that Cushman was ok.
The *Fortune* had been robbed but reached the port
    and all the crew and passengers were safe.

They thanked the man for his intelligence
    in bringing them the message Cushman wrote.
They all were in a big predicament
    but they had some assurance from the note.

The Council then discussed the situation
    and all decided to house Weston's men
and hopefully the kind accommodations
    would kindle the warm goodness within them.

As Fuller would assist the sick to mend
    they'd help the men to set off on their own
and soon they'd move to their own settlement
    as they set out exploring on the coast.

They lost contact with Wampanoag tribes
    but other matters forced them to attend.
They would rebuild relations in due time
    and would confirm the Compact with their friends.

The blockhouse on the mount had been complete.
    They'd feel more safe out working in the fields.
They had to clear the crops of choking weeds
    and hopefully ensure their harvest's yield.

So setting fretful worries to the side
    and focusing on what they truly need
and with their love dismissed the groans and gripes
    and welcomed the men in their company.

The sick amongst them rapidly improved
    and even though they were profane and rude,
they seemed to recognize that they were loved
    and all the jagged coarseness seemed to smooth.

In fact the kindness that the Pilgrims gave
    was well received and neighborly instilled
as many of the men seemed well behaved
    and volunteered to help out in the fields.

Chapter 47

Discovery
August 1622

Soon after, a small group of Weston's men
   sailed on the *Swan* to set off and explore
and find a new place for their settlement
   up north while they were coasting on the shore.

Of those who had remained in Plymouth town
   the Pilgrims gave the best accommodations
and though there were some frowsy matters found
   they took the brunt to maintain good relations.

But as they diligently tended corn
   they noticed damage to their growing crops.
The ears still green were broken off and torn,
   that looked suspiciously like sabotage.

And of those who had volunteered to help
   the Pilgrims saw them breaking ears from stems
as if ensuring that the harvest failed
   as spoiled green corn could never ripen then.

They secretly reviled the grace received
   and thought the succor proved the Pilgrims weak,
absurdly credulous beyond belief,
   too dumb to know the company they keep.

Then growing bold the men would smear the town
   and criticize the gross incompetence
of everything that was already done,
   dismissing it as insignificant.

While learning more about the men's contempt,
   the Pilgrims chose to focus on their work.
It served no purpose for them to resent.
   They simply took the measures to preserve.

They'd burn themselves if they became enraged
   and this would sorely take them from their toils
and what they did not carefully maintain
   would bitterly and negligently spoil.

If they were mocked for honoring their wives
   and caring for their family and friends,
they knew the criticism was from spite,
   such criticism is its own offense.

If others hold contempt for unity
   and disregard the proper thoughtfulness
then they can build their own community
   and comfort themselves in resentfulness.

The Pilgrims patiently endured the men
   and let them be decently entertained
so when they had found their own settlement
   they merrily could go on their own way.

In time the *Swan* and *Charity* returned
   and moved the men to Massachusetts Bay
but left to rest those that remained infirmed
   whom Fuller mended till their health regained.

The others soon recovered strength and health
   through hospitality and Fuller's care
but gave no thanks for any of the help
   and wellness seemed to agitate them more.

The *Charity* had left the men supplied
    with loads of food, commodities and tools
and even though the Pilgrims were denied
    they would not dither and be Weston's fools.

The men had plotted out a new location
    and would need their supplies to settle down
but without leadership and sound relations
    they'd have a struggle to maintain the town.

And groups without a trusted leadership
    that stir within confusion of a crowd
can storm to take control of a sound ship
    but soon will ask for help in bailing out.

The Pilgrims faithfully plod on their own
    and built themselves up for the next harvest
but rationed bread they had was almost gone
    and crops were shot from the men's viciousness.

Then Plymouth had a fortunate surprise
    as the lean Pilgrims faced more famished straits,
the English ship *Discovery* arrived
    and dropped the anchor in the Plymouth Bay.

Some say the ship was sent by Providence,
    to answer prayers for the town's benefit
and others say it was sheer stubbornness
    — the Pilgrims' staunch refusal to give in.

But Andrew Weston ranted bitterly
    when *Charity* sailed to Virginia
and railed on Plymouth with disparity
    and how the company had given up.

And on the way to England in return
   the Gentleman John Pory was aboard
who served Virginia a three year term
   as Secretary of the Governor.

With all that Weston said about the town
   he thought that he would check it out himself
to see if it was really falling down
   and if the colony was beyond help.

And while he toured the town he was impressed
   and recognized the planning and the skill.
Of all the new towns he had visited
   he had not seen another better built.

And entertained in Elder Brewster's house
   he browsed the studied titles of the books
and Brewster gave him one he pointed out
   — a commentary on the *Pentateuch.*

And after speaking with the Council men
   along with the town's faithful Governor
he said he would speak honestly of them
   and properly inform the investors.

And with the ship the Pilgrims made some trade
   although the prices were extremely high
and with the beaver pelts they made exchange
   for trade commodities to help get by.

And with the challenges that were imposed
   and hardships dumped upon the settlement
the slander Weston openly had told
   turned out to be the best advertisement.

Chapter 48

Thankless Giving
Autumn 1622

In time, the autumn harvest yields were low
    and as they gathered the surviving ears
they had the seed for the next time they sow
    but faced another famine the next year.

Recalling harvest time the year before
    with the abundance and the festival
they shared in plenty and packed full the store
    and were prepared for winter's interval.

But all that they had done responsibly
    to settle down and slowly pay their debt
was given in return calamity
    and now ill will had spoiled the fields they set.

Each day they rose to do their tasks and toils
    and saw the slow development each day
but as they nurtured fruits from gritty soil
    the promise of a prize was snatched away.

And from the Compacts they had made before
    relations with the local tribes were strained
and Weston's men had started stealing corn
    and so the Massachusetts were enraged.

But as they patiently worked through the fields
    the Governor in front to lead them on
the baskets for the corn were slowly filled
    but scarcely would sustain them till next fall.

The Governor could not dismiss the need
    as they were still confronting starvation
but could not simply coddle misery
    but strengthened their resolve to overcome.

So when the harvesting had been complete
    and they put seed and surplus in the store
they gathered for a spare Thanksgiving feast
    far from the opulence the year before.

Yet after the strict rationing that year
    with grumbling bellies that could not be filled
they gathered family and friends up near
    and once in a long time had a full meal.

Then soon thereafter Weston's men returned.
    They sailed into the harbor on the *Swan*
and even with the bridges they had burned
    they had to tell the Pilgrims of their want.

Of the provisions *Charity* had left
    they had begun to run low on supplies.
The buildings in the town were almost set
    but they would need more food in the meantime.

They also heard the Pilgrims had been furnished
    with fresh new stock of trade commodities.
They needed those supplies to make some commerce
    and Thomas Weston would repay the fees.

Some people hold the Pilgrims were austere
    but in the face of this absurdity
this wild proposal would have stirred up laughter
    if this was not too sad for comedy.

As Weston's men were waiting for reply
   the Plymouth Governor clearly explained
that their supplies were purchased at a price
   and they refused to throw them all away.

The men were offered kindness while they stayed.
   The Pilgrims had respected goods they brought
and in return the Pilgrims had been paid
   sour malice of a sabotaging plot.

And although Weston's men were critical
   and made a mockery of Pilgrim ways
their own ways were not proving viable
   as all their goods were squandered into waste.

And from their settled town at Wessagusset
   the men caused trouble with the Native tribes
and they were stealing corn from Massachusetts
   and burning friendships with their flagrant crimes.

The Pilgrims did not want the men to starve
   but Weston's men needed to change their ways.
They needed to take matters in regard
   and operate so they could be sustained.

The Pilgrims offered to make an agreement
   that by combining their commodities
they'd show the profits they had been achieving
   through benefits of honest courtesy.

They'd take the *Swan* out on the trip for trade,
   the boat of Weston's men was much more large,
but for the trip that they agreed to make
   the Pilgrims would direct and be in charge.

The Governor was sure to make the point
    that they would take the others as a favor.
They did not need to take this trip in joint
    but hoped they all could learn to work together.

So Standish was appointed to command,
    Tisquantum was the group's interpreter
and with the volunteers of the good men
    they fitted up the *Swan* for the venture.

Then loading up they would sail to the south
    off of the Cape and in the open sea
and find a passage they had heard about
    through the Cape shoals for their further journeys.

Chapter 49

The Shoals
November 1622

Two times they tried to venture on the *Swan*
    and two times they were turned back for delays,
the first time they were blown back by fierce winds
    the second – sickness caused Standish to stay.

Persistently, the joint group tried a third
    and while stout Captain Standish had been ill
the trip was led by Plymouth's Governor
    and they left in November's autumn chill.

Then sailing on the *Swan* out to the sea
    with Plymouth's shallop tied behind in tow
they sought to broaden opportunities
    and hoped to sail beyond the Cape Cod shoals.

Tisquantum said there was a passage through
    as he had sailed on French and English ships
and this would give them an efficient route
    to broaden their expanding partnerships.

Then venturing beyond the sheltered cape
    they sailed along the edge of the deep sea
and set off from the roar of the surf's break
    they tacked their course and zigzagged steadily.

Then when they had approached the Cape Cod shoals
    a group climbed in the shallop to explore
and nimbly sound the depths as the crew rowed
    to find the place Tisquantum passed before.

It was a tedious and baffling task
　　to venture out and find a novel way
where often forward steps redouble back
　　and disappointment wearily frustrates.

To plot and chart a safe and steady path
　　through situations that remain unknown
requires a patient and persistent tact
　　in hope to do what has not yet been done.

If one insists on rushing to desire
　　one is advised to stick with well-worn roads
and in conventional ways to retire
　　to find the well-established set of goals.

But in accepting greater challenges
　　persistence is required for the bold quest
while keeping balance that is delicate,
　　with no assurance there will be success.

Yet through devotion something is achieved
　　although it may not be intended aims
and in some way each venture is received
　　and the exertion strengthens all the same.

Although the Pilgrims found this to be true,
　　this was the way they managed to survive,
this was not recognized by Weston's group
　　and without patience they began to gripe.

Without a vision for a greater goal
　　they sought to gratify their simple needs
and satisfied with their short-sighted spoils
　　demanded everything immediately.

As Weston's men were nagging tirelessly
   and quibbled about every single thing
the Pilgrims worked the task methodically
   and tried to bear the others gracefully.

Then as the light of day began to wane
   Tisquantum guided them far from the shoals
and harbored in the Manamoyick Bay
   to find a place to make a camp on shore.

Tisquantum and the Governor then set
   out on the tiny boat off of the *Swan*
and on the land they courteously met
   some of the area's inhabitants.

At first, the people skittishly would flee,
   they'd never met the Pilgrim's group before
but then Tisquantum was able to greet
   them pleasantly as a friendly neighbor.

The leaders were soon welcomed at the village
   and offered gracious hospitality
and in the pleasantry that they were given
   the Pilgrims offered gifts respectively.

And as they were together entertained,
   enjoying one another's company,
they soon began negotiating trade
   and offered and received agreeably.

Then soon the leaders had returned to camp
   and brought some venison as a warm treat
to illustrate a point to Weston's men
   of ways to conduct business properly.

All day while carefully sounding the shoals
    they mocked the Pilgrims for incompetence
but then while Weston's men sat on the shore
    they couldn't even cook their own corn mush.

Then with the contact that the Pilgrims made
    for dinner they could enjoy venison
and this itself would properly explain
    how good relations serve their benefit.

And even if that meal did not convince
    the next day they would have nothing to say
while they were busy loading up the ship
    with barrels full of corn they made in trade.

The Pilgrims would not fret in argument.
    They did not tease or rile in childish fun.
They simply worked in earnest diligence
    and answered quietly with what they'd done.

So in the evening they enjoyed the meal.
    The next day offered more tasks to complete.
And through the obligations that they filled,
    they found fulfillment in their industry.

Chapter 50

Tisquantum, the Passing of a Friend
November 1622

On the next morning, they arose from sleep
  with prospects for some gratifying work.
They needed to retrieve the corn and beans
  and then deliver trade goods in return.

The volume made for a demanding task
  to load the food into the vessel's hold.
They had enough to fill at least eight casks,
  each one held over sixty gallons full.

They filled the shallop on the beach with ease.
  The challenge was to load this on the ship.
They lifted bags to other's downward reach
  while balancing so the boat didn't tip.

And getting them all to cooperate,
  completing tasks indeed for their own good,
the leaders hoped the others would refrain
  from arguing and have respect for food.

They fastened down the cargo on the ship
  and diligently worked in the fair day
so that the food stayed dry for the long trip
  — when storms arrived, it would then be too late.

Conditions of the weather always change
  beyond prediction and anticipation
but negligence is how defeat is made,
  the victories are won through preparation.

The evening arrived with finished work.
The men were resting from their busy day.
The load of food was carefully secure
but still they needed to search out more trade.

They planned to try to find the pass again
so they could navigate through the Cape shoals
and to the south more partners could be made
and they could fill the ship with a full load.

Although this trade had brought a hefty haul
it couldn't nourish the two colonies
till harvest time in the next distant fall.
They had a lot of hungry mouths to feed.

In morning light the camp began to stir
as they arose from their recovered rest
but Bradford heard Tisquantum's feeble word
about his aching body and his head.

He tried to rise but barely sat upright
and was too weak to stand upon his feet.
He had been suffering through the whole night
and shivered as his clothes were soaked with sweat.

They brought fresh water so that he could drink
and let him drift back into gentle sleep
in hope to aid in his recovery
before continuing on their journey.

So they decided to stay one more day
and let their guide and friend Tisquantum rest
and they could mend their gear in the delay
while they allowed their friend to convalesce.

But on the next day he was still unwell,
　in fact his sore condition seemed the worse.
They gave him sassafras and other salves
　in hope to break his fever that had surged.

While they were waiting some complaints were heard
　and Weston's men insisted they should leave
— delaying for Tisquantum was absurd
　and they had heard of his past treachery.

They had protested about the Cape shoals
　and did not want to travel there again.
But now they argued that they need to go.
　They seemed unsatisfied with everything.

And Weston's men could skulk away and judge
　and they could all condemn him with abuse
but if they wanted to trudge with a grudge
　Tisquantum knew of their treachery too.

The Governor then pulled these men aside
　and told them they were acting coarse and rude.
Considering their friend Tisquantum's life
　he had more value than all of them proved.

Although he had offended with his faults
　he had assisted in ways of great worth.
Two days before they loaded corn they bought
　with his assistance as interpreter.

The Pilgrims focused on self-management
　and concentrated on development.
They had no place to caustically condemn.
　The strongest soul is able to forgive.

Tisquantum then was bleeding from his nose
and he pulled Bradford closer to his side
and Bradford carefully inscribed the notes
of last requests before his dear friend died.

Tisquantum's passing was a somber loss
to his close family and Pilgrim friends
and even though his death came as a shock
the bridge that his life opened did not end.

From distances they could not comprehend
the English and the Wampanoag Nations
approached and through a solitary man
two worlds were opened in communications.

On the next day the Pilgrims gathered round
and softly set Tisquantum in a grave
and as they covered him in the moist ground
his spirit rose in memories and prayer.

And in the sentience of passing time
of every moment's intersecting rays
there is a gentle resonance of life
as he is spoken of this very day.

Chapter 51

Returning from the Shoals
November 1622

With frequent storms and the loss of their guide
    the search for the passage would have to wait.
On icy winds, the winter had arrived
    and they returned to shelter in the Cape.

But needing to make more substantial trade
    before returning to the settlements
they stopped at common places on the way
    to pay some visits to established friends.

The first, their visit to the Massachusetts
    turned sour upon the sight of Weston's men
and Massachusetts spoke at length accusing
    the way the group had been abusing them.

Although the Massachusetts had received them
    the thought of Weston's men made them enraged.
The Pilgrims still attempted to appease them
    however trade could not be made that day.

So next they sailed across the Cape Cod Bay,
    a distance from the town of Wessagusset,
in hope that they succeed again in trade
    with Sachem Aspinet who governed Nauset.

And here they were received hospitably,
    sustaining trade for common benefit.
They had resolved the past hostilities
    and were confirming worth in partnership.

Then loading up at least eight casks of corn,
    they packed the shallop on the sandy beach
and mentioning the troubles from before,
    the Pilgrims showed the benefits of peace.

The Pilgrims then described the First Contact,
    the Nausets had assumed they were a threat,
then fending off an earlier attack,
    the Pilgrims turned the Nausets into friends.

They chose the ways to meet and interact
    in countless ways they could communicate.
They could destroy each other with attacks
    or build together through their honest trade.

At Nauset they had gained about the same
    as they had gained before at Manamoyick
and normally the same could have been made
    in trade with people of the Massachusetts.

Since Weston's men destroyed what had been built
    by acting desperately as wanton thieves,
they filled their bellies with their rotten guilt
    instead of wholesome food that they all need.

The patient Pilgrims then would need to work
    so good relations could again be raised
from what the Wessagusset men had burned
    then beneficial trade could be regained.

The Pilgrims were resolved for moving on
    and hoped to make with everyone they meet
relationships that each side could build on
    by finding ways where both sides could agree.

Then next they sailed to visit Mattachiest
    upon the southern shore of Cape Cod Bay
and towed the shallop filled with corn from Nauset
    and hoped that they continued making trade.

Then on the tiny boat off of the *Swan*
    Winslow accompanied the Governor
although the boat's repairs were so forgone
    they feared they'd sink before they reached the shore.

Then meeting with the Sachem of the town
    they sat together to negotiate
and passing terms of the discussions round
    they were able to make another trade.

But then before they could communicate
    to bring the Pilgrims' shallop to the shore
the pressure of the air dropped with a weight
    in heavy clouds of an approaching storm.

They saw the water rearing up with waves
    and then the *Swan* tried to make an escape
and cut the shallop as a castaway
    to clear far from the shore's wave crashing break.

Although the storm brought heavy pounding rain
    the Governor and Winslow did not run
both drenched, they stood at the edge of the bay
    to keep sight of the shallop and the *Swan*.

But in the veil of distance blurred with grey
    the two began to fear the men were lost
and as the storm cleared later on that day
    the *Swan* and Plymouth's shallop both were gone.

The locals helped them search along the shore
 and found the place the shallop ran aground.
The careful packing of the beans and corn
 was fortunately dry and snuggly bound.

They asked the Sachem if his town could watch
 the corn and shallop until they returned.
They'd need to bring some tools so they could patch
 the damaged shallop with their carpenter.

They said that they would pay a nice reward
 if people in the town kept the corn safe
and asked if someone could guide them toward
 their town a distance fifty miles away.

And with a guide, both of the men walked back
 and in their town after three worried days
like facing headwinds with a skillful tack
 they saw the *Swan* return to Plymouth Bay.

Then from the numbing sense of loss they felt
 the blocking wall was suddenly transformed
into the welcome of a festival
 as they divided up the beans and corn.

1623

Chapter 52

Weston's Settlement Fractures
February 1623

In February there was more bad news
  of Weston's settlement at Wessagusset.
The settlement was a disastrous ruin
  and they had problems with the Massachusetts.

The *Charity* had left them with supplies
  — tools, victuals and commodities for trade
but that was squandered in a few months' time
  and all they had was lost in desperate waste.

The Pilgrims took them on a trade journey
  in hope to help them with necessities
and used all of their own commodities
  they purchased from the ship *Discovery*.

All Weston's men were capable and strong
  and they were given fair and equal shares
but then their portions were already gone
  and they had fewer people in their care.

In fact the Wessagusset settlement
  was at a better site than Plymouth town
— a better harbor to receive shipments
  more fishing, hunting and more fertile ground.

The Pilgrims hoped to teach diplomacy
  and proper ways of trade for sustenance.
These lessons proved out of the rude men's reach.
  They first needed to learn self-management.

And since they could not hold themselves together
   and couldn't finish anything they'd start
with buffets from the changing of the weather
   inevitably they had fell apart.

As Hobomock relayed what he had heard
   from rumors that had passed from town to town
the Pilgrims were both saddened and disturbed
   how Weston's settlement had fallen down.

They sounded to be truly destitute.
   Some men were dying, exposed to the cold
as they were in such wont for lack of food
   they stripped themselves and then they sold their clothes.

Some had begun to do the simplest tasks,
   out fetching water, chopping wood and more,
and answered lazy whims that they were asked
   for nothing more than a cap full of corn.

Others continued flagrantly to steal
   and creeped through night and sneaked throughout the day
and they were pressed to hang one of their men
   to pacify the Massachusetts' rage.

Some had abandoned houses that were built
   to forage ground nuts on the forest floor
and dug through summer's leaves that long had fell
   and scrounged subsistence desperately outdoors.

Others were digging clams up at the shore
   and one had been so weak trudging through mud
he couldn't pick his feet up anymore
   and others found him dead where he got stuck.

The Massachusetts held them in contempt
   and made a mockery of their sad ways
and treated them with caustic insolence
   and made a comedy of their disgrace.

The food some stashed and selfishly had kept,
   the Massachusetts dug up and then stole,
then snatched their blankets from them while they slept
   and left them shivering out in the cold.

In February, Plymouth had received
   a letter from the chief of Weston's men
that stated Wessagusset's desperate need
   and written with John Sander's script and pen.

John Sanders said he'd travel for some help
   at Eastward on the island Monhegan
but as they fit the *Swan* so it could sail
   there was some more advice that he had needed.

He said that he had tried to borrow corn
   so he'd provide his starving men with food
till he could bring more back to keep in store
   but then the Massachusetts had refused.

He asked the Governor for his advice.
   The Massachusetts would not loan the corn
and did not care if they were going to die.
   He thought that they should take the corn by force.

Then they would gain the food they sorely need
   and he could keep his men all pacified
and then upon the *Swan* he could retrieve
   a boat load more to keep them satisfied.

By this the Governor was quite incensed
    at the impertinence that Sanders showed
as his men piled offense upon offense
    with everything they spoiled and filched and stole.

So Bradford wrote John Sanders a reply
    that Weston's men must act responsibly
and buckle their own straps until they're tight.
    They've made enough disruptions of the peace.

The Massachusetts were already mad
    that Weston's men were pilfering their crops.
They were destroying partnerships they had
    and their disgraceful ways needed to stop.

Then Bradford wrote that Sanders should soon sail
    to Eastward where he can obtain supplies
then carefully ration the food until
    they could provide for themselves to get by.

They did not want to ignore Weston's men
    but like the ships caught in the storms at sea
if they are tied, they begin battering,
    and both will be at risk of foundering.

Chapter 53

Visit to Sowams
March 1623

In March a messenger ran into Plymouth
  and urgently requested Hobomock
as the Pilgrims' friend carefully listened
  they saw him sadden as the other spoke.

Then when the messenger swiftly departed
  with words that Hobomock gave in return
the noble Pniese stood silently despondent
  and pondered heavy news that he had heard.

The Governor and Winslow stood nearby
  as Captain Standish had gone to Pamet
and waited for their friend to make reply
  and tell them of the news that troubled him.

Then Hobomock lifted one of his hands
  and held the shoulder of the Governor
and from his gaze the men could understand
  the weight of news brought by the messenger.

Relaying what had touched him with a chill
  the somber voice of Hobomock then said
that Ousamequin had been gravely ill
  and some feared he may already be dead.

He said they needed to go to Sowams.
  It was a matter of dire urgency
and as they learned more of local customs
  the Governor and Winslow both agreed.

They must show their respect to their close friend
    and reach his home before it is too late
and with the others they could strengthen him
    providing love and their medical aid.

So Hobomock and Winslow were prepared
    and then John Hampden also volunteered
— from London, he stayed with them for a year
    and proved to be a worthy visitor.

Then surgeon Fuller gave them some advice
    and handed them a bottle they would need
and Winslow's wife also pulled him aside
    and gave him a confection remedy.

Then having everything that they would need,
    they set off on the trail without delay.
They had before them a lengthy journey
    and needed to make time in light of day.

And as they hurried through the forest trees
    that stood upon the rolling rounds of hills
they hopped the fallen logs and leaped the streams
    and kept a pace as brisk as mountain rills.

Then crossing on the mud of a hill's bank
    on the slick steps Winslow fell on his pack
and sadly they heard Fuller's bottle break
    but at that point they could not double back.

By night they reached the town of Nemasket,
    a place where Winslow frequently had been
and they were able to stop for a rest
    before they rushed off on the path again.

And then within a few miles of Sowams
   they reached a ferry at the waterway
and they looked for someone who could boat them
   — the water was too wide and deep to wade.

Then Winslow fired his musket to announce
   and summon anyone out of their view
and some men who lived in a nearby house
   arrived to carry them in a canoe.

They knew the Sachem Corbitant lived close
   and they were travelling through his domain
and felt that he still thought them to be foes
   although they did not think of him the same.

They were not there because they looked for trouble,
   they came with hope that they could help their friend
and honoring the noble Massasoit
   they'd keep the peace in their respect for him.

But when the men with the canoe arrived
   they bore some mournful news along the way
— the Massasoit had already died
   and he was buried earlier that day.

This news then struck them like a thunderbolt.
   The sudden shock set their hair up on end.
Of any blast, by far the hardest blow
   is from the loss of family and friends.

They also knew that Corbitant was next
   to be appointed as the Massasoit.
They knew that this would probably upset
   the Pilgrims' Compact with the Wampanoags.

They were nearby the village Mattapoisett,
    the town governed by Sachem Corbitant
and Winslow said that they should make a visit
    in hopes that they could make their peace with him.

Both Hobomock and Winslow knew the risk.
    They were attacked by Corbitant before
and he took Hobomock as a captive
    yet fortunately peace had been restored.

But Winslow felt they shouldn't back away.
    They had this single opportunity
to meet and hopefully communicate
    and peacefully divert hostility.

Then Edward Winslow carefully explained
    to make sure that John Hampden understood
that they were stepping into danger's way
    and they may be walking straight to their doom.

Then Hampden said he fully understood
    and that he must stay carefully composed
and knew that any nervous misstep could
    send everything veering out of control.

Then Winslow emphasized their stay of arms.
    They'd only fight if they were attacked first.
They'd make no signs to cause others alarm
    but were prepared to entertain the worst.

Then Winslow said that if they were ambushed
    then Hobomock should try to get away
and if they had to face a sudden rush
    he'd be the one most able to escape.

Then he could warn the people back at Plymouth
   so they would know to make themselves prepared
until they knew who would be Massasoit
   in hopes that the Compact could be repaired.

But this was all a careful preparation
   and hopefully there would not be a need
to scatter in a frantic separation
   — this venture was in hopes to keep the peace.

Then with this explanation the men turned
   committed all together to move on
and without certainty to feel assured
   their courage and their faith carried them on.

They knew this was a very narrow path
   and it was doubtful that they would survive
but in their efforts to maintain the peace
   they willingly put their lives on the line.

As they were on the trail to Mattapoisett
   the noble Hobomock abruptly stopped
and he began a grieving lamentation
   as if there was a vision that he saw.

"Neen womasu Sagimus" he called out
   as if the words were burning in his heart
"My loving Sachem" again — sad and proud,
   as if the words were tearing him apart.

Then turning, Hobomock said to Winslow
   in tones that were both noble and lamenting
that there were many Sachems he had known
   but never anyone like Ousamequin.

He praised the Massasoit's honesty
  who never worked in ways of treachery.
He was a leader of integrity,
  a lofty Sachem of nobility.

He was not bloody like so many others.
  He did not punish in ways that were cruel.
He did not rage about with fiery temper
  and thoughtfully and fairly made his rule.

He was not easily disturbed or riled
  at times when others had caused him offense.
He would stay open to be reconciled
  and was not driven mad to seek revenge.

He governed others with far fewer strokes
  and led his people with his reasoned mind
and listened carefully when wisdom spoke
  and was attentive to hear good advice.

With those he loved, he truly gave his love
  and they could trust each statement that he made
and everyone relied on his resolve
  and were assured he never would forsake.

Then Hobomock said that he dearly feared
  the Pilgrims may not have another friend
as animosity was often heard
  he had restrained the malice against them.

When Hobomock had carefully explained
  a quiet sadness settled on the men
then Winslow looked up at the Pniese and said,
  "Hobomock, you too have been our faithful friend."

In early spring the branches were still bare,
  the ground was covered with the fallen leaves
and in the pause while they were standing there
  they heard the sweetened music of birds sing.

The situation that they faced was grave
  but nature had a lesson in the songs,
they must bear this and could not back away
  life has no choice but to continue on.

After a few more miles they reached the town
  and Hobomock saluted those he saw
but Sachem Corbitant was not around
  and he was with the others at Sowams.

They did not meet any hostility
  and as the villagers around them spoke
while Hobomock led them respectfully,
  they visited the Sachem's stately home.

Then briefly speaking with the Sachem's wife
  they asked if she had heard any new word
and if the Massasoit was alive
  and whether Corbitant would soon return.

She said she heard the Massasoit died
  and would know more later that afternoon.
They thought they'd know for sure before the night
  and they expected Corbitant back soon.

So Winslow and the others thought they'd wait
  and meet with Corbitant when he returned
but as the hours of day began to wane
  no one with news arrived or could be heard.

So Winslow hired someone as messenger
   to quickly run to Sowams and find out
and then hopefully they would know for sure
   right when the messenger returned to town.

They watched the sun descending from the sky,
   enduring the excruciating wait,
and they were thinking of the chill of night
   as it was getting later in the day.

The sun approached the low and flat horizon
   and shadows were outstretching on the ground
and as the day about them was expiring
   the messenger came running back to town.

He said the Massasoit was alive
   when he had spoken with those at Sowams
but they expected that he soon would die
   and wouldn't live to see tomorrow's dawn.

The men leaped up and stood upon their feet
   and grabbed their packs and other sundry things
then Winslow filled the man's hands full of beads
   and they were on their way at breakneck speed.

With daylight gone they travelled through the night
   and Hobomock led them through memory
along the path on threads of soft moonlight
   responding to a friend in urgent need.

Then out into the open at the town
   they ran up to the Massasoit's home
and they could hear the people wail out loud
   and the whole place was steeped with grieving moans.

The house was packed with crowds that stood around,
  the Sachems and the Pnieses from the tribes
and Hobomock led Winslow in the house
  and the crowd turned and parted in surprise.

The Massasoit lay fearfully weak.
  Then women desperately rubbed on his limbs
and Powahs danced and made spine chilling screams
  to scare the evil spirits out of him.

The Massasoit could no longer see
  and some nearby were whispering to him.
Then everyone was quiet suddenly
  and they said that it was the Englishmen.

Then as the crowd was clearing round the men
  so they stood out in Ousamequin's home
the Massasoit spoke to those near him
  demanding that they tell him who had come.

When Ousamequin heard Winslow was there
  he said that he desired to speak with him
and as Winslow began approaching near
  the Massasoit reached his hand to him.

When Winslow knelt by Ousamequin's bed
  the Massasoit blindly searched for him,
"Keen Winsnow" – "Art thou Winslow?" – he then asked
  to find out if it truly was his friend.

And as he made a clear response "Ahhe"
  to tell him "Yes" it was in fact Winslow
so that the Massasoit heard his speech
  and recognized the sound of his friend's voice.

Then wearily and somberly intoned
  he said, "Matta neen wonckanet namen
Winsnow" which was the saddened statement, "Oh,
  Winslow, I shall never see you again."

Then Winslow asked for Hobomock to come
  to translate all that needed to be said
and make sure Ousamequin understood
  the Governor had sent them with some aid.

Then as the trusted Hobomock explained
  the Massasoit thankfully agreed
and Winslow grabbed the small jar that contained
  his wife's confectionary remedy.

Then carefully on the tip of his knife
  the Pilgrim gave the blend of herbs and berries
between his clenching teeth to save his life
  as Ousamequin's health was sore despairing.

Inside his mouth the jam slowly dissolved
  and Ousamequin swallowed the sweet juice
and everyone was standing round enthralled
  as they could see how the confection soothed.

They'd been dejected in depressed dismay
  while watching Ousamequin suffering.
He hadn't eaten anything for days
  and this was the first hopeful sign they'd seen.

Then Winslow gently looked inside his mouth
  and saw it furred with swelling of the tongue
and Winslow scraped it clean and helped wash out
  to clear away corruption and the crud.

Then Winslow offered more of the preserves
   that Ousamequin ate with greater ease
and feeling the rough parching of his thirst
   the Massasoit asked to have a drink.

So Winslow mixed the remedy with water
   and stirred it carefully till it dissolved
and in a sipping bowl he tipped to offer
   refreshment for the Massasoit's pall.

In half an hour a noted change was made
   in how much Ousamequin had improved
and everyone who gathered was amazed
   and hope began to lift their downcast mood.

Then Ousamequin said that his lost sight
   had slowly started to return to him
and as he could discern the twinkling light
   this bolstered his strength with encouragement.

Then Winslow mentioned Fuller's medicine
   that had been in the bottle that was broke
and there were other things that would help him
   and he asked if some messengers could go.

He needed Fuller's medical advice
   and chickens so they could make a warm broth
to make sure Ousamequin was revived
   and fully cured of ailments he had caught.

Then while the messenger retrieved these things,
   if Ousamequin wished, Winslow would stay
until the messengers returned to bring
   what Ousamequin needed for his aid.

Then Ousamequin gratefully agreed
    and chose some messengers to send away
and Winslow wrote a list of what he'd need
    and the swift men would be back in two days.

The men were off some hours before the dawn
    and Winslow, Hobomock and Hampden stayed
and Winslow tried to make a simmered stock
    by cooking up the meal of native maize.

The Sachem had regained his appetite
    and asked for pottage that the English made
but he had not recovered yet that night
    — the Sachem's stomach was still delicate.

So with the help of ladies in the town
    they cracked the corn to boil a pot of meal
and Winslow searched until some things were found
    with properties that were medicinal.

He found some sassafras and dug the root
    and gathered handfuls of strawberry leaves
and made an herbal relish for the soup
    then strained it through his laundered handkerchief.

Then drinking all the bowl of broth they filled
    the Massasoit was regaining health
and then he mentioned others who were ill
    and asked if Winslow would provide them help.

Then Winslow went around the town that night
    and did the same for all that had been ill
and cured the infirmed from their ailing plight
    as dawn began to glow upon the hills.

Then later Ousamequin was asleep,
    the others said he hadn't slept for days
and when Winslow sat down off his tired feet
    he then collapsed exhausted just the same.

The great Sachem continued to improve
    and everyone was thankful for his health.
Then in the afternoon he had more food
    as he was hungry after his long rest.

Then later Winslow hunted goose and duck
    to make a batch of pottage for his friend
and with his steady aim and some good luck
    he bagged a duck and then returned again.

While Winslow slowly cooked the savory soup
    the Massasoit's appetite was piqued
with the aroma wafting through the room
    and scrumptious prospects of the meal to eat.

And as it proved the duck was very fat
    Winslow suggested that they skim the pot.
Although the Sachem's appetite was back
    his stomach was too tender for thick broth.

With this the others said they disagree
    and wanted to fill up the Sachem's bowl.
The Massasoit was especially
    insistent that he have the pottage whole.

Although Winslow thought it would be unwise
    he wouldn't tell the Massasoit – no.
He couldn't say something that would imply
    the Sachem didn't know of what he spoke.

Then Ousamequin had a hardy meal,
   a sight that pleased all those who stood around
and though the Sachem's appetite was filled
   he found he could not hold the supper down.

Then as he heaved the meal up violently
   the happiness was once again distressed
as Ousamequin's nose began to bleed
   which many of them thought the touch of death.

The Massasoit's nose then bled for hours
   and they all tried to make the bleeding stay
and as his health again was looking dour
   they said the Sachem should have been restrained.

Then Winslow was able to staunch the wound
   and everyone was settled with relief.
The quiet peace began to calm the room
   and Ousamequin drifted off to sleep.

Then Ousamequin slept for hours that day
   and when he woke he felt he was revived
and for refreshment Winslow washed his face
   with cloth sopped with fresh water from outside.

But when the Sachem leaned over the bowl
   to dip his face in water from the spring
he breathed the water up into his nose
   and coughing once again, began to bleed.

This time the Massasoit feared he'd die
   and once again the people were distressed
but Winslow reassured his friend this time
   it only was his nose's tenderness.

Then after Winslow stayed the blood again
   the Massasoit settled to relax.
He did not feel the soreness, aches and pains
   and all his strength and health was coming back.

The messenger returned later that day
   whom Ousamequin gratefully received
and since his full recovery was made
   he saved the chickens to keep them to breed.

And then with all his Sachems in attendance
   with Pnieses and the Powahs that he leads
the Massasoit focused their attention
   uniting them with his impassioned speech.

He said that only a few days before
   they told him to distrust the Englishmen
and that they could not be held to their word
   and that they never have been his true friends.

And just the day before they had arrived
   to help him when he was in the most need
their love was said to be but wind and lies
   and that they did not truly love in deeds.

He heard the bitter and the poisonous talk
   that friendship with them was no benefit
and simply let them bumble, slip and fall
   and give way to the others against them.

And then he said they proved their love was true
   in all the kindness they had given him
not just in what they say but what they do
   and for his life he will not forget them.

Then after he had made his noble speech
   he held a private council in his house
and keeping Hobomock and three close Pniese
   he then commanded everyone else out.

Winslow and Hampden were both standing round
   while Ousamequin counselled privately,
two English oddities mixed in a crowd
   with Wampanoag's own nobility.

Then Corbitant approached the Englishmen
   and Winslow did not know what to expect.
He might resent them more for what they did
   or maybe what they did earned his respect.

And speaking so Winslow could understand
   slowly pronouncing the Algonquin words
he asked the Englishmen to visit him
   before they needed to make their return.

Then my great uncle cordially agreed
   although he wondered if it was a trick.
The invitation was made trustfully
   and seemed to be in genuine friendship.

And as they felt to be with peers and friends
   they stood with all the others through the day
and waited for the private council's end
   to hear what Hobomock would have to say.

Chapter 54

Guests of Sachem Corbitant
March 1623

After the private council was complete
   the Sachems and the Englishmen were called
back in the Massasoit's house to meet
   so Ousamequin could speak with them all.

And reaffirming his commitment to
   the Compact with the Pilgrims that was made
he said their friendship had proved to be true
   and then bade that his Sachems do the same.

Then Ousamequin asked the Englishmen
   to thank the Governor for his kind love
and then offered his thanks to all of them
   as his health had dramatically improved.

Then Hobomock, Winslow and Hampden joined
   the Sachem Corbitant for a short visit,
and walked along the path back to his home
   nearby at his own village Mattapoisett.

Then Corbitant surprised them with a change.
   Before his character seemed made of stone,
imposing like a distant mountain range
   but now he showed more subtleties of tone.

He proved to be an entertaining wit
   and gestured to them in a jesting way
and tickled them with clever jokes and quips
   and reveled when the others did the same.

And then he made a direct inquiry
   and asked them what the Governor would do
if he was sick or suffered injury.
   Would Winslow also come and help him too?

And then without a slightest hesitation
   Winslow declared that without doubt he would.
They were friends with the Wampanoag Nation
   and they would prove their friendship for the good.

The Pilgrims wanted Corbitant's friendship
   extending neighborly development
and they hoped to confirm their fellowship
   in commerce, trade and mutual respect.

Then Corbitant welcomed them in his home
   and let them settle on the offered seats
and as he proved to be a proper host
   he then continued with his inquiry.

He asked Winslow if he had any fear
   for two of them to venture out alone
and journey distantly removed from far
   Patuxet where they built their town and homes.

And Winslow said there was no sense of fear.
   It was their love that was compelling them
and all that they had felt was deep concern
   for the well-being of their dearest friend.

Then curiously Corbitant observed
   if they were truly fearless as he said
then times before why did they stand at guard
   when Wampanoags visited their place?

And why would they fire muskets in the air
  at times before when they approached to meet.
He thought that it was signs that they were scared
  and did not know a better way to speak.

Winslow then said it was a salutation,
  a signal that their arms had been discharged,
a notifying message for attention
  in due respect and not to cause alarm.

He said it was a hail often conducted
  and ships would do the same on open sea
and times before Tisquantum had instructed
  to fire their pieces as a way to greet.

Then Corbitant made an important point
  — Tisquantum had said many different things
and he said things intended to distort
  and had said many things meant to deceive.

Of this Winslow acknowledged and agreed
  but then comparatively he explained
the Pnieses dress in their regalia,
  and greet extravagantly their own way.

Each man attended to the other's speech
  and Corbitant then offered his opinion
and shook his head to show he disagreed
  and said he did not like those salutations.

Soon after food was brought in for a meal
  and bowls were first set down before the guests
and Corbitant observed the men sat still
  and did not grab the food that had been set.

Instead they thanked the Sachem for the food
  and waited properly till he was served
and then they asked if Corbitant approved
  and gave the holy blessings they observed.

When food is offered in congenial treats
  and tasty flavors waft up with the steam
the most compelling instinct is to reach
  and grab and tear away something to eat.

But Corbitant was watching carefully
  and through the different customs and beliefs
he waited patiently so he could see
  the ways the English showed civility.

The English both sat with their heads bowed down
  and Edward Winslow said a solemn prayer
in the expressions humble and devout
  — a thankfulness for the attended care.

Then when the English lifted up their eyes
  they saw that Corbitant was watching them.
But Sachem Corbitant did not inquire,
  he nodded his head to acknowledge them.

Then lifting up his head with his closed eyes
  he raised his hands with broadly opened palms
and offered up his own thanks to the skies
  in sacred chanting of his native songs.

When Corbitant had finished his own prayer
  he opened his arms with a welcome wave
and as they all partook upon the fare
  the Sachem asked to whom the English pray.

Then Winslow told him stories about God
  and of creation and their preservation
and of devotion to the sacred laws,
  of grace and faith, forgiveness and salvation.

He told the Sachem of the Ten Commandments
  and Corbitant agreed that they were wise
although he had some questions of the seventh
  as he could not see having just one wife.

Then Winslow drew upon the verse of scripture
  for what the Ten Commandments truly said,
"Love thine God with all thine heart. Love thine neighbor
  as thyself." and then continued to explain:

"A husband would refuse to share his wife
  with any other man,
then how could man ever expect his wife
  to want to share him with another woman?"

And through the supper they discussed as friends
  each one's beliefs and then compared the two
and found that they had more agreements than
  the differences that others might construe.

Then Sachem Corbitant said that the God
  of which his friend Edward Winslow had spoken
was similar to what his people sought
  whom they called Kiehtan of the Wampanoags.

After they ate they passed the Calumet
  that circled round where they agreed to meet
and then contented, they retired to bed
  and softly settled down to sleep in peace.

At dawn the group quickly prepared to go
   and thanked the Sachem before heading back,
then Hobomock nodded to show Winslow
   an eagle feather was stuck in his hat.

Chapter 55

Hobomock Reveals the Plot against the Pilgrims
March 1623

After the group had travelled many miles
    then Hobomock came to a sudden stop
and carefully he pulled them to the side
    and said they urgently needed to talk.

During the private council that they had
    the Massasoit had instructed him
to let them know of a plot to attack
    all Weston's men and their own settlement.

He could not speak of this until assured
    they were alone in certain privacy
and not to say a word that could be heard
    by anyone outside the colony.

A group of Sachems of the Massachusetts
    was plotting with many surrounding tribes.
They're planning an attack on Wessagusset
    to kill all Weston's men whom they despise.

Since they're concerned the Pilgrims will defend
    the fractured settlement at Wessagusset
they have coordinated an offense
    that will destroy their settlement at Plymouth.

They have coordinated the attacks
    with Nausets, Pamets and the Succonets
of Mattachiests, then the Capawaks
    and also Agawoms from Manomet.

They had solicited the Massasoit
  to get him to join their conspiracy
and then commit all of the Wampanoags
  but he refused them all vehemently.

The Massasoit Ousamequin said
  they must attack the plotting principals.
Their sole defense was to cut off the head.
  This snake was large enough to crush them all.

This plot could risk the start of all-out war
  and they would weaken as their numbers fall
and breaking compacts they had made before
  the Narragansetts would destroy them all.

He knew the Pilgrims would resist to fight
  and patiently and peacefully endure.
They would refuse to be the first to strike
  and only fight if they were attacked first.

But as they hope for peace to be preserved
  this time there simply was no other way.
If this conspiracy attacked them first
  by then it would already be too late.

He said the Massasoit had been clear,
  without the principals the plot would cease.
They had to act for war to be deterred.
  This was the only way to keep the peace.

Then after Hobomock gave them the message,
  they knew they had to hurry to get back.
They had a two day journey still ahead
  and needed to reach the town Nemasket.

Then after resting anxiously that night
   they set off swiftly with first light of day
and heard some news that sped them in their flight
   that Standish sailed for Massachusetts Bay.

They were relieved when they returned that day.
   The shallop had not sailed upon the voyage.
The counter winds had held them at the bay
   and they were waiting till they could deploy.

They met a Pamet man who visited
   and he insisted on abounding trade
and he was pressuring insistently
   that Standish sail to Massachusetts Bay.

Then Winslow cordially dismissed the man
   without an indication that he knew.
There was no doubt an ambush had been planned
   to cut off Standish with a plotting ruse.

Then when the man departed peacefully
   Winslow and Hobomock told them the news
and touched upon the details carefully
   so all the leaders of the village knew.

Chapter 56

Captain Standish Rescues Weston's Men
March 1623

There was a general reluctance to act
  and many were opposed to the campaign.
They wanted to see if they were attacked
  and hoped the problem would just go away.

But messages continued to confirm
  that there was trouble looming up ahead
and this would turn into a massacre
  if some deterrent wasn't done instead.

They did not doubt the Massasoit's word.
  He said the threat was imminent and real
and there were other messages they heard
  that said the plot was to destroy and kill.

They heard from Sachem Wassapinewat
  whose brother was the Sachem Obtakiest
and he refused to join into the plot
  that organized in the conspiracy.

It seemed the Pilgrims did not have a choice
  so they decided to make a campaign
and then they organized a solid force
  to venture up to Massachusetts Bay.

The Captain would command the hardy group
  and Standish chose eight of his bravest men
and they would sail the shallop as a troop
  and noble Hobomock would go with them.

Then on the day that they were set to sail
    a desperate man who staggered with a pack
came into town appearing weak and frail
    — a Wessagusset man, Phineas Pratt.

Then speaking with the others gathered round
    Pratt tried explaining why he had to leave
and told of dangers at the other town
    and reasons why he felt he had to flee.

He said that while he had ran down to them
    he lost the path somewhere along the way
and this by chance had happened to save him
    or he'd been killed before he could escape.

He said the Massachusetts came in town
    and they would take the food from cooking pots
and ate it while the others stood around
    while shouting out insults and making taunts.

And if the settlers made any complaint
    the Natives held sharp knives up to their chests
and he was certain that on any day
    a club would strike his head and knock him dead.

And Pratt was sorry that he came to them
    but had to tell them of his company
and of the dangers pressed on Weston's men
    and he came to them for security.

So Pratt was welcome to stay in the town
    and Standish and his army then set sail.
They couldn't just desert the other town
    and helplessly await to be assailed.

When Standish and the others reached the bay
    they saw the *Swan* was moored without a watch
and then they felt concern they were too late
    and Weston's men already had been lost.

Then on the shore the Captain fired a shot
    to signal anyone near to report,
then two men came not wearing any clothes
    and said they sold them weeks ago for corn.

The Captain asked what did they have to eat.
    They said they eat the nuts upon the ground.
Then Standish asked them where they go to sleep.
    They said they live with nature not in town.

The men said they had found a purity
    and bounced like happy squirrels on limbs of trees
with lots of nuts and clams that they could eat
    — they'd found an Eden of tranquility.

Then Standish asked them what they'd do for clothes,
    they'd need something for warmth out in the snow.
And then they said there wasn't any snow,
    it's spring and flowers everywhere they go.

Then one began to whistle like a bird
    and flapped his arms like he was going to fly
but as he tried the air was not disturbed
    except in vacant spaces of his mind.

Then Standish and the others led the men
    to Wessagusset where they would be safe
and tried to gather all of Weston's men
    to tell them of the danger that they faced.

Then Standish asked them why they left the *Swan*
    tied to the shore without a man on guard.
He thought that Sanders sailed to Monhegan
    for victuals and supplies before they starved.

Then one of Weston's men tried to explain
    that Sanders had set sail upon the shallop.
None of them wanted to sail out that day
    so he could only man the smaller boat.

Then Standish had become exasperated
    — they wouldn't even sail for food they need
as if all they desired would soon be shaken
    to fall into their laps from out of trees?

Then Captain Standish asked all of the men
    if any of them wanted to survive
and told them that the Massachusetts planned
    to rush the town and take all of their lives.

Then as they spoke a native came to town
    and carried beaver pelts in search of trade
and Standish cooled and softened his tone down
    to hear what offers that the man would make.

But Captain Standish saw within his eyes
    a deep resentment harbored in the man
as if the Captain saw his heart on fire
    that burned with spite and fierce belligerence.

The Captain said he had so little corn
    that he could not make any sort of trade
but he would let them know when he had more
    and calmly sent the man upon his way.

After the man walked out of Wessagusset
   others appeared at the outskirts of town.
One was a Sachem of the Massachusetts
   and others dashed and flitted all around.

Then one began to yell at Hobomock
   and stood out in the open to be seen,
a Massachusetts Pniese name Pecksuot,
   a principal of the conspiracy.

He said he knew why Standish had come there
   and they had waited for the group to come
and they would not be taken unawares
   and he cannot be hurt by English guns.

Then Pecksuot began to taunt the men
   and fondled his knife in his Wampum beads
then gestured with a mocking, leering grin
   and said that soon he'd watch the English bleed.

Then redirecting to the other side
   the Sachem Wituwamat called out loud
and said that he has many deadly knives
   that tasted both the French and English blood.

But as the Massachusetts taunted him
   the Captain exercised his self-control
and carefully instructed all his men
   to disregard the childish, teasing ploy.

He said the insults from the enemy
   should never be received as an offense.
They show the lack of any discipline
   and he gave no regard to sour weakness.

And Standish said they had to stay together
   and not to let the taunts lure them away.
The Massachusetts meant to prod and pester
   and bait them in an ambush they had laid.

Then Captain Standish tried maneuvering
   so they could fight directly in the field
but found the others kept eluding them
   and fled and scattered in the wooded hills.

Then Pecksuot began to tease again
   and called out Captain Standish by his name
and said that he was just a little man
   and Pecksuot was big and strong and brave.

So this continued throughout the whole day.
   Then taunts and howls continued through the night
and Standish had an idea of a way
   how they could face for a decisive fight.

In morning Standish gave the careful plans
   and led some of the men out of the town
and cinched and buckled with his loyal band
   he stood outside an isolated house.

The plotting Natives began to appear
   and stepped out at the edge of the dense woods
and of the scatter of men in the clear
   both Pecksuot and Wituwamat stood.

Then Hobomock announced for them to hear
   that Standish wanted to speak privately.
There were so many Massachusetts near,
   the Sachem was assured security.

He said that Pecksuot should not be scared
   and didn't need to run away in fright
and hoped the talk won't cause him any fear
   since he continued fleeing from a fight.

Then so that everyone could clearly see
   the Captain then removed his sheath and sword
and without arms he stood defenselessly
   and waved to bring the Massachusetts forth.

At the abandoned and decrepit house
   the Captain stood at the open doorway
and Pecksuot thought this would be a trounce
   and him and Wituwamat led the way.

With daggers hid in Wampum necklaces
   the Pniese and Sachem came with two more men
but they could not conceal their grinning faces
   despite the stoicism known of them.

Then Captain Standish came with three more men
   and with his signal they closed fast the door
and Standish had no fear than would a spear
   and no remorse this time than would a sword.

He was no brawler and no rabble rouser.
   The Captain was an awesome polished soldier
and even if his stature did not tower
   he's built as solid as a granite boulder.

And with the Pniese's brash complacency
   the sudden moment caught him off his guard
and Standish charged like shot artillery
   and struck with the force of a cannon ball.

One hand clamped down upon the Pniese's throat
the other grabbed the knife hung on his neck
and with the knife the Pniese had made his boasts
the Captain stabbed his chest till he was dead.

The other men inside were overcome
and Standish cut off Witawamat's head
and then outside the others turned to run
with Standish brandishing the face of death.

Later some minor skirmishes occurred
but soon the scorch of war was cooled to peace
and as the rival plotters had dispersed
then Weston's men agreed that they should leave.

Although the Pilgrims said they'd welcome them
and they could live in Plymouth settlement
the men wanted to go to Monhegan
and sail on fishing boats back home again.

And from the little corn the Pilgrims had
they gave the men some victuals for their trip
and walking from the venture that collapsed
the men disbanded Weston's settlement.

Chapter 57

An Unexpected Visitor
April 1623

The plot was ended, Weston's men had gone
  and Standish did not stoop for spoils of war.
They left the Massachusetts on their own
  and did not try to pillage for reward.

The campaign was not made for an advantage
  but they were forced by dire necessity
— resolved, they sailed back to their families,
  addressing their responsibilities.

And even though the threat had been removed
  they were still facing other enemies,
not from hostilities, but lack of food
  while struggling in severe extremities.

What corn was left they had to keep for seed
  and although everyone wanted to eat,
they wouldn't have a crop next year to reap
  if they engorged themselves for short term need.

And even with no surplus in the store
  they stayed engaged with all their daily tasks
and while some gathered shellfish at the shore
  they spotted an approaching shallop's mast.

Then some of them ran back into the town
  to notify the faithful Governor
and then announce to everyone around
  to greet the unexpected visitors.

Some men then waded out into the bay
 and helped to pull the shallop to the shore
and noticed one onboard who backed away,
 a timid and embarrassed passenger.

Then as the shallop hull was dragged on land
 the man pulled down his hat as to conceal
and they became intrigued about this man
 by what he clearly tried not to reveal.

Then Bradford bent to look beneath the brim
 to try and peek to see the man in question
and when he got a better look at him
 announced out loud, "Is that you Thomas Weston?"

Then Weston cringed when he was recognized
 and looked like he might run back to the boat.
He feared that his arrival might incite
 their anger from agreements that he broke.

But as he seemed to brace against the blows
 that he expected he would soon receive
his barricades were quickly over thrown
 when he found he was welcomed graciously.

When Thomas Weston looked he saw the bad
 and craved all that he wanted desperately
but mindful of what little that they had
 the Pilgrims seemed to see things differently.

They chose to focus on what they could do
 and did not dwell upon what had been done.
They managed tasks to put their skills to use
 and worked for good so they could overcome.

So Weston was led into Plymouth town
    and taken as a welcome visitor,
an honored guest they brought into the house
    of their esteemed and worthy Governor.

Then seated, Weston spoke of the demands
    he had addressed and dangers he had faced
and knew the Pilgrims could not understand
    the perils he endured as he explained.

"As soon as I arrived I heard the news
    of troubles in the town of Wessagusset
so then I found a shallop I could use
    to travel to the bay of Massachusetts.

"And I feel it is unforgivable
    that people here refused my sound advice
to help them build a town more tenable
    and give them what they needed for supplies.

"So since you all refused to help those men
    I sailed to see what salvage may remain
but on the course there was a tempest wind
    and then we feared we would be castaway.

"The men I hired to sail the boat for me
    all proved to be sadly incompetent.
I told them that stupidity was free
    and I should not be made to pay for it.

"They didn't know how to do their own jobs
    and kept insisting I help bail the boat
— as if the wind and waves were all my fault!
    and then of course the boat sunk like a stone.

"And then while they were helping me to shore
    they nearly drown me in the breaking waves
  and then refused to swim back in the storm
    to check the wreck for things that might be saved.

"So then we had to walk to Piscataqua
    and sand kept getting in the boots I wore
  then an angry band of Natives robbed us
    and left me with the one shirt that was torn.

"Then suffering the gross humility
    of walking into town with just a shirt
  I gallantly endured indignity
    and screamed and shouted until I was heard.

"Then finally someone loaned me a suit
    but it's too big and doesn't even fit.
  And then someone gave me a pair of boots
    but I can tell he had been wearing them.

"And then they said they'd loan a tiny boat
    and they would sail me to the colony,
  there were some men who would agree to go
    because the others had abandoned me!

"I don't expect for you to pity me.
    I only told you this so you will see
  the conquests I have made intrepidly
    while you've been sitting in your shacks to read.

"And hopefully I'll be an inspiration
    to help correct the ways you are conducting
  and then provide some needed motivation
    to make your operations more productive.

"Although I am no longer an investor.
    You can't deny my generosity.
I simply hope that you all can do better
    and so I give priceless advice for free.

"And while I'm here I need to take a loan.
    I need some beaver pelts to buy supplies
and then I'll pay the men who loaned this boat
    the wages for the sailing trade they plied.

"I have another ship that's on the way
    and it is loaded with commodities
and I'll make sure they harbor at your bay
    and give you everything that you all need."

While standing in astonished disbelief
    the Pilgrim leaders listened patiently
and suffered Weston sympathetically
    and then the Governor said gracefully:

"Although we are aggrieved with your ordeals
    and all the difficulties you endured
we have responsibilities to fill
    of which we all have made by oath and word.

"As you have seen we have but meager means.
    We need the pelts to trade for food and clothes.
We feel the town would have a mutiny
    if we gave out the goods that we had stored."

Enraged the visitor began go bawl:
    "Is it my fault you can't manage supplies
or that your people are out of control!"
    And then the Governor kindly replied,

"But in the desperation of your case
   we will not leave you stranded without means.
We know the difficulties of this place
   and wish to offer kindness in extremes.

"We have decided to provide some pelts
   – a hundred that our earnest work had won –
and with these you can satisfy your debts
   along with means to carry you back home."

The Pilgrim leaders then led Weston out
   and grabbed a hundred beaver pelts for him
and then politely led him through the town
   while careful not to make a show of this.

Then when the shallop was about to leave
   the Pilgrims heard some statements Weston said
and they were staggering beyond belief
   that kindness had so quickly been betrayed.

Then as they pushed the shallop from the shore
   then Weston yelled he'd set them all on ear
and insolently said he was abhorred
   with each and every Plymouth villager.

Then fading, Weston ranted on as if
   he hoped to fill the sail with slandering.
And so the Pilgrims let him jib the skiff
   and turned their minds to more productive things.

Chapter 58

Private Enterprise
April 1623

Then later as the Pilgrims worked the fields
   to clear the grounds before the seeds were sown
the irritation of some was revealed
   as they began expressing frustration.

They said that they were working in the sun
   while others sat all day in the cool shade
and when something was needed to be done
   the others always turned and ran away.

They all relied upon community
   and shared the fruits of annual harvests
but they felt some were not contributing
   and always needed more for their own rest.

Once this disgruntled issue had been broached
   each person in the village was perturbed
as everyone condemned the other's sloth
   and each one claimed to do all of the work.

No doubt they all had suffered through the dearth,
   yet through the hardships they had been convinced
they weren't appreciated for their worth
   and they felt others were exploiting them.

The others could not recognize their trials
   and all the hardships they endured at home
without considering that all the while
   the others dealt with hardships of their own.

So they assembled in the Meetinghouse
  then openly their voices could be heard
and then attentively with the whole town
  find a consensus with each one in turn.

The Governor and leaders of the town
  stood facing the entire community
and people waited for their turn to sound
  their own position in the colony.

And quite a number stood to make their peace
  so others knew their isolated qualms
and others spoke about their unity
  in ways they thought the problems could be solved.

And all together they devised a means
  that liberated private enterprise
without neglecting the necessity
  of managing civil stability.

Each family would have a plot of land
  according to what they proved to maintain
and they must satisfy their own demand
  to harvest what they sow and cultivate.

They would decide the plots of land by lots
  in fairness without any preference.
Each was responsible for their own spot
  and would rely on their own governance.

That year they drew the lots for private use
  and if this system proved to benefit
then in the coming years it may be proved
  that they could draw the lots for ownership.

As each was then provided open means
  to prove what they could privately produce
the urgencies of the necessities
  pressed on them months before the harvest moon.

The only corn they had was kept for seed.
  Through winter they consumed all they had stored
and there was nothing more they had to eat.
  They faced a famine as the year before.

Some messages arrived by fishing boats
  and the investors were sending supplies.
John Peirce had sent the *Paragon* of note
  and they had hoped that it would soon arrive.

Then they divided up in equal groups
  to send on alternating fishing trips
and then with the returning catch each brought
  they divvied into portions to subsist.

When tide was out they dug the sand for clams.
  Some hunted and divided up the game.
Impoverished yet still living off the land
  and in their unity they were sustained.

Chapter 59

The Courage to Carry On
May – July 1623

The Pilgrims' choice to change communal planting
    to private enterprise proved a success
so through their own direction they could manage
    their destiny with sense of ownership.

More corn was planted than ever before
    and everyone was far more gratified
when they could see the sprouting of the corn
    resulting from the work that they had plied.

And there were friendly rivals of contest
    and some would brag about who set the most
and others would compare who set the best
    and all together they watched the crops grow.

And as the crops were flourishing in growth
    and all the crops of each plot were combined,
each one held in account the work they owned
    and what their work would earn at harvest time.

And they compared the parcels of the plan
    while corn and beans were growing all together
as all of them had planted the same land
    and they were all exposed to the same weather.

And as each person planted privately,
    each had their own responsibility
to give a share to the community
    that was the basis of their industry.

For the time being their best means of food
  so they could all survive till harvest time
was fishing in the bay in their small boat
  with the rotations of their groups in line.

So every group would sail out on their turn
  and cast the net in hopes of bass and cod
and when they hauled a load they would return
  as heroes celebrated with applause.

But fishing was sometimes a fickle trade
  and schools of fish could not always be found
and groups would stay out on the bay for days
  until they had a catch to bring to town.

There were no victuals waiting at their homes
  so they stayed out until they caught some food.
The shame that they would disappoint the town
  was hungry motive for each of the groups.

So through this they found that they were sustained
  and checked each day as their crops slowly grew
and waited for the shipment on the way
  as blossoms turned to buds promising fruit.

But even with their careful discipline
  and the reliance binding them together
the world was larger than their heart's intent
  and they had no control over the weather.

For days they did not have a drop of rain
  and all the growth they watched came to a halt
and then for weeks the drought remained the same
  and leaves were withering on drooping stalks.

And each day they felt helpless and forlorn
    as they were watching their crops slowly die
and all their work for sweet and meaty corn
    was somehow being tragically denied.

Then when a fishing trip out on the bay
    returned and pulled the shallop on the shore
they said they met a ship along the way
    that had a letter for the Governor.

Then as the Governor read out the note
    all of their growing hope turned to a void
as every person's tender heart was broke
    and all they worked for felt to be destroyed.

The ship John Peirce had chartered for the town
    had failed on two attempts across the sea
and on the third they feared the ship went down
    and all was tragically lost to the deep.

The ship was loaded with their families
    and friends who were embarking to join them
and then they heard the ship was lost at sea
    and all they built was tumbling down on them.

And even those who had the strongest will
    and character that seemed carved out of stone
felt cracks that fractured with the brittle chills
    then shattered with the force of a cold blow.

Yet still they picked the scattered pieces up
    and bundled close so they could carry on
and desolate in humbleness and love
    they placed their faith into the hand of God.

And on one day they gathered on the hill
   and all together in devotion prayed
and by coincidence or miracle
   the heavy clouds blew in with gentle rain.

And then the rain continued for two weeks
   so that the life of their crops was restored
and gently showers came so soft and sweet
   there was no damage from a gusty storm.

And in addition to the Sabbath day
   the Pilgrims always honored piously,
they gathered once again to congregate
   for faithful prayer and staid humility.

And then for some in rapt astonishment,
   for others — confirmation of belief,
a letter was sent to the settlement
   retrieved by Standish on a trade journey.

When Bradford read the letter with the news
   the hope of everyone was quite revived
as every word was read as gospel true
   as all the passengers were still alive.

The letter said the ship named *Paragon*
   commissioned by John Peirce of the investors
was almost castaway in a sea storm
   but everyone had safely been delivered.

The damaged ship docked at an English port,
   the passengers and goods were all transferred
and soon the ship the *Anne* would be unmoored
   and then to Plymouth they would all venture.

Then from the date the letter was composed,
    the *Anne* had certainly already sailed
and they could then expect the ship was close
    and could arrive at Plymouth any day.

Then late in June a ship came in the bay
    but they found that the ship was not the *Anne*
and Captain Francis West made shore to say
    that he was chasing poaching fishermen.

The Pilgrims had a patent from the King
    so they were clear to have the colony
and were conforming with legalities
    and operating with integrity.

And then they learned the ship had casks of peas
    that Captain West said he would gladly trade
but when he saw the Pilgrims' scanty means
    he charged more than they would agree to pay.

And even though the Pilgrims' means were lean,
    they felt assured of their resilience.
They felt that they would hold out for the *Anne*
    and proved they could endure their circumstance.

And Captain West said that they'd seen a ship
    that had been castaway upon a shore
and didn't mean to cause alarm in them
    but hoped it wasn't who they waited for.

Still they refused the Captain's gouging terms
    as he would not budge from the price he set
and in response the Pilgrims remained firm
    and although meek, they were not desperate.

Chapter 60

The Anne's Arrival
July 1623

Late in July, another ship arrived
    that brought the Pilgrims promise of relief
and as the ship dropped anchor at high tide
    they saw the *Anne* had crossed the northern sea.

Then on a tiny boat rowed to the shore
    the *Anne's* commander Master William Peirce
hailed all the people with the Governor
    upon the rock where the small boat was steered.

Once on the shore then William Peirce explained
    the ship had been commissioned by investors
and there were sixty passengers who came
    and stowed inside were stores of their provisions.

The news was like the lapping on the shore
    that soothed the pressing crowds persistent woes.
Then Peirce gave letters to the Governor
    and they made plans for how they would unload.

Most of the passengers were family
    with friends from Holland where they had their church
but Pastor Robinson could not be seen
    and many of the members had been spurned.

And in the group were some they did not know
    who would be separate from the colony
as they were sent to work upon their own
    Particulars from the community.

The Pilgrims also found no shipped supplies.
   Investors did not have financial means.
The trade commodities were sacrificed
   to send the passengers with their own things.

Although this ship brought more help than before
   and passengers came with their store of food,
this wasn't quite the ship they had hoped for
   as they were planning to receive more goods.

The Pilgrims still received them heartily.
   They certainly had learned how to make do.
The dearth inspired their ingenuity
   and they remained resolved and resolute.

But as the Pilgrims stood with open arms
   the passengers responded differently.
The friends and family were kind and warm
   but others stepped on shore reluctantly.

In fact, some passengers began to cry
   and then refused to go into the town
as if condemned to wretched misery
   and said the place would drag their proud lives down.

And then a man named John Oldham announced
   that their arrival would help to improve
the pitiful conditions of the town
   the Pilgrims had neglected and abused.

The Pilgrims certainly could not deny
   that their appearance showed some wear from work
but in a span of less than three years time
   they built this town from a bare patch of dirt.

But they were hardened from flippant offense
   and welcomed others in their settlement.
The others did not have experience
   to recognize their past accomplishments.

So as the leaders spoke with William Peirce
   the Pilgrims kept the others entertained
and with their means, they set a supper's course
   to share the food of which they were sustained.

Some of the passengers partook the meal
   and cordially received the offered food
but the disgust from some was not concealed
   and they were blatant with ingratitude.

They were appalled the Pilgrims had no beer
   and wondered how they managed to survive.
The thought of drinking water made them fear
   they'd soon fall ill in misery and die.

The Pilgrims reassured them it was safe.
   They had been drinking water for three years.
The water from the spring was free from taint
   and always proved refreshing, sweet and clear.

But then John Oldham barked out in reply,
   "How can you say the water's safe to drink
when you all live in sick infirmity.
   You cannot smell for how badly you stink!"

And then the Pilgrims gave apology,
   they did not have the barley, means or craft
and they were living in simplicity
   and the spring water was all that they had.

Then others said they cannot eat the food.
  The Pilgrims didn't have a crumb of bread.
The others feared becoming destitute
  if fish and lobster was all they were fed.

The Pilgrims were aware of their coarse means
  and friends and family that had arrived
were trying to adjust to the extremes
  they recognized the Pilgrims had survived.

But the Particulars of the new group
  refused to look at the reality
and would not be aggrieved to stop and stoop
  to think of what the Pilgrims had achieved.

They had envisioned the place differently
  and felt the failure of their expectations
was not of their accountability
  but to be blamed on other's faulty stations.

Then the Particulars said they would leave.
  They thought they'd build a bigger, better town.
They didn't come to live in misery
  and feared the Pilgrims would hold them all down.

They also feared the food that they had brought
  would be purloined without any regard.
They thought they had been brought there to be robbed
  and then they would be coldly left to starve.

And at the tables set for them to eat
  all the Particulars expressed their grief
and then John Oldham stood to take the lead
  with fussing quibbles spewing endlessly.

So the Particulars made rivalry
    and failed to take account for other's roles
and only saw particularities,
    denying their reliance on the whole.

With the commotion that was heard outside
    the Governor came promptly to address
and as the bickering calmed he inquired
    to find the cause of the riled argument.

Then after Oldham made his rank complaints
    the Governor spoke in a soothing voice
assuring him that all their things were safe
    and would be kept secure when brought to shore.

Then Bradford said a meeting would convene
    so the arising issues were addressed
and they could settle on the terms agreed
    to find a way they all could be content.

Chapter 61

Reaching an Agreement at the Town Meeting
July 1623

Within ten days the people were assembled
    upon the hill in Plymouth's Meetinghouse
to find a way addressing the contention
    and then resolve dissension in the town.

Then after Brewster led them all in prayer
    the formal meeting of the town convened
and at the front stood Plymouth's Governor
    addressing the whole body with his speech:

"As I begin, I'm happy to announce
    that Plymouth welcomes the new settlers,
receiving you into our humble town
    as *Anne* arrived with the new passengers.

"As you have noticed, our means here are meek
    yet have no doubt, our spirits remain strong.
We have contended with adversities
    and held ourselves together all along.

"And in our little town's community
    we are provided opportunities
established on our love and unity
    to benefit our wholesome families.

"But we must keep in mind extremities
    that we have had to face repeatedly
as we are dwelling in severity
    and are beset with countless tragedies.

"Some of the passengers upon the *Anne*
    had also sailed upon the *Paragon*
and storms had kept that ship from reaching land
    and times we feared you all were wrecked and gone.

"The *Anne's* Commander Master William Peirce
    was also Captain of the *Paragon*
and he described how the ship's masts were sheared
    and many times they thought that all was lost.

"Yet, fortunately you all made it through,
    still on this journey in another storm
the pinnace that had sailed along with you
    was lost and may not be seen ever more.

"And this reminds us of the lessons learned
    — instead of craving what we want to take
we cherish what we have for love preserved
    as in an instant it may dash away.

"And if the pinnace *Little James* is lost
    we will devoutly pray for those poor souls
and hope that somewhere they have reached a coast
    where they may live their lives fulfilled and whole.

"We were relying on that pinnace too
    as we have been subsisting on the fish.
That boat could have provided us more food
    until our fields have ripened for harvest.

"And on this matter we have been convened
    as the new planters have expressed concern
that they would not have all the food they need
    if victuals that they brought were all dispersed.

"The new-comers can safely be assured
    all their supplies they brought will be respected.
With our devoted deeds and honest words
    the whole community will be protected.

"And although most of us have tattered clothes.
    We have not lost our decent dignity.
We have preserved our love and righteous souls.
    The rough has polished our civility.

"For several days we have pursued discussion
    to focus on the points we disagree
in hopes that we may find the best solution
    and from the problems find a remedy.

"Some of the people had a great idea
    of which they graciously explained to me
and now I call them so they may repeat
    their idea to the whole community."

With this the Governor stepped to the side
    and from the crowd one of the people stood
and then he slowly began to describe
    his own solution for the common good.

"Considering the problems from before
    when ships arrived and brought new passengers
we didn't have enough food in our store
    for new and unexpected settlers.

"Before the *Anne* arrived we could subsist
    and we have sown our fields with growing corn
and since the new-comers do not like fish
    we'll let them keep the food they brought to shore.

"The new-comers have their supply of food,
 the rest of us will eat the summer's fish
and we will honor and respect their stuff
 but they must do the same for our harvest.

"The corn we reap at growing season's end
 will be reserved as our private supply
exactly as reserves of our new friends
 allowing for the choice to sell and buy.

"The food they brought could last them through the year
 and of the corn, we'll help them grow their own
and recognizing what we have done here
 we pray they will respect our town and homes."

The goodman then sat back into his seat
 and then they asked consensus of the group
and everyone had reason to agree
 this is how they should manage all their food.

Then after nodding their assured consent
 as everyone felt satisfied and pleased
the Governor confirmed the agreement
 and then continued with his stately speech.

"Arriving with our friends and family
 are several independent passengers
– Particulars to the community –
 who had agreed to the investor's terms.

"We all embrace you in our colony.
 We will provide you space to live and work.
You can expect respect from us and we
 expect to be respected in return."

And then the Governor read out the terms
of which Particulars before agreed
— the duties charged allowing them to work
as their own planters independently.

And as the terms were read for all to hear
the group of the Particulars was stirred
as Oldham seemed to poke and prod and jeer
as he excited them with whispered slurs.

The leaders noted how the group behaved
although surprised to see this from grown men
and kept a distance from the childish play
to draw the meeting to a sober end.

Concluding, all the people walked outside
and looked upon the harbor from the hill
and it appeared the pinnace had arrived
and this gave everyone a hopeful thrill.

The pinnace proved to be the *Little James*.
The storm had blown the little ship off course
but cleared they were able to find the bay
and dropped the anchor to make a safe port.

Chapter 62

Wedding Day
August 14, 1623

Aug.
14 In radiant light of the august month
    they set sometime aside to celebrate
the prospects prompted through what they had done
    with festivals set for a wedding day.

The *Anne* was riding anchor on the bay
    and twenty houses had been built in town
and in the settlement that they had made
    the Pilgrims had good reason to be proud.

The fields around were flourishing with corn
    and they felt organized and diligent
with affirmation from the solid core
    of sturdy growth in their development.

And through the heavy labors of their time
    and pious faith in holy sanctity
they cherished moments they could set aside
    to lift in joy their gathered families.

And witnessed with the warm community
    the oaths and vows provided testimony
to be fulfilled in loving unity
    through the devotion of sweet matrimony.

Upon the *Anne* one of the new-comers
    was of the Leyden church's laity
Isaac Southwell's wife, Alice Carpenter,
    who sadly had been widowed recently.

And ever since the goodwife came to shore
    some of the Pilgrims could not help but note
the Governor was subtly transformed
    with touches of the tenderness of love.

The Governor had been unwavering,
    a guiding figure of the Pilgrim's strength,
and his close friends found it astonishing
    as if they heard his heart in secret sing.

The love he had was never held in doubt
    but since he sadly lost dear Dorothy
he gave his life to everyone in town
    and loved them all in service selflessly.

As they held marriage as a civil bond
    and Bradford governed from the civil helm
he had been razzed by his devoted friends
    that Bradford would have to marry himself.

The Governor's assistant Allerton
    was happy to preside as magistrate
and Elder Brewster's reverent eloquence
    would bless the ceremony with his grace.

And as each person in the town prepared
    to share enjoyment in the revelry
a group of new-comers came running scared
    of something in the distance they had seen.

They said they spotted out beyond the fields
    a warlike army of the Native men.
They were descending from surrounding hills
    and were approaching the town's settlement.

They said the fearsome men were armed with bows
  and arrow quivers strapped upon their backs
and gathered in a mass for an approach
  preparing to make a surprise attack.

Then Captain Standish jumped up from his seat
  and Edward Winslow stood up to attend
and they walked up the hill so they could see
  the slow approach of Wampanoag men.

Then many climbed up on the town's bulwark
  and watched in safety behind the ramparts
and on the hill some stood around the fort
  to watch in fear of an approaching war.

Some tried to count the number of the men
  who then were walking through the nearby fields
and pressure felt to push on all of them
  as nervous tension teetered as it built.

Then filing from the fields outside of town
  the group gathered over a hundred strong
and no one said a word or made a sound
  when Standish and Winslow walked out alone.

And from the Wampanoags one stood out
  bedecked in feathers with a painted face
and the new-comers stared in speechless doubt
  as they watched the men cordially embrace.

And as they watched their tension was released
  as stoic faces began flashing smiles
and the only disturbance of the peace
  was happy laughter affable and kind.

Then they held up the venison they brought,
    four bucks they must have bagged along the way
along with a wild turkey that they caught
    to share in their friends' festival that day.

Then Standish waved them all back into town
    and they were welcomed through the bulwark gate
and when they stored their bows in Bradford's house
    the new-comers stood speechless and amazed.

The Governor received the Massasoit
    as honored guest and dear and faithful friend
along with Pnieses of the Wampanoag
    who had accompanied four more Sachem.

Along with what the Massasoit brought
    the Pilgrims had a dozen deer to eat
with baskets filled with plums and grapes and nuts
    as they all shared enjoyment in the feast.

And laughter, music, dancing filled the day
    until the dusky cloud blushed up above
then through their lifetimes they may celebrate
    the bride and groom's vows of devoted love.

Chapter 63

Negotiating Wages for the Crew of the Little James
September 1623

The crew of the new pinnace *Little James*
    appeared to be a rude and rowdy bunch
and after Weston's froward men were saved
    the town had a new surge of insolence.

But earnest efforts for establishment
    with thoughtful care for service to protect
provide stability that draws dissent
    that can erupt with what no one expects.

The Pilgrims felt assured that what they had
    was able to endure the passing storms
and their assurance was cast iron clad
    with lessons from what they withstood before.

But the assurance can also beguile
    into complacency and negligence
and Pilgrim leaders knew from fiery trial
    to keep up with the heedful maintenance.

And the new pinnace could give needed help
    for fishing and exploring for more trade
and this would benefit the Commonwealth
    if only the crew would cooperate.

There were some promising and hopeful signs
    while listening to stories from the crew
who strung some fishing tales on a long line
    from open sea before land was in view.

They told some stories from their faring ship
    when they had made their transatlantic way
and times at sea the fog became so thick
    they had to lie at hull and furl their sails.

And while they waited for the fog to clear
    they passed their time by fishing the deep sea
and were surprised by the abundance here
    and had some catches they could not believe.

They said they had at least a thousand fish,
    they even had to throw three hundred out
and they looked at their captive audience
    who gathered close in a large, hungry crowd.

They said one cod had weighed a hundred pounds,
    far bigger than what they had ever seen
and huge flatfish that could have fed the town
    that they had hooked and wrestled from the deep.

The sailors held a captivating spell,
    more than from stories that were read in books,
but this was not from any artful skill
    — the crowd was simply starved to hear of food.

With the attention that the crew received
    from tales of catches they had on their trip
they would become the town celebrities
    when they returned from sea with loads of fish.

The *Little James* was fit and well equipped,
    far more than the small shallop in the bay.
The Pilgrims had been struggling to fish
    with ill sized hooks and one old torn up seine.

But when they tried to organize the crew
   to venture out on the first fishing trip
the sailors then contentiously refused
   and said they'd just as soon destroy the ship.

They said that they decided to be pirates
   and that they had been cozened and deceived
and they refused to work for mindless tyrants
   and would rather be hung than work for free.

They said they were not offered any pay
   and they would gain their earning with the spoils.
They had no interest venturing for trade
   or plying with the stinky fishing toils.

They then refused to listen to command.
   They'd rather buccaneer the loot for free
and have no loyalty to any land
   and take the vessel in a mutiny.

The Governor spoke to the angry crew
   and told of virtues gained through honest work
and that the pinnace certainly would lose
   when met by French and Spanish man-o'-wars.

He never would expect their work for free
   but they should have been paid before they left.
The colony is not a treasury.
   They're in the middle of a wilderness.

So Bradford spoke with Master William Peirce
   and they were able to work out a deal
that Peirce would tell the London investors
   they'd have to pay the wages on a bill.

The *Anne* was set to sail to England soon
  with fur and sundry items gained in trade
and when the next commissioned ship returned
  Peirce would make sure the sailors would be paid.

The sailors had good reason to complain
  but seemed to take the deal reluctantly.
They had good reason to demand their wage
  but sadly they seemed set on piracy.

Then in September the *Anne* set to sail
  with loads of clapboard and plush fur from trade.
The Pilgrims made sure that they didn't fail
  to work at making sure their debt was paid.

Sept.
10

And Winslow sailed with the ship's passengers
  to make sure to procure commodities
and give account to London investors
  so the next shipment brought supplies they need.

By then the fields were filled with ripened corn,
  the disagreements had all settled down
and this year's harvest would fill up their stores
  and pleasant promise shined upon the town.

Chapter 64

A Visit from the Governor General
September 1623

In the same month after the *Anne* departed
    a letter came with an official stamp
the Parliament in London had appointed
    a general Governor for New England.

The Captain Robert Gorges held the position,
    the son of Knighted Ferdinando Gorges
and planned to settle at the same location
    where Weston's group had built a town before.

The note was sent from Massachusetts Bay
    and shortly after the message arrived
a stately ship sailed into Plymouth Bay
    and Gorges' boat rowed to the town's shore side.

The leaders of the town lined up to meet
    the formal visit of the dignitary
and they had all heard of his father's feats
    as his discoveries were legendary.

The general Governor and his escorts
    were shown around the settlement of Plymouth.
He was impressed with how they'd been employed
    compared to shambles left at Wessagusset.

Then Captain Gorges decided he would stay
    at Plymouth for at least a couple weeks
enjoying both his evenings and his days
    in the uprightness of the company.

He recognized the richness of insight
   that had been gained in long experience.
The Pilgrim leaders were glad to provide
   to aid the Captain in his governance.

So Captain Gorges decided to assign
   the Plymouth Governor to his counsel
and Bradford would officially preside
   with Captain Francis West – the admiral.

Then in the Governor of Plymouth's home
   as Captain Gorges – the general Governor –
discussed the matters of officialdom
   there was a knock at William Bradford's door.

Politely then a goodman stepped inside
   who had been posted at the watch in turn.
He gave report as he had been assigned
   and said that Thomas Weston had returned.

The Pilgrims heard the name with a slight grudge
   but dared not make a single moan or groan.
The poise of their composure did not budge
   but still they dreaded what could then unfold.

But what had made the Pilgrims feel intrigued
   was how the general Governor behaved
as everyone who stood around could see
   that Gorges delighted hearing Weston's name.

He then turned to the Plymouth Governor
   and asked for Master Weston to be sent
and they wondered if Captain Robert Gorges
   and Thomas Weston could be longtime friends.

Weston had managed to regain his ship
    and sailed into the harbor on the *Swan*
and stepped on shore with brazen confidence
    to show the Pilgrims that they had been wrong.

Then marching to the Governor's own home
    he triumphed in his glorious return
and with his struggles and his battles won
    he relished thoughts of how the town would burn.

Then barging through the Governor's front door
    he was surprised to see the group of men
and Captain Gorges – the general Governor –
    with William Bradford standing next to him.

Then Captain Robert Gorges stood from the chair
    while all the others waited silently
and sternly he officially declared
    of Thomas Weston's criminality.

The first charge was for flagrant negligence
    of men left at the town of Wessagusset
and lacking any rule of management
    they had disturbed the peace of the whole region.

Then Weston answered in outraged protest
    — he left the men with victuals and supplies.
He can't be blamed for their mismanagement
    of articles that they had been consigned.

Then Bradford stood up in Weston's defense
    confirming that the men could not be helped
as they had lent aid to their settlement
    and even with support the town still failed.

So Captain Gorges allowed the charge to pass
   then raised another which he was aggrieved
as it abused the state and civil class
   and gave dishonor to his family.

He said that Thomas Weston had insisted
   the noble man Sir Ferdinando Gorges
procure for him a transportation license
   for ordnances to arm New England forts.

Then Weston took the shipment overseas
   and sold the ordnances as pilfered loot
and violated the state property
   and caused his father a royal rebuke.

Then Weston tried denying with excuse
   and claimed the shipments had been castaway
but Captain Gorges had undisputed proof
   and Weston then confessed he had been paid.

Then Captain Gorges gave a berated speech
   how Thomas Weston acted through his greed,
endangering the English colonies,
   abusing State and Gorges' family.

Then in the scolding Thomas Weston sunk
   as if he lost all sense of dignity
and in the deep despair that Weston plunged
   Gorges questioned his lack of integrity.

Then Captain Gorges turned to his counsel's side
   and asked the Plymouth Governor to say
if sentencing was for him to decide
   what would his conscience have him magistrate.

Then Bradford took a careful, thoughtful pause
　　to weigh his judgement with a steady hand
and governed himself from impulsive thought
　　and did not want to punish the poor man.

There was no question Weston had helped them
　　and ventured the endeavors premier funds
so Bradford thinks it best to recommend
　　what benefits the lives of everyone.

So for the general Governor's request
　　the Governor of Plymouth calmly said,
"There is no question of Weston's offense
　　and the abuse he has brought to the state

"and we are all aggrieved to hear about
　　the general Governor's good family
and this wrong doing is without a doubt
　　an act that has been done despicably.

"I feel we should not make haste to condemn
　　there are still services that may be gained.
As surgeons know, we try to mend the limb
　　before deciding we must amputate.

"I think that Master Weston sees his fault
　　and consequences are well understood
and through the lessons that he has been taught
　　he'll know it best to work for common good."

And all the Pilgrim leaders then agreed
　　and vouched for Thomas Weston's character
and a good sign of gracious clemency
　　was signaled from the general Governor.

And in the instant Weston felt some slack
   he lunged up shouting out his heated grief
as if he was the one who was attacked
   and started ranting argumentatively:

"The problem is the Plymouth Colony!
   They squandered wastefully all that I gave
and I don't need their righteous sympathy
   when I know they are all deceitful knaves.

"They built this settlement with my supplies
   then all they do is sit around and read.
I sent them help but they don't even try
   and only speak of Christian purity.

"Then after they were seated in their town
   they broke agreement for the shares they owe
and from what I had principally paid down
   they cut me from the stocks I had controlled.

"And then I sent the other group of men
   to help this town in its pathetic need
and then the Puritans abandoned them
   so Wessagusset foundered tragically.

"I have been suffering financial loss
   from Plymouth's lack of productivity
and with my payments for their idle costs
   I needed to secure some currency.

"So I had asked Sir Ferdinando Gorges
   along with the Council of New England
if they could lend my honest aim support
   for ordnances defending settled land.

"And with the careful plans I had arranged
   Sir Gorges would not provide sufficient means
so I was forced to keep the shipment safe
   by selling it less it be lost at sea."

If left unchecked than Weston's crooked speech
   would have continued twisting into knots
but Captain Gorges then stood up from his seat
   to make sure Weston knew he better stop.

The general Governor put his foot down
   on the rat's tail before it got away
and ordered Weston curb his snippy pouts
   or he would stand before the magistrate.

Then weary of the snide contentiousness
   the general Governor adjourned the day
and for the night he let the issues rest
   and so retired to his own lodging place.

Weston then pleaded to the colony
   if they had planned to turn him over to
the general Governor's authority,
   as he was scared they had condemned him too.

And Bradford said he could not bar the way
   that would be taken by Sir Gorges' son
and from outbursts of comments he had made
   he complicated this for everyone.

But Bradford said he'd see what he could do
   to try to make amendments for the wrong
and later Gorges made the agreement to
   release the culprit upon his own bond.

Then Gorges returned to Massachusetts Bay
accepting Weston's release on his word
and Weston was kept ready while he stayed
until a summons for him had been heard.

In the accommodations that were made
Weston continued to cause more offense.
The Pilgrims' advocation was repaid
with slander, calumny and bitterness.

And Weston's enmity grew as he stayed
as John Oldham and the Particulars
with the unruly crew of *Little James*
all snubbed the Pilgrims and the Governor.

They even heard when Thomas Weston said
that Gorges had been appointed by a favor
and Pilgrims may be Justices a day
but he had made them his appellant beggars.

Chapter 65

The Great Fire
November 5, 1623

The harvest for the year was a success
  and proved more bountiful than years before
and the sense of retaining ownership
  made work more gratifying than before.

And every basket that each family filled
  along the standing rows that they had sown
was toted with a produce they could feel
  — a true account of the work that they owned.

And through the skill and care that they had earned
  and in devoted time they gave to work
the labors of their lives were slowly turned
  to ripen sweetness through the toils endured.

And as they hauled the bushels into town
  with husky ears of overflowing corn
they tallied all the numbers that they count
  when they brought their work to the Common Store.

With the abundance of that harvest year
  they all felt they were stable and sustained
but without care, strong confidence can veer
  where circumstances suddenly can change.

The crews of the *Swan* and the *Little James*
  were lacking aim and bouncing all around
and flailing with no want to be engaged
  their dithering disturbed the rest of town.

The Pilgrims loaned a house where they could stay
   and on a freezing cold November night
the men decided they would celebrate
   and fed their discontent into a fire.

Nov 5

They stoked the fire into a raging blaze
   so sparks were flying from the chimney top
and set the thatch upon the roof aflame
   and lit the whole town from the single lot.

Some others ran to clear them from the house
   – the sailors didn't know it was on fire –
and as the Pilgrims were running about
   the bitter sailors stood off to the side.

The Pilgrims raised alarm for everyone
   and fell in line along their practiced drill
engaged in exercises they had done
   as men began to fetch the water pails.

The Governor and Captain took command
   as everyone awakened to report
and they all recognized the threat at hand
   — the house on fire adjoined the Common Store.

The Common Store held all their gathered food
   they'd need to carry them for the whole year
and if they lost all of the common good
   it would be more than anyone could bear.

Some of the Pilgrims said to clear the store
   but Bradford feared they only would be robbed
as he saw some were watching the fires roar
   and grinning at the flames while families sobbed.

So as the others worked to douse the fires
    that now were burning several houses' roofs
the Governor pulled some men to the side
    and said to gather bundles of their clothes.

They dunked the clothes so they were sopping wet
    and ran into the store beneath the flames
and covered all the storage to protect
    from burning cinders falling overhead.

After all of the soaking clothes were set
    and as the men walked from the building's door
someone then dumped a pail on Bradford's head
    — his hat caught fire while rescuing the store.

Then once outside they joined the passing line
    with sloshing pails of water from the bay
then shouted out by someone in the night
    they heard the voice of someone clearly say:

"Be careful of some others who are near.
    Not all of those amongst you are your friends."
And as the pails of water quenched the fire
    the fiery glow began to cool and dim.

There were four houses that completely burned
    and everything inside lost to the flames
but no one had been seriously hurt
    and all the common storage had been saved.

And when they checked the damage all around
    more smoke began to rise from a small shed
on the far wall of the town's storage house
    after they thought all of the fires were dead.

But this fire looked especially suspicious
   with leaves and twigs placed in a kindling pile
and a firebrand was set as by intention
   to spark the store house from the other side.

The Pilgrim's preparations kept them safe
   but now there seemed some troubles pressing them
what had incited the fire and the flames
   was from some animosity within.

A warrant for arrest soon came to them
   for Thomas Weston to be sent away.
The general Governor demanded him
   be brought up to the Massachusetts Bay.

They also sent the *Little James* for trade
   but they returned with little fur and corn
and then upon returning to the bay
   the ship was damaged in a sudden storm.

But through their troubles they had persevered
   and their supply of food had been secured
and with the close of yet another year
   their families and town had been preserved.

1624

Chapter 66

Annual Elections
March 1624

In winter Captain Gorges returned to England
    as Wessagusset did not suit his tastes
and so the settlement packed up again
    and Weston was released to sail away.

The Pilgrims also fixed the *Little James*
    from damages inflicted by the storm
and sent the pinnace out for fish and trade
    with fresh provisions from their season's corn.

Yet through the winter some contention grew
    in hissing whispers that were going round
as some were stirring an unsavory stew
    of discontentment through the settled town.

The new-comer Particulars were set
    with John Oldham seeming to take the lead
to form a faction in the settlement
    that was against the general company.

They told the others there'd be no supplies
    and the investors had abandoned them
and sowed the seeds of bitterness with lies
    to tangle up the towns accomplishments.

Then luring others with wild fantasy
    that they would never have to work again,
all the Particulars were promising
    the opulence of the most wishful dreams.

And even though the town had modest gains,
　　all the accomplishments were real and true,
but some could not resist an offered way
　　that promised easy streets to plentitude.

And some convinced themselves they could believe,
　　despite the honest work that they had done,
that they could sink the ship while out at sea
　　and this new group would build a better one.

So a small group of the old settlers
　　thought they should break with Plymouth colony
and join the faction of Particulars
　　to gain all that the group was promising.

Then late in March for the election day
　　the people gathered on the hill to meet
to make consensus for the populace
　　their choice to lead the general company.

Before they voted Bradford stood to speak.
　　As he had served as Governor that year
he noted issues of the company
　　of relevance for the upcoming year.

He wanted to make sure they were informed
　　to make the best choice for their common good
and then before them he made his report
　　so everyone who voted understood:

"As we have now completed our third year
　　upon our settlement at Plymouth Bay,
we have endured the trials that met us here
　　to meet again for our election day.

"Of course our trials are not completely won
    because each time demands are satisfied
another task arises to be done
    and so we diligently work through life.

"But keep in mind that joy is not sustained,
    as love cannot be preciously retained,
except as our devotion stays engaged
    in labor for what we fulfill to make.

"We know the happiness of families
    just as success of the community
cannot be passively set to receive
    but actively and carefully achieved.

"And individual accomplishments
    that have been reached through ventures and endeavors
have all arisen from our settlement
    that our determination built together.

"And through the years our little town has grown
    so have demands in public management
and we must draw forth more throughout our own
    for leaders in our civil government.

"Until we learn to live a perfect way
    so no act causes any detriment,
for the security of private gains
    we must provide for public benefit.

"If governing be honored and esteemed
    then there should be more who partake in it.
If governing be deemed a burdening
    then there should be more willing to bear it.

"I thus propose increasing the held posts
    of the assistants to the Governor
and bring this for this year's election vote
    to help maintain community accord.

"There is another issue that arose,
    some members of the general company
expressed a wish to close the shares they hold
    and free themselves from Plymouth Colony.

"For this the general body has agreed
    but as we know the gift of liberty
also accrues responsibilities
    that cannot be dismissed so easily.

"We all agreed to a full seven years
    to pay investors for our ventured share.
Pursuit of freedom is why we moved here
    but for this there are burdens we must bear.

"Those wishing to join the Particulars
    will be allowed to leave the company
but they must wait for the full seven years
    or payments to the store must be increased.

"And then for the remaining time agreed
    they'll pay half of their grown commodities
– beside what their household will need to eat –
    in contribution for their tenancy."

Then William Bradford won another term
    in the election for the Governor
and five assistants were also confirmed
    to represent the public whom they served.

The fractious group stayed with the company.
   They only wanted to get things for free
then with an open door to liberty
   they found that staying was the greater ease.

Chapter 67

Winslow Returns
March 1624

Soon after the election had been held
  another ship arrived at Plymouth Bay
and as the tide inside the harbor swelled
  the Pilgrims kept their rosy hope restrained.

Some of them recognized the *Charity,*
  the ship had visited the former year,
and had brought Pilgrim friends and families
  along with the dissenting new-comers.

With all the ships that had arrived before
  the Pilgrims set their hearts upon relief
but every time the ships came to harbor
  the ships delivered burdens of more grief.

Then as a group stood at the harbor shore
  a musket shot saluted from the ship
and they could hear as Winslow made report
  and waved his hat in joy from the distance.

So Bradford and some others took the boat
  and pulled the oars to row across the bay
and they saw Winslow from their slow approach
  and clearly a bright smile was on his face.

And as the shallop drew next to the hull
  they recognized Commander William Peirce
who proudly stood upon the deck above
  with Winslow greeting with abundant cheer.

And with permission granted to the men
   the Governor began to climb on board
and stepping up the ladder in ascent
   he heard the sound of cattle's mooing joy.

Then when he saw the cattle on the deck
   the Governor embraced Winslow's return
with a strong sense the trip was a success
   before the gathered group could say a word.

Then Winslow made a quick apology
   for the delays before returning home
and said that he could speak more openly
   when they could talk more privately alone.

The Governor reacted with surprise,
   the voyage seemed to be a great success.
Winslow did not need to apologize
   and Bradford smiled at his friend's humbleness.

Then Winslow gave the Governor a pack
   of letters in a bundle neatly tied
and Bradford set them gently in his bag
   and said the council would view them that night.

Then Master Peirce led them below the deck
   to see the cargo they had in the hold
and William Bradford saw what they brought back
   — all the supplies they held more worth than gold.

And then returning to the upper deck
   and speaking to the other men on board
they cheered to hear of labors coming next
   with heavy work hauling supplies to shore.

Then Winslow introduced the Governor
   to three men who were waiting on the side.
Each one was brought to aid the endeavor
   with expertise in the crafts that they plied.

The first man was a fisher of the sea
   they'd send up to Cape Ann to settle down
and he would work with the ship *Charity*
   where the best fishing places could be found.

Another was a salter by his trade
   and from the water of the open sea
there would be boundless profit they could make
   by selling salt to fishing ships they see.

The third man was a master carpenter
   and building ships was his trade's specialty
and he was eager to begin his work
   constructing Plymouth its own sailing fleet.

Then more than bringing trade commodities
   and a supply of fresh necessities
Winslow made sure that he brought back the means
   for them to gain more self-sufficiency.

After the Governor met the trade men
   a meek and humble voice begged reverently
and then a cringing man came up to them
   who struck the Pilgrims with humility.

Then Winslow told the other Pilgrim leaders
   the man was an anointed minister
whom Winslow knew by the name of John Lyford
   who had been sent by pushy investors.

Then Lyford stepped forward with his head bowed
   and his whole body trembled where he stood
and he kept his face solemnly turned down
   as if he dare not lift his eyes to look.

Then Bradford graciously addressed the man
   with a kind voice yet loud enough to hear
and looking up as a poor supplicant
   John Lyford's eyes were brimming with his tears.

Then suddenly he burst in howling sobs,
   no longer able to restrain himself,
and praised the mercy of the Holy God
   for his deliverance and sacred help.

And graciously the Pilgrims all received
   the man who stood and made a solemn plead
not doubting his aggrieved sincerity
   while hoping they could help the man find peace.

Then through the day the Pilgrims toiled and worked
   unloading the supplies off of the ship
and each time that the shallop came to shore
   the loads were cheered with rife astonishment.

Chapter 68

Plymouth Council / Oldham's Confession
March 1624

The same night that the *Charity* arrived
    the council met inside the Meetinghouse
and Edward Winslow carefully described
    what had transpired while he was gone from town.

He mentioned problems with the investors
    who had resisted sending some supplies
and as he mentioned to the Governor
    they had delayed the ship's departure time.

There was a factious group opposing them
    amongst investors of the company.
They were a small number of merchant men
    but they were set against the colony.

They seemed intent to tear the venture down
    but there were questions to the men's design
and why they wanted to destroy the town
    — they were invested in the enterprise.

Some others offered to buy the joint stock
    – the faction must not want what they abuse –
and then they could get their investments back
    or else all of them would abjectly lose.

The council said that while Winslow was gone
    they were addressing the same situation
and the Particular group that had come
    seemed set upon the public's agitation.

Then Winslow made one more important point
that after him and Cushman found a ship
the opposition seemed to find accord
and then they acquiesced to give consent.

But they insisted that some of their men
were sent with them to Plymouth on the boat
and with no reason to object to them
Cushman and him gave way to let them go.

The letters that Edward Winslow had brought
confirmed the information that he gave
and there appeared to be subversive plots
against the little town at Plymouth Bay.

A group was set to see the Pilgrims fail
yet some wanted the Pilgrims to succeed
and the conflict to tip the balanced scales
had cleaved in half the London company.

And then a letter from the treasurer
gave indication of uncertainties
that caused concern within the investors
about the Pilgrims' instability.

But as they read the list of the complaints
they were astonished at the things they heard.
This bold endeavor was not for the faint,
and the complaints were baseless and absurd.

Some who had left complained there was no beer
and said they could not bear to drink the water
but they did not have any market stores
and they were nowhere near a local tavern.

There were the matters of reality,
   they were not on a flight of dalliance.
This was the pressing work of industry
   and they had known there would be challenges.

Winslow said he had thoroughly explained
   but they all knew the only way to prove
what they were doing for the venture's gain
   was from the fruits that their work could produce.

Reflecting on what they had overcome
   and the stability they had achieved
the substance and the sense of what they'd done
   was irrefutable reality.

No doubt Winslow delivered from his trip.
   He brought some cattle and commodities.
Cushman and him had found the three trade men
   and they were set for self-sufficiency.

They knew that situations always change.
   They knew the dangers of complacency
and vigilance allowed them to manage
   diverting devastating tragedies.

And from production of their industry
   they would be able to settle their debts
and the investors of the company
   would have no reason for their arguments.

So they resolved to focus on their work.
   They had no time for the cantankerous.
Raffish contentiousness does not endure.
   They wanted to build up their settlement.

And then agreeing to stay on their course
    they thought they could retire for the good night
and then there was a knock upon the door
    and they beheld John Oldham walk inside.

But listening the council was surprised
    when Oldham meekly asked if he could speak.
He wanted to confess that very night
    what weighed upon his conscience heavily.

He said he wronged them by his words and deeds
    and slandered them in letters that he wrote
and had been hired in animosity
    so that the colony was overthrown.

But now he sees with the commodities
    and the arrival of the fresh supplies,
the competency of the company
    and recognized that he had been beguiled.

He said he would not be an instrument
    against the Pilgrims and the colony
and hoped to benefit the settlement
    and be forgiven by them decently.

The instance seemed an answer to their prayers
    as they had hoped they could reach an accord
and work together in ways that were fair
    resolving qualms of the Particulars.

And since the leader of the factious group
    expressed desire to join the company
the others could decide to join in suit
    and work together in sweet harmony.

Chapter 69

Hopes and Joys
Spring and Summer 1624

Before the yearly lots had been assigned
  so everyone could start to sow their crops
the planters asked for a change of design
  so they could be assigned permanent lots.

The year before had been their best harvest
  where they held ownership of their own work
and they felt they could build on this progress
  if ownership of lots was also firm.

Then they could manage their own property
  and the devotion to their acre lots
would be their own responsibility
  instead of skipping from plot after plot.

The corn became more valuable than silver
  through satisfaction found in wholesome meals,
and quarts of kernels became the gold standard
  and tasteful trade was purchased at the till.

No one in town had money anyway
  and without stores where money could be spent
the budgets they maintained and fees they paid
  were all devoted to true nourishment.

The Governor and Council all agreed
  that each should hold account upon themselves
and caring for their private property
  maintain the source of their enriching health.

So every person was assigned a lot
   to hold and maintain as their property
— an acre each could cultivate with crops
   and reap the fruits of their own industry.

And as the planters diligently sowed
   for what they cultivated privately
there were some other specializing roles
   applying to the general company.

And everyone paid tribute to the town
   to cover the community expense,
a small percentage of what they each grew,
   their shares providing general betterment.

And the three men upon the *Charity*
   were promptly given stations for their work
and they were all provided parity
   to pay their trades out of the common purse.

But with each hope of means the town may gain
   that had arrived upon the *Charity*
none of them were able to be sustained
   as each one foundered disappointingly.

The *Charity* dispatched north to Cape Ann
   to build the fishing stages on the coast
to clean and salt the fish that they had planned
   the fisher would haul back with each caught load.

And several of the planters volunteered
   to help the venture at their own expense
as building permanent processing tiers
   would later be to the town's benefit.

The fisher on whom the endeavor hinged
　then proved to be a laggard and a drunk
and the supplies and service sent to him
　were lost as the whole enterprise was sunk.

But all of the endeavor wasn't lost
　as the men were able to compensate
recovering the company's spent cost
　with loads of fur through their established trade.

The salter also proved of little worth
　although he gushed how much he would produce
but when it boiled down to the earnest work
　the braggadocio proved little use.

He scouted all around for a good site
　and took samples of soil methodically
as if performing alchemy divines
　for incantations of a mystery.

Enchanting upon an ideal location
　he had ten of the men dig him big holes
that would hold water for the operation
　fulfilling all the fortunes he foretold.

And then he had them build him a large house
　where the arising piles of salt would stay
but of the reservoirs dug from the ground
　the water they poured in just drained away.

The third man differed from the other two
　and earnestly began to build them boats
and his capacity and skill were proved
　in the production that his work bestowed.

There were two sturdy shallops that he made,
    a lighter they could use as a small barge
and he was teaching the skills of his trade
    to Francis Eaton — Plymouth's carpenter.

Then next, two ketches were planned to be built
    but after they had hewn the oaken boards
in the hot days the ship builder fell ill
    and his health's vigor could not be restored.

Then Samuel Fuller and the others tried
    to help and cure the man at any cost
but in the summer heat he slowly died
    and they were all heartbroken with the loss.

Then news came from distant Damariscove
    where *Little James*, the town's pinnace had gone.
The ship was wrecked while harbored at the cove
    and the ship's master and two sailors drowned.

A storm had broken the ship from its ties
    and smashed the hull upon the rocky beach.
And then the ship was dragged out with the tide
    and sunk so only the masts could be seen.

So many hopes and joys that they received
    were taken from them just as easily
and as they strove for self-sufficiency
    their self-reliance proved the remedy.

Chapter 70

John Lyford
Spring and Summer 1624

Of those who came upon the *Charity*
   John Lyford did not have a standard trade.
His calling was within the ministry
   and as a pastor he had been ordained.

The letters that the Pilgrims had received
   presented several reasons for concern
and there were many curiosities
   they were not fully able to discern.

In London there was clear hostility,
   the different letters all stated the same
as some investors in the company
   seemed to oppose the Pilgrims in the main.

The Pilgrims hoped to bring those from their church
   from whom they parted at the town of Leyden
but each attempt was hampered and deferred
   and friends and family were stuck in Holland.

Then every time the ships brought passengers
   many arrivals were opposed to them
as if they were receiving saboteurs
   who had been sent in sore malevolence.

Even the letter from John Robinson,
   their reverend Pastor who remained in Leyden,
made the suggestion they were blocking him
   from coming to be minister of Plymouth.

And Cushman stated in his letter sent
  that the opposing group had pushed instead
for Lyford to go to the settlement
  which he had hinted as cause for suspect.

Although the Pilgrims took note from their friends
  the messages were offering advice
and did not go so far as to condemn
  and they preferred to see with their own eyes.

So Master Lyford was received in town
  and warmly welcomed with sincerity
and choosing to refrain from skittish doubt
  the Pilgrims trusted to be neighborly.

The first impression that John Lyford gave
  was gushing reverence and modesty
and sympathetically they had been swayed
  with streaming tears that streaked upon his cheeks.

And they had spent some time talking with him
  for more insight into his ministry
and spoke of verses that gave light to them
  and raptured in the scriptures' sanctity.

And Lyford cheered the town's accomplishments
  and loved the services on Sabbath day
and dove-like lighted on the settlement
  and filled the air with his uplifting praise.

And he confessed transgressions from his past
  and of the pangs his conscience sorely hurt
and yearned for pure simplicity at last
  and hoped that one day he could join the church.

And through devotion that they found they shared
    and in accord with the beliefs they lived,
they welcomed to receive with love and care
    in humble comforts that they had to give.

And in respect of Lyford's acumen
    and honoring his wisdom's clear insight
they told him matters of the settlement
    and then consulted him for his advice.

Although they warmly had accepted him
    in time they noticed Lyford drift away
and then to further their astonishment
    he spent his time with Oldham on most days.

And then the faction of Particulars
    gathered again in a contentious group
and Lyford and John Oldham seemed to stir
    them as the leaders of a raucous crew.

And then some heard John Lyford make the claim
    the church at Plymouth was a heresy
and that their Sabbath service was profane
    and was devoid of any piety.

He said they did not have a minister
    and with no Pastor there could be no church.
Without a shepherd to instruct the herd
    the flock of the lost sheep would never learn.

Then Lyford said he volunteered to serve
    but then the Pilgrim leaders had refused,
he was anointed at a proper church
    whose sanctity the Pilgrims had abused.

Then as the Pilgrim leaders walked through town
   and when they gathered for their common work
the hissing whispers slithered all around
   and chortles from snide mockeries were heard.

And if another honestly inquired
   about the secret silliness they teased
their faces would turn plane in blank denial
   as if offended by the inquiry.

Then as the *Charity* readied to sail
   John Lyford seemed especially withdrawn
and as he had been keeping to himself
   he wrote all night until each morning's dawn.

He busily was writing secret letters
   some noticed he kept carefully concealed
and then he slipped them to one of the sailors
   with coins in payment for a slippery deal.

Then with this sly and clandestine exchange
   the sailor was seen laughing in his sleeve
and glimpsed by Pilgrims passing on their way
   they thought this was a curiosity.

Chapter 71

For One and All
Summer and Autumn 1624

The Pilgrims noted Lyford's sly exchange
    and they coordinated a quick plan.
The *Charity* was ready to voyage back
    and Winslow would sail with the ship again.

And Master William Peirce was well aware
    of treacheries he had seen taking place.
He'd seen the shuffling on the English pier
    and the frustrations and absurd delays.

His competency of the ship's command
    required attention to minute details.
He saw some things that had passed underhand
    both in the harbors and when they set sail.

And any good commander worth his salt
    could not allow such happenings to slip.
There must be actions to correct the fault
    or else the perfidy could sink the ship.

So when the ship had sailed out in the sea
    then Master Peirce commanded them to hold
and out from harbor at about three leagues
    the Pilgrims reached the ship in their small boat.

The Governor and others came on board
    and Lyford's letters were quickly retrieved
and in John Lyford's hand they saw record
    of wicked treachery and ill deceit.

The twenty letters John Lyford had sent
  were filled with rancorous dishonesty
and plans to ruin the small settlement
  were written boldly and explicitly.

And in one letter to John Pemberton,
  a foe to their small Reformation church,
they found two letters Lyford had purloined
  and made copies with annotated slurs.

One letter was to Brewster from before,
  the other written to John Robinson
that Lyford copied on the former voyage
  before they left the English port Gravesend.

Then Winslow noted earlier that year
  while loading shipments to the colony,
he left the cabin to attend affairs
  and then found someone rummaged through his things.

This added scope to the conspiracy
  and proved how far back Lyford's acts began
as he connived upon the *Charity*
  before the ship had even left England.

The Pilgrim leaders then made careful records
  of contents from the letters Lyford wrote
and with fair copies from all of the letters
  they let most of John Lyford's letters go.

However those of most material
  they sent fair copies to the addressees
and kept as evidence originals
  in Lyford's hand to prove his treachery.

There were some letters by John Oldham too
    whose scrawl of script was difficult to read
but they could see his deep involvement to
    the evil aims of the conspiracy.

And then the ship continued sailing out
    preventing those on board who were in league
from notifying villains in the town
    who planned to ruin the community.

Then on the little boat the leaders turned
    and rowed the shallop back to Plymouth Bay
to see what more they were able to learn
    before they chose a criminal court date.

Upon returning not a word was said
    and then they waited till the time was ripe
to let the traitors build their confidence
    and carefully observe what would transpire.

And then the faction began to grow bold
    with bitterness and animosity
and looked for ways to bait and to provoke
    and tried to quarrel about everything.

Then once when Oldham was called to his watch
    to serve his civil duty in his turn
he insolently began talking back
    and tried inciting Standish with barbed spurns.

So Oldham began calling Standish names
    as if his rubbish could cause injury
and stooping to the vulgar and profane
    he needled for some sensitivity.

But Captain Standish could not be aroused
    and stood and stared in utter disbelief
at foolish gestures from a silly clown
    who seemed infirmed with an absurdity.

Then finding Standish too firm of a man
    he held a knife up to the Captain's chest
but when the Captain grabbed it from his hand
    he screamed the Captain was hurting his wrist.

On Sabbath, Lyford gathered his own group
    and damned others for heathen practices
and said the Plymouth church to be untrue
    and only he could hold church services.

And the Particulars began to pick
    at everything within the settlement
and called the Pilgrims evil heretics
    demanding the church members banishment.

And then the leaders thought that it was time
    to gather in the Plymouth Meetinghouse
and to conduct an open, public trial
    to set the evidence before the town.

Chapter 72

The Trial
Autumn 1624

The people gathered in the Meetinghouse
    and although they did not know of the trial
as everyone assembled from the town
    they felt the weightiness of the called time.

And as the day's assembly settled down
    and everyone had found a place to sit
the Governor stood facing the whole town
    and brought to order for the fellowship.

Then Brewster was asked to lead them in prayer,
    an invocation before they began,
and eloquently he prayed for repair
    through wisdom in hope they may understand.

Then after Brewster's gracious eloquence,
    a blessing for the civil gathering,
the Governor stood in the front again
    and opened his explanatory speech.

"I thank you all for your faithful attendance
    and taking time from duties of your day
but there arose a matter of importance
    that jeopardizes the whole company.

"We all have our own obligated tasks
    providing for ourselves and families
and the reality of which I ask
    diverts us from responsibilities.

"And as we all pursue our private lives
    so much depends upon the Commonwealth
as all the work we do and trade we ply
    relies upon what others do as well.

"We make no claim for wealth gained without work
    and do not shirk from life's adversities.
Our trust in one another is our worth.
    Our greatest asset is community.

"So with the time you all have set aside
    with our attention in our unity,
our separate lives may thoughtfully align
    for our well-being and stability.

"Together we maintain this settlement.
    The Commonwealth depends upon us all
and every service for our betterment
    in diverse ways does service for us all.

"We do not claim to have a perfect state
    but persevere in practicality
as through the years we have managed to make
    a town through honest work and industry.

"And as we rise upon what we achieve
    we broaden vision with fresh inspiration
but sadly each success and victory
    will be frustrated with jealous contention.

"Last year many arrived upon the *Anne*
    and all were welcomed in our settlement
and we agreed upon an honest plan
    for those who came upon their own expense.

"Yet through the year a faction has been formed
    that is attacking our town's unity
and peevishness of the Particulars
    is discomposing the community.

"We all know well we went without supplies
    and this required our careful management
and for another year we have survived
    and further strengthen our establishment.

"The new-comers should know we went for years
    and the investors never sent us help
and the town that the new-comers found here
    we painstakingly built all by ourselves.

"In fact we have learned that there is a group
    of the investors who oppose the town
and we have learned that some are being used
    to try to tear the whole colony down.

"And thus today we have assembled here
    and formally present the allegations
so the community can see and hear
    the presentation of the accusations.

"As Governor of Plymouth colony
    I call John Oldham and John Lyford forth
with allegations of conspiracy
    in acts intent to harm the Commonwealth."

The two men sat within the factious group
    that hissed and sneered with insolent disdain
and leaping to his feet John Oldham stood
    and shouted out disgracefully profane:

"That is a lie and you're a bunch of rascals.
    I've never been against this stupid town
and you all just like causing people hassles
    and then attack to hold a good man down!"

John Lyford was a little more composed
    and looked around him in shocked disbelief
and as he stood he straightened his wool coat
    and weighed his words for a responsive speech.

"There certainly will be a reckoning
    with charges brought against a man ordained
who came to save you all from suffering
    in wicked misery and sinful shame.

"You Puritans have blocked me from the church
    and have denied me of my ministry
and are rejecting the true, sacred word
    to make this place a heathen colony.

"I bear these vile offenses of abuse
    with graciousness that is the gift of God
and all these allegations are untrue
    just as this trial is an egregious fraud."

After the two Particulars' rebuke
    John Oldham and John Lyford took their seats.
They said the allegations were untrue.
    That's all the others needed to believe.

Yet others who were sitting all around
    knew contrary to what the two denied
as they had heard their bitterness in town
    and knew the two men's statements were both lies.

And some of their most loyal followers
    were shocked to hear what both of the men said,
their statements changed when they addressed the court
    from what they'd say inside their group's enclaves.

Then Bradford nodded at the men's replies
    confirming that he understood them both
and seeming unperturbed by any guise
    he kept his calm composure as he spoke:

"I thank you both for the two statements made
    before the town's entire community
and first I will address what Oldham said
    and see if I can jog his memory.

"I'm sure each person here heard Oldham say
    — 'He's never been against this stupid town'
yet there was a confession that he made
    and said he wanted to burn the town down.

"The very night the *Charity* arrived
    the Council held a meeting in this Hall
and Goodman Oldham entered quite contrite
    and openly confessed before us all.

"He said that he had tried to hurt the town
    in words and deeds and acts of treachery
and everyone has witnessed him around
    and with their own eyes they have clearly seen."

Then staying in his seat John Oldham yelled,
    "That's a lie! I never said anything!"
and so the irony spoke for itself
    and Bradford then continued with his speech.

"But then you were befriended by John Lyford
    and joined into the thinly veiled rebellion
and everyone has seen that you are spiteful
    and sowing prickly seeds of sour contention.

"And we were notified of opposition
    in London of some company investors
and we have learned of their secret intention
    to force our little town to fail and falter.

"Some of the members of the company
    said they were blocking shipments of supplies
and the group was against the colony
    and did not care about the settlers' lives.

"That's why the town had sent Winslow before
    and he returned upon the *Charity*
and that is how we heard of their reports
    and the supplies we needed desperately.

"Then the opposing group had to relent
    so the supplies could finally be shipped
but then on board they made sure they had sent
    someone who had a poisonous intent.

"Now Master Lyford previously said
    that we would not admit him in our church
but somehow sadly he has been misled
    from conversations we had earlier.

"John Lyford said that he wanted to join
    our church after arriving on the ship
and all the deacons had been overjoyed
    for him to join our Sabbath fellowship.

"Then as we learned what only time could tell
    we had to wait before we let him preach
but then on Sabbath while our church was held
    John Lyford started meetings secretly.

"He claimed that he was giving sacrament
    and we withheld and did not interfere.
We would have loved him at our services
    as we admired him as a minister.

"The seeds of discontentment have been sown
    and tangled brambles snag our every step
as prickly briars and poisonous berries grow
    to choke the open fields our labors kept.

"John Oldham pulled a knife on Captain Standish
    and threatened to plunge it into his heart
yet the defenses that the Captain managed
    have saved our lives more times than we can mark.

"And from the secret meetings Lyford holds
    and twisted whispers that are malice bent
we all have seen this plot as it unfolds
    and recognize the damage it intends.

"And Lyford's actions perfectly coincide
    with what the opposition group has done
and we know he is working on their side
    an instrument of their malevolence."

Again John Lyford delicately stood
    and carefully made his formal address
while managing the comfort of his mood
    with smoothness that he easily expressed:

"I bear to witness what the Governor
    and Council have indecently proclaimed
but graciously I'll give my honest answer
    to these defamatory statements made.

"My wife and I came to this colony
    in hopes to find a godly fellowship,
for sanctuary and for purity
    in pious prayer and heavenly worship.

"I see my services as minister
    are needed by this testimonial
as statements made by our poor Governor
    are self-deceptive and delusional.

"I am a shepherd come for the lost sheep
    and underneath the soot of burnt deceit
I see the tenderness of purity
    that still remains untouched from what misleads.

"I am a man of God, not business
    and lead the way to save and to redeem.
I don't spend time hobnobbing with merchants.
    My calling is divine, not market schemes.

"This whole idea is quite ridiculous.
    I'm not in league with some conspirators.
I do not have time for this foolishness.
    I do not even know the investors.

"I hope you will appoint me minister
    as I can see these leaders are confused.
The statements here are vile and sinister.
    You cannot make these claims, you have no proof!"

Smugly satisfied Lyford sat back down
    as the assembly shuffled in unrest.
The barbed contention they had seen in town
    was now confronted in civil contest.

Then the attention of the company
    turned to the front to wait for a response
and William Bradford nodded silently
    and members of the Council correspond.

They brought a bunch of letters to the front,
    all bundled neatly with a single string,
and murmurs turned as matters came undone
    while Bradford drew the knot's unfastening.

Then carefully he sorted through the bunch
    and took the time to organize his thoughts.
He was not going to lurch into a lung
    and smudge the lines of the uncovered plot.

There was a change in the Particulars
    who looked at Lyford in astonishment
and then the town's elected Governor
    resumed his speech to the whole settlement.

"We find it interesting that Lyford claims
    he does not know the opposition's plan
when we have letters that were sent to them
    and they were written in John Lyford's hand."

And then the Governor began to read
    straight from the letters to the Company
and all the people could together see
    the letters smeared and smudged with falsity.

All the descriptions that Lyford had wrote
    were clear distortions of reality
and some thought they could even be a joke
    if they were not such a sad travesty.

And Lyford wrote about the Leyden church
    and said they should not come and must be blocked
because the Pastor and their friends would hurt
    the execution of their secret plot.

And as they listened to the Governor
    reading the letters no one could believe
even members of the Particulars
    objected and openly disagreed.

Then Oldham jumped up and began to scream:
    "It's evil to have read my private letters!
You Puritans are just a bunch of fiends!"
    And then he tried inciting all the others:

"My Masters! Where are your hearts and your rage!
    You have often complained! Now is the time!
Have courage and seize this moment to charge!
    With what you do, I will be at your side."

But all his group looked in bewilderment.
    They heard what both of the men had denied
and then they heard the letters they had sent
    and they could see the slander and the lies.

Then seeing that he had no more support
    he turned to leaders of the colony
and in his rage said that the Governor
    had violated the group's privacy.

Now that the squall had seemed to settle down
   John Oldham could no longer stir up hate
and Master Lyford sat with his head bowed,
   not in devotion but to hide his face.

An then the Governor began to speak:
   "We thank you Goodman Oldham for your say
and if you please, now kindly take your seat
   or else we will have to keep you restrained.

"Now we can see your previous denial
   of trying to incite a mutiny
has been presented to us in this trial
   and witnessed by the whole community.

"And now a question for Master John Lyford,
   do you agree with what John Oldham said,
that the investigation of your letters
   intended to harm in an evil way?"

Then in the pause John Lyford didn't move,
   in fact, he didn't even lift his head.
He was the one who had demanded proof
   and now his insolence seemed to be dead.

And then the Governor went on to say,
   "It seems that Master Lyford cannot speak.
Perhaps I may be able to explain
   for why he chooses to sit quietly.

"He probably realizes we discovered
   he stole some letters from the colony
as our investigation has uncovered
   his malice and his jealous treachery.

"We have two letters of our brethren
    taken from Winslow on the *Charity*
that Lyford had copied in his own hand
    before they set sail to the colony.

"It's true I intercepted Lyford's letters
    and him and Oldham both gave us good cause
and I had done this for the town's protection
    yet he had done it to cause us all harm.

"As Governor of our Community
    I gathered the supporting evidence
and in performing my civil duty
    presented it in court for the public."

Eventually John Lyford stood to speak
    but pointed at Particulars to blame
and as he carried on indignantly
    he filled the room with bitterness and shame.

The year before the colony established
    a jury system for their public court
and there was no lengthy deliberation
    before they reached a verdict to report.

Both Lyford and John Oldham were convicted
    and were expelled from the community.
John Lyford had six months before eviction
    and Oldham had to leave immediately.

Of course the Pilgrims offered clemency
    if the men could prove that they were reformed
but they would have to bear this patiently
    for status in the town to be restored.

Then Lyford suddenly broke down in tears
   and made confessions of his dreadful guilt
and said his conscience could no longer bear
   the wickedness he had tried to conceal.

He said that he could never make amends
   and had done Plymouth and its people wrong
and tried to ruin the whole settlement
   and all that he had wrote was false and naught.

So Oldham had to get ready to leave,
   his family could stay for six more months,
until he had made comfortable means
   to give them proper accommodations.

And Lyford could remain for six more months
   but if he then refused to be reformed
they would expel him from the settlement
   and move his family to be restored.

Chapter 73

Constantly Inconstant

John Lyford had withdrawn to meditate
    and for some weeks kept wholly to himself.
He seemed resigned as the town's reprobate
    and others felt how sadly he had fell.

Then as sometime had passed John Lyford asked
    if he could make a statement at the church.
He wanted to apologize at last
    to all the people in the town he hurt.

The Council of the town and Governor
    had been observing Lyford for some weeks
and felt that he was trying to reform
    and they decided they would let him speak.

So they determined the next Sabbath day
    when all the people gathered in the church
they granted that his conscience that he weighed
    would have a chance to be graciously heard.

Then after sacred worship had been held
    where Elder Brewster preached then closed with prayer
John Lyford was led to the front to tell
    the people of the weight he could not bear.

Then standing up before the congregation
    John Lyford was completely overwhelmed.
Even before he could make his first statement
    he sobbed and trembled so he almost fell.

Then someone stood and helped to steady him
   and slowly Lyford became more composed.
Then Lyford nodded meekly to the man
   after he balanced from his bawling throes.

Then sniveling and with a trembling voice
   John Lyford spoke before the gathered town,
"I will confess I have been this town's foe
   and both in word and deed done you all wrong.

"And with my evil words and treachery
   I thought I could stir rancor in this town
and fiendishly and diabolically
   bring the whole village violently down.

"Hospitably I was received in town
   and then I offered bitterness in turn.
I shut my eyes to kindness I was shown
   and closed my ears to goodness I had heard.

"And now I stray about without a home
   from the malicious envy I had sinned,
now cursed as Cain to be a vagabond
   from my infliction on my brethren.

"I wasted all and now all has been lost,
   forsaking grace in friends and God above,
and the three things I know to be the cause
   — vainglory, pride and glutinous self-love."

And then collapsing down upon his knees —
   "I know you all could never forgive me.
All I can ask is that you pray for me."
   as he continued to profusely weep.

With this some of the Pilgrim's tender hearts
   were moved to help this wretched suffering
and Samuel Fuller was the first to start
   to coax the poor man's sad infirmity.

As surgeon he could not allow such pain
   without attempting ways to heal and mend
and as a deacon he professed his faith
   by trying to forgive and not condemn.

Then others joined with Fuller in a plead
   believing his repentance was sincere
and begged that Lyford's censure be released
   and for his harsh expulsion to be cleared.

And then the members of the church agreed
   that Reverend Lyford fully be absolved.
He turned away from his iniquity
   and once again followed a higher call.

Then formally accepting his repentance
   they lifted punishment that he had bore
and welcomed him in town with sweet forgiveness
   and he could teach amongst them as before.

But then despite his numerous confessions,
   convictions and announced acknowledgements
he turned back to his treacherous aggressions
   and diabolical belligerence.

He stood before the members of the church
   and before God confessed to the whole town
and after all his crying they had heard
   he tried to justify what he had done.

They found that he had written once again
   and tried to get another letter through
confirming all he previously said
   to prove to them again he was untrue.

He carried himself as a godly man.
   He knew the scriptures and could quote from them
and by the orders he had been ordained.
   But Lyford kept the devil inside him.

The Pilgrims would return to their decision
   expelling Lyford for his punishment.
They hoped that he could prove to be repentant
   but Lyford's wickedness would not relent.

Chapter 74

Raising the Pinnace

From Eastward came a boat bearing good news
    regarding the wreck of the *Little James*,
the ship had been abandoned by the crew
    but these men said they knew it could be saved.

The ship had sunk while at Damariscove,
    a storm had battered it against the shore
and no more than the masts were seen above
    the water where it sat on the sea floor.

But then the fishermen explained a plan
    to raise the ship so it could be reclaimed.
From what the ship was able to withstand
    to lose the vessel would be a sad shame.

So then the Pilgrims organized a group
    to join the fishermen by Monhegan
and all together see what they could do
    to raise the ship for carpenters to mend.

With ample store of victuals to provide
    and beaver pelts to help defray the cost,
the men set sail with their tools and supplies
    with buoyant spirits to save what was lost.

Then at the cove the men set to their work,
    John Alden, the town's cooper trimmed the casks
and others helped by hewing needed boards
    so that the ship could be repaired at last.

They worked for weeks and watched the turn of tide
   that ebbed and flooded in and out the cove
and like the lapping on the water line
   there was the constant pulsing through the flow.

And as the water level slowly fell
   the wreckage of the ship was then exposed
and they could see the damage to the hull
   and splintered boards were smashed at a large hole.

And as the glut was pouring from the ship
   as ebbing tides receded every day
the precious food and goods that the ship kept
   were washed away in a dejected waste.

Then when the ship appeared completely drained
   they saw the flotsam strewn out in the mud
and then the coming tide would slowly raise
   and drown the ship again beneath the flood.

Upon the massive movement of the world
   and with the rise and fall of constant change
the Pilgrims held fast to their busy work
   and were affirmed in how they stayed engaged.

The *Little James* could be raised in a day
   between the low and high marks of the tide
but preparations needed to be made
   before their machinations could be tried.

The sea is a profound immensity
   where soaring mountain ranges can be drowned
but with a little ingenuity
   solutions for all problems can be found.

And the relentless changes of the tide
    that tirelessly erode the *Little James*
could be hitched as a horse with proper ties
    if they learned how a harness could be made.

Yet still to know does not make something done
    and grappling with the task is the sole way
and then one finds the engine of invention
    is powered by disruptions from the change.

Then working to prepare what they would need
    they made themselves prepared to do the task,
then sail the unseen opportunities
    as massive ships are moved by canvassed masts.

Then organized, they all knew what to do
    and waited for the ripeness of the time
and in the morning of the newest moon
    they'd have the broadest range of different tides.

They tied the buoyant casks in fastened lines
    and hauled them where the *Little James* had sunk
and riding on the dropping of the tide
    the ship was harnessed with the strings of tuns.

Then checking and rechecking the cinched knots
    they made sure everything had been secured
then waited to see if what they had thought
    would pass the test and actually work.

For months the ship had sunk repeatedly
    and had been inundated countless times
but then they hoped their creativity
    would help the ship to rise up with the tide.

And as the ocean tide came flooding in
    the ropes and wood began to creak and moan
which was a good sign to all of the men
    because they knew their work carried a load.

Then as the flowing tide steadily rose
    the ship that had been listing on its side
was moving as if it began to float
    and slowly pitching began to turn right.

Through this the taut suspense began to build,
    the project seemed to move in the right way
but this brimmed bowl could accidentally spill
    and wreck again if anything gave way.

And then the *Little James* was floating free
    and as the tide continued flowing high
they had to work even more urgently
    to set her at the shore to fit her tight.

Then at the shore they worked on the repairs
    and weeks went by before the work was done
but when the *Little James* was fit to sail
    they gloriously steered her back to home.

1625

Chapter 75

John Oldham's Return
Spring 1625

In the next spring around election time
    John Oldham waltzed in with some other men
as if he wasn't ready to resign
    from causing a commotion with offense.

They dragged their boat up on the sandy beach
    and Oldham did not show any compunction
as he could not return without a leave
    but he was not one to regard instructions.

In fact he raged as if he had been wronged
    and had convinced the men who came with him
that some unscrupulous line had been drawn
    and they had come to set things right again.

And as the small group marched into the town
    John Oldham led them with his yelling voice
and slowly people gathered all around
    with a short pause of each one's daily chores.

And although Oldham didn't seem to mind
    the other men were struck with disbelief
when children began scattering in fright
    from gathered lessons learning how to read.

The Deaconess and Goodwife Mary Brewster
    had been conducting school outside that day
and Oldham with his group of rude intruders
    had scattered all the children in a fray.

But Oldham had been blinded by his rage
   and lost all sense of rationality
and from the village that he had portrayed
   the other men then saw things differently.

John Oldham said the town had been oppressive
   and all the people lived in misery
but they saw nothing tyrannous or dreadful
   just a small town with cheery families.

So keeping careful watch upon the men
   then Mary Brewster had someone retrieve
the others who were working in the fields
   as it was time for sowing the year's seeds.

And promptly others returned to the town
   and then the Plymouth Council all arrived
and Oldham raged on like an angry clown
   and pointed out each person he despised.

And when he saw the Governor had come
   while rushing from the fields with all the others,
John Oldham jumped up on his knotty stump
   and raved and railed as if he had no druthers.

And all the men who Oldham brought with him
   became embarrassed with all that they heard
as Oldham seemed to rant on without end
   with bitter, hateful statements that he slurred.

And there was no loss in the irony
   as Oldham made his vitriolic stand
and used the vilest language hatefully
   declaring Bradford an ungodly man.

Then after everyone had heard enough
　　and Bradford was about to interject
one of the ladies in the group spoke up
　　and suddenly John Oldham was silent.

The one and only person in the crowd
　　who seemed to part the storm with sunny light
and bring to peace John Oldham's ranting bout
　　were the stern words of Oldham's scolding wife.

"John, you should be embarrassed and ashamed.
　　The people here gave us a place to live
and then provided means to keep us safe
　　but then you keep attacking all of them.

"And even after you had been expelled
　　they let your family stay to keep us safe
to give you time to settle somewhere else
　　and find a place where we could relocate."

But this attempt to quench the fearsome fire
　　was like she had thrown oil upon the flame
and quickly Oldham turned back to his ire
　　and once again began to rant in rage.

"You see how evil all these people are
　　and how they all behave despicably
as now they have done the most wicked harm
　　by turning my own family on me!"

And through the rife commotion that ensued
　　no one had noticed that a ship arrived
and although it was clearly within view
　　this squall diverted every person's eyes.

And graciously the ship was not of pirates
    or a belligerent invading force
but this absurd affair of wild defiance
    had certainly turned all of them off course.

Then everyone was suddenly surprised
    as they saw two men standing, looking on
as Winslow and Commander Peirce arrived
    and no one even noticed them approach.

And then the Governor spoke with the men
    whom Oldham had recruited and deceived
and they said they would take him back with them
    as they could clearly see his falsity.

The musketeers were all lined up at last
    and with the butt of each gun gave a thump
on Oldham's britches while he cowered past
    and sent him back to where he had come from.

John Oldham tried to burn the colony
    but Pilgrims trusted formal governance
and hoped a lesson of humility
    would help to mend the manners of the man.

Chapter 76

Gaining Independence

Through Edward Winslow's second trip to England
a lot transpired in London and in town
and with the formal parting of John Oldham
the Council gathered in the Meetinghouse.

Winslow had managed to bring more supplies
yet fees they paid kept plunging them in debt
and Council members told him of the trial
and how a mutiny was held in check.

Then Winslow told them of the bitter row
when the investors of the company
received the letters that John Lyford wrote
and split in angry partiality.

The group opposing Plymouth Colony
condemned the censure of the godly man
and said the Puritans were hindering
a righteous ministry with silly shams.

And even though the letters all described
the plotters working to destroy the town
the opposition faction all replied
their dealings were legitimately sound.

So the investors then agreed to hold
some meetings so they could investigate
and they selected of impartial note
two men of eminence to moderate.

But from examining the evidence
   and all the people Lyford had betrayed
the opposition group had no defense
   and realized there was nothing they could say.

So Lyford's friends were dealt a sound defeat
   and they had to withdraw their harsh attacks
and they abandoned the whole company
   and froze finances that caused a setback.

The colony still had their loyal friends
   and the small group stayed with the company
but there was no support that they could send
   as they had been fatigued financially.

The London friends sent their encouragement
   but now the company was in dour debt
and with the loss of other investments
   they had no means to offer any help.

They said that fourteen hundred Sterling Pounds
   was needed to clear all the debt they owed
and for the perseverance of the town
   the Pilgrims had to make this on their own.

But even past disruptions they endured
   the fees for goods and shipments that they made
increased the debt accrued by the venture
   and any hope of profit was erased.

And from the work of their successful year
   they filled their stores with goods that they would ship
and with the pounds of pelts they felt for sure
   they would pay down some of the deficit.

They loaded up their ship the *Little James*
  and planned to sell the ship upon return.
Their fishing ventures never seemed to pay.
  They found more profit growing their own corn.

They also loaded up the other ship
  upon which Winslow recently returned
and then sent Captain Standish on the trip
  to help negotiate financial terms.

The setback from the opposition's schemes
  had been endured and turned to victory
and now the ships sent back across the sea
  were laden with their trade and industry.

With Standish and two ships with loads of pelts
  returning to a port across the sea
there was a confidence the Pilgrims felt
  they had achieved their viability.

The London merchants were both stretched and strained
  and debts delayed the shipments of relief.
The loyal and devoted group had stayed
  but spiteful breaches had decreased their means.

So then the Pilgrims had made a response
  and answered with a proof of worth and use
and gave assurance for the venture's cause
  with two ships loaded with what they produced.

And after the ships sailed the former year
  they did not rest, but reaped their summer's yield
and they had plenty corn for every share
  and stores for trade from cultivated fields.

Then loading up their shallop they sailed east
   to trade their corn along the northern coast
and traveling for more than thirty leagues
   they bartered for the pelts to fill the boat.

Instead of trading with commodities
   they bartered corn they raised upon their own
and found reliance in their industry
   instead of waiting for supplies on loan.

There was a danger taking the long trip,
   the boat could not withstand the season's storms
and in the open sea there was a risk
   the boat would sink and they would lose the corn.

But they were pressed by the necessity
   and took the chance to venture out on faith
but knew this course put them in jeopardy
   and more reliant means were wisely made.

So Francis Eaton used the skills he learned
   while working with the craft master before
and built a ship that was more strong and stern
   for trading ventures with surplus of corn.

He had to saw the shallop in two halves
   and trimmed some boards about six feet in length
and fit them to extend a greater craft
   then reinforced the hull and built a deck.

With affirmation of devoted work
   they found contentment and enjoyed the peace
sufficiently producing their own worth
   determined to live independently.

Epilogue

Epilogue

1626 & 1627

In early April Sixteen Twenty-Six
   the Pilgrims heard that Standish had returned
but he did not come on a merchant ship
   but rode a fishing boat from what they heard.

They fetched him from a nearby fishing camp
   and they were grateful for him to be back
but sadly heard of the misfortunes slammed
   relentlessly upon the venture's path.

Some pirates captured *Little James* at sea,
   the Master, crew and laden all were lost
and that was just the start of tragedies
   that fell upon the journey at great cost.

Upon his ship returning to a port
   England was stricken with a deadly plague
and all the ship had laden was sold short
   as multitudes were dying every day.

He couldn't meet the merchant company
   and sadly Deacon Robert Cushman died
and then their fountain of wise ministry
   Revered John Robinson had also died.

King James had died and Holland's Prince Maurice
   and all the past they had, felt to be gone.
They heard the news and bore it ruggedly
   but they felt isolated and alone.

And with the loss of the entire shipment
    the Captain felt a heaviness of guilt.
But he was of no blame for negligence.
    They took the losses as a test of will.

They took the Captain then so he could see
    what they already built up in their store
and on the next vessel across the sea
    they were prepared to ship back even more.

Then in the year of Sixteen Twenty-Seven
    the Deacon Isaac Allerton returned
and he worked out with Company investors
    a new agreement and new set of terms.

For the amount of eighteen hundred Pounds
    they'd sell their stock of Plymouth Colony
and as installments yearly were paid down
    the faithful Pilgrims owned the company.

The Beginning

Appendixes

Mayflower Compact

In the name of God Amen. We whose names are underwritten, the loyal subjects of our dread sovereign Lord King James, by the grace of God, of Great Britain, France, & Ireland King, defender of the faith, &c.

Having undertaken, for the glory of God, and advancement of the Christian faith and honour of our king & country, a voyage to plant the first Colony in the northern parts of Virginia. Do by these presents solemnly & mutually in the presence of God, and one of another, Covenant, & Combine ourselves together into a Civil body politic; for our better ordering, & preservation & furtherance of the ends aforesaid; and by vertue hereof to Enact, Constitute, and frame such just & and equal laws, ordinances, Acts, constitutions, & offices, from time to time as shall be thought most meet & convenient for the general good of the Colony: unto which we promise all due submission and obedience. In witness whereof we have here undersubscribed our names at Cape Cod the 11th of November, in the year of the reign of our Sovereign Lord King James of England, France, & Ireland the eighteenth, and of Scotland the fifty-fourth. Anno Domini 1620.

Copy of the Mayflower Compact from:

Bradford, William. *Of Plimoth Plantation*, edited by Kenneth P. Minkema, Francis J. Bremer and Jeremy D. Bangs. Boston: Colonial Society of Massachusetts and New England Historic Genealogical Society, 2020.

Signatories of the Mayflower Compact from Nathaniel Morton's *New-Englands memoriall* (referenced in the Colonial Society of Massachusetts and New England Genealogical Society's edition of William Bradford's *Of Plimoth Plantation*):

John Alden, John Allerton, John Billington, William Bradford, William Brewster, Richard Britteridge, Peter Brown, John Carver, James Chilton, Richard Clark, Francis Cook, John Crackstone, Edward Doten, Francis Eaton, Thomas English, Moses Fletcher, Edward Fuller, Samuel Fuller, Richard Gardiner, John Goodman, Stephen Hopkins, John Howland, Edward Leister, Edmond Margesson, Christopher Martin, William Mullins, Digory Priest, John Ridgedale, Thomas Rogers, George Soule, Miles Standish, Edward Tilley, John Tilley, Thomas Tinker, John Turner, Richard Warren, William White, Thomas Williams, Edward Winslow, and Gilbert Winslow.

The names of those which came over first, in the year <u>1620</u>, and were (by the blessing of God) the first beginners, and (in a sort) the foundation, of all the plantations, and Colonies, in New England (And their families).

8   Mr. John Carver, Katherine his wife, Desire Minter, & 2 manservants, John Howland, Roger Wilder. William Latham, a boy, & a maidservant, & a child that was put to him Called, Jasper More.

———————

6   Mr. William Brewster. Mary his wife, with 2 sons, whose names were Love, & Wrestling, and a boy was put to him Called Richard More; and another of his brothers. The rest of his children were left behind & came over afterwards.

———————

5   Mr. Edward Winslow, Elizabeth his wife, & 2 menservants, Called George Soule, and Elias Story; also a little girl was put to him called Ellen, the sister of Richard More.

———————

2   William Bradford, and Dorothy his wife, having but one child, a son left behind, who came afterward.

———————

6   Mr. Isaac Allerton, and Mary his wife; with 3 children Bartholomew Remember, & Mary. And a servant boy, John Hooke.

———————

2   Mr. Samuel Fuller; and a servant, called William Butten. His wife was left behind & a child, which came afterwards.

———————

2   John Crackston, and his son John Crackston.

———————

2   Captain Myles Standish and Rose his wife.

———————

4   Mr. Christopher Martin, and his wife; and 2 servants, Solomon Prower, and John Langmore.

———————

5   Mr. William Mullins, and his wife; and 2 children, Joseph, & Priscilla; and a servant, Robert Carter.

---

6   Mr. William White, and Susanna his wife; and one son Called Resolved, and one born a-shipboard called Peregrine; & 2 servants, named William Holbeck, & Edward Thompson.

---

8   Mr. Stephen Hopkins, & Elizabeth his wife; and 2 Children, called Giles, and Constanta a daughter, both by a former wife. And 2 more by his wife, called Damaris, & Oceanus; the last was born at Sea. And 2 servants, called Edward Doty, and Edward Lester.

---

1   Mr. Richard Warren, but his wife and children were left behind and came afterwards.

---

4   John Billington, and Ellen his wife; and 2 sons, John, & Francis.

---

4   Edward Tilley, and Ann his wife; and 2 children that were their Cousins; Henry Sampson, and Humility Cooper.

---

3   John Tilley, and his wife; and Elizabeth their daughter.

---

2   Francis Cooke, and his son John; but his wife, & other children came afterwards.

---

2   Thomas Rogers, and Joseph his son; his other children came afterwards.

---

2   Thomas Tinker, and his wife, and a Son.

---

2   John Rigdale; and Alice his wife.

---

3   James Chilton, and his wife, and Mary their daughter; they had another daughter that was married came afterward.

---

3   Edward Fuller, and his wife; and Samuel their son.

---

3   John Turner, and 2 sons; he had a daughter came some years after to Salem, where she is now living.

---

3   Francis Eaton, and Sarah his wife, and Samuel their Son, a young Child.

---

10   Moses Fletcher, John Goodman, Thomas Williams, Digory Priest, Edmond Margesson, Peter Browne, Richard Britteridge, Richard Clarke, Richard Gardiner, Gilbert Winslow

---

1   John Alden was hired for a Cooper, at Southampton, where the ship Victualed; and being a hopeful young man was much desired, but left to his own liking to go, or stay when he came here, but he stayed and married here.

---

2   John Allerton, and Thomas English were both hired, the Latter to go master of a shallop here; and the other was reputed as one of the company, but was to go back (being a seaman) for the help of others behind. But they both died here, before the ship returned.

---

2   There were also another 2 seamen hired to stay a year here in the Country, William Trevor, and one Ely. But when their time was out they both returned.

Copy of "The names of those which came over first," from:
Bradford, William. *Of Plimoth Plantation*, edited by Kenneth P. Minkema, Francis J. Bremer and Jeremy D. Bangs. Boston: Colonial Society of Massachusetts and New England Historic Genealogical Society, 2020.

Maps

Maps based upon *The National Map* produced by the United States Geological Survey.

Other books and maps consulted for historical information:

Ames, Azel. *The May-Flower and Her Log.* Boston and New York: Houghton, Mifflin, 1907.

Bangs, Jeremy Dupertuis. *Pilgrim Edward Winslow, New England's First International Diplomat.* Boston, New England Historic Genealogical Society, 2004.

Raize, Erwin from William Bradford. *Of Plymouth Plantation 1620-1647,* edited by Samuel Eliot Morison. New York: Alfred A. Knopf, 1970.

Smith, Andrew C. from John G. Turner. *They Knew They Were Pilgrims.* New Haven and London, Yale University Press, 2020.

Mayflower's Arrival at Cape Cod

Map for Chapter 6 & 7

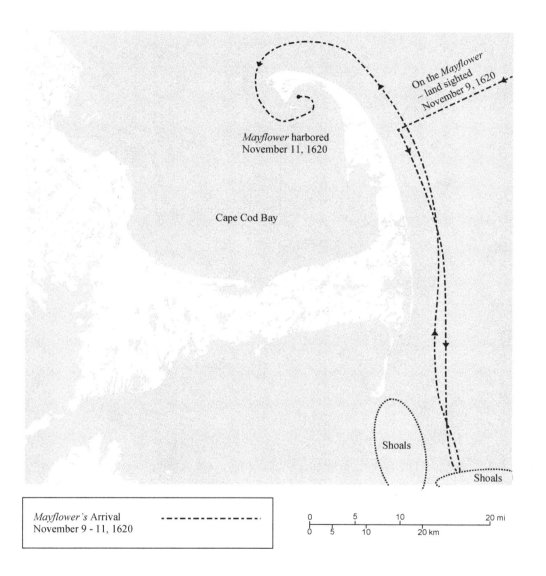

On the *Mayflower*
– land sighted
November 9, 1620

Mayflower harbored
November 11, 1620

Cape Cod Bay

Shoals

Shoals

Mayflower's Arrival
November 9 - 11, 1620

0   5   10   20 mi
0 5   10   20 km

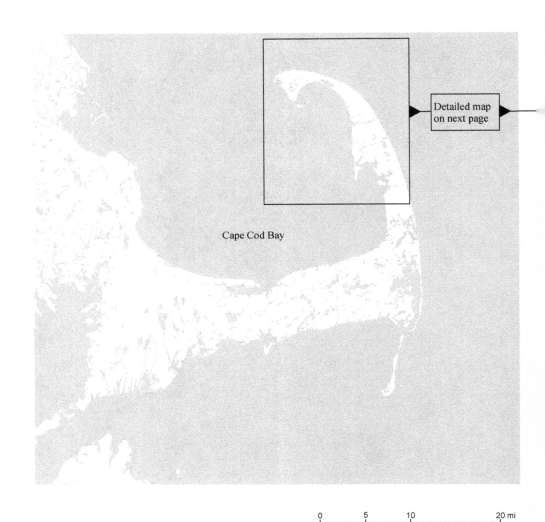

Detailed map
on next page

Cape Cod Bay

| 0 | 5 | 10 | 20 mi |
| 0 | 5 | 10 | 20 km |

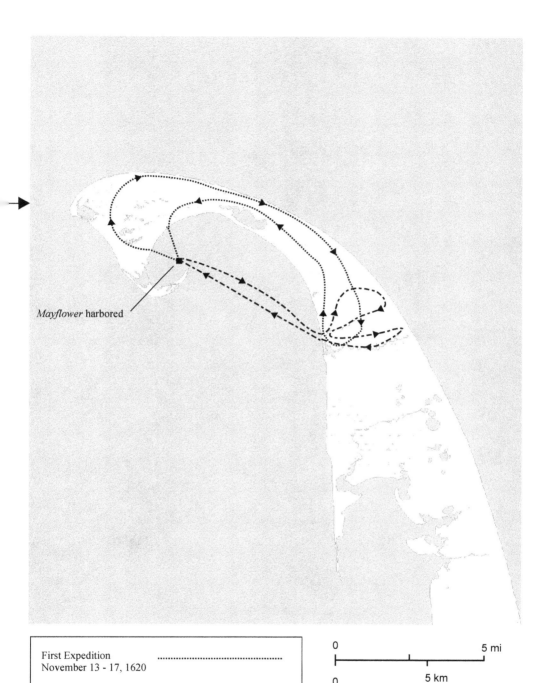

Mayflower harbored

First Expedition
November 13 - 17, 1620

Second Expedition
November 27 - 30, 1620

0   5 mi

0   5 km

Third Expedition

Chapter 12

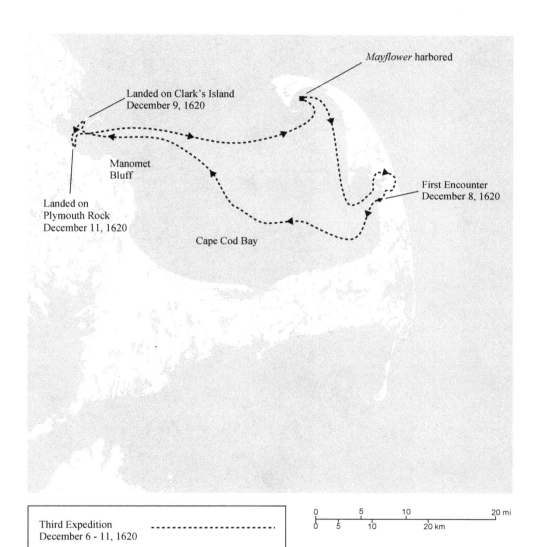

Mayflower harbored

Landed on Clark's Island
December 9, 1620

Manomet
Bluff

Landed on
Plymouth Rock
December 11, 1620

First Encounter
December 8, 1620

Cape Cod Bay

| Third Expedition |
| December 6 - 11, 1620 |

0   5   10   20 mi
0   5   10   20 km

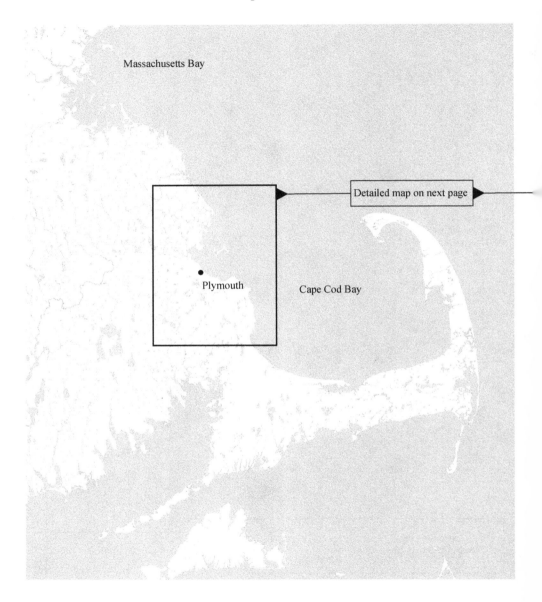

Massachusetts Bay

Detailed map on next page

Plymouth

Cape Cod Bay

| 0 | 4.5 | 9 | 18 mi |
| 0 | 5 | 10 | 20 km |

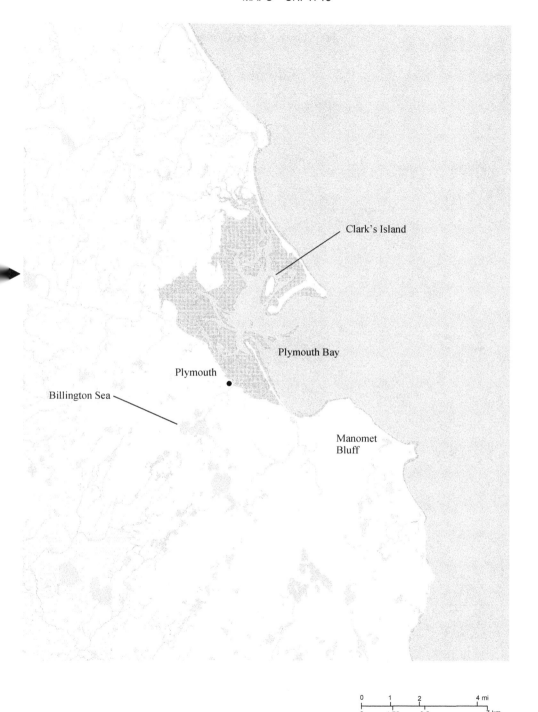

Clark's Island

Plymouth Bay

Plymouth

Billington Sea

Manomet
Bluff

0	1	2		4 mi
0	1.75	3.5		7 km

Envoy to Ousamequin

Chapter 27

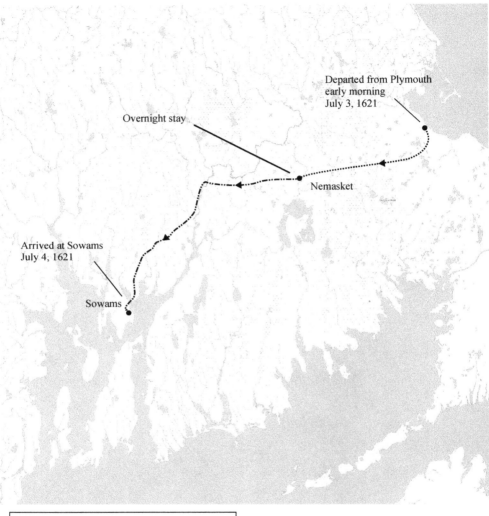

Departed from Plymouth
early morning
July 3, 1621

Overnight stay

Nemasket

Arrived at Sowams
July 4, 1621

Sowams

Envoy to Ousamequin
July 3, 1621

July 4, 1621

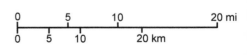

0   5   10   20 mi

0   5   10   20 km

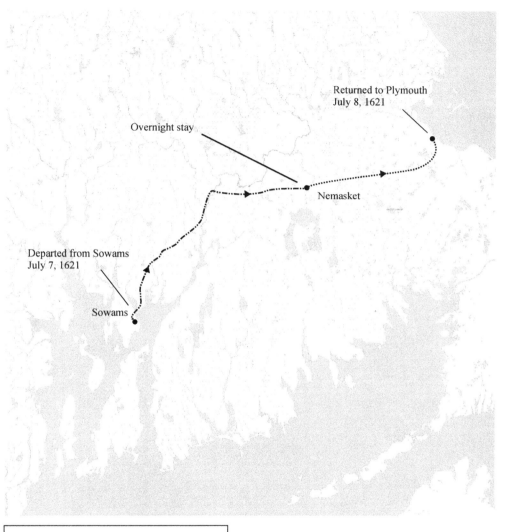

Returned to Plymouth
July 8, 1621

Overnight stay

Nemasket

Departed from Sowams
July 7, 1621

Sowams

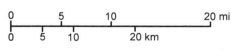

Return from Sowams
July 7, 1621

July 8, 1621

0   5   10   20 mi

0   5   10   20 km

Journey to Nauset

Chapter 28

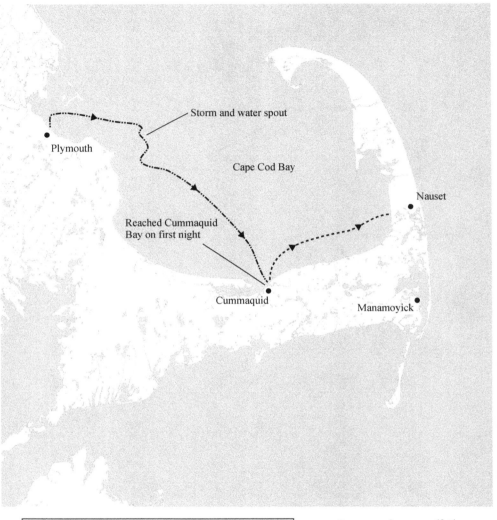

Storm and water spout

Plymouth

Cape Cod Bay

Reached Cummaquid
Bay on first night

Cummaquid

Nauset

Manamoyick

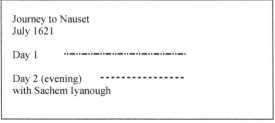

Journey to Nauset
July 1621

Day 1

Day 2 (evening)
with Sachem Iyanough

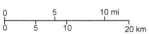

0		5		10 mi
0	5		10	
				20 km

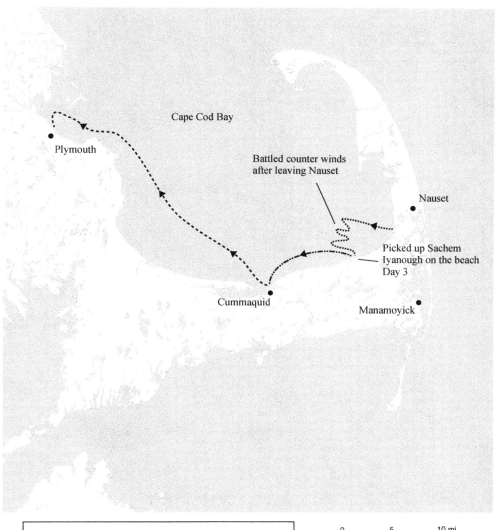

Cape Cod Bay

Plymouth

Battled counter winds
after leaving Nauset

Nauset

Picked up Sachem
Iyanough on the beach
Day 3

Cummaquid

Manamoyick

Return from Nauset
July 1621

Departed Nauset on 2nd Night ·······································

Returned to Cummaquid
with Sachem Iyanough

Returned to Plymouth
with John Billington's boy

0   5   10 mi

0   5   10   20 km

437

Envoy to the Massachusetts

Chapter 30

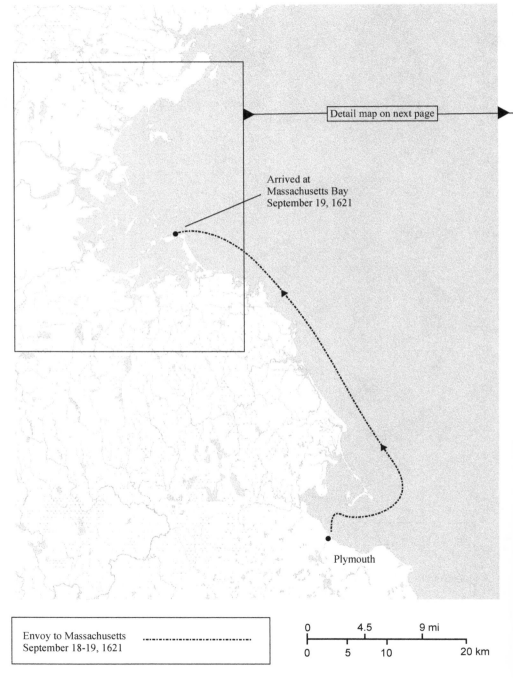

Detail map on next page

Arrived at
Massachusetts Bay
September 19, 1621

Plymouth

| Envoy to Massachusetts September 18-19, 1621 | .... |

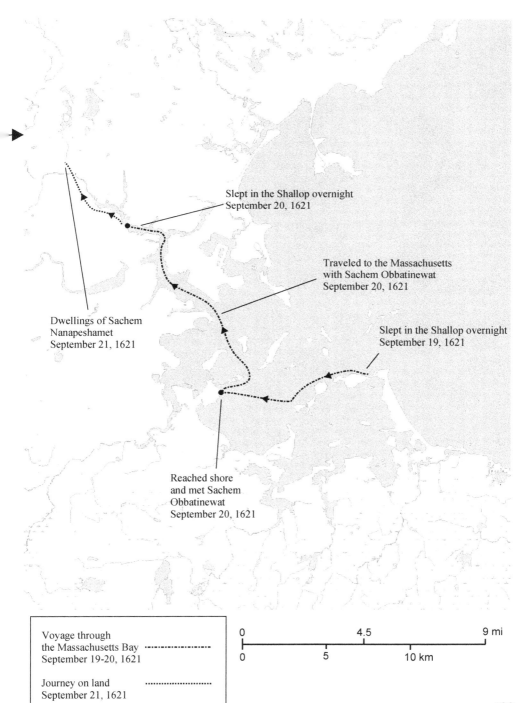

Slept in the Shallop overnight
September 20, 1621

Traveled to the Massachusetts
with Sachem Obbatinewat
September 20, 1621

Slept in the Shallop overnight
September 19, 1621

Dwellings of Sachem
Nanapeshamet
September 21, 1621

Reached shore
and met Sachem
Obbatinewat
September 20, 1621

Voyage through
the Massachusetts Bay
September 19-20, 1621

Journey on land
September 21, 1621

0		4.5		9 mi
0	5		10 km	

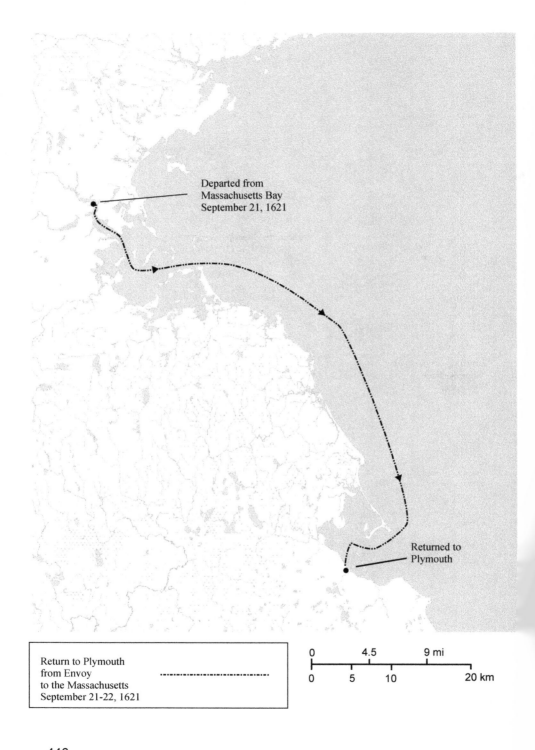

Departed from
Massachusetts Bay
September 21, 1621

Returned to
Plymouth

Return to Plymouth
from Envoy
to the Massachusetts
September 21-22, 1621

0   4.5   9 mi

0   5   10   20 km

The Shoals
Tisquantum, the Passing of a Friend
Returning from the Shoals

Chapter 49, 50 & 51

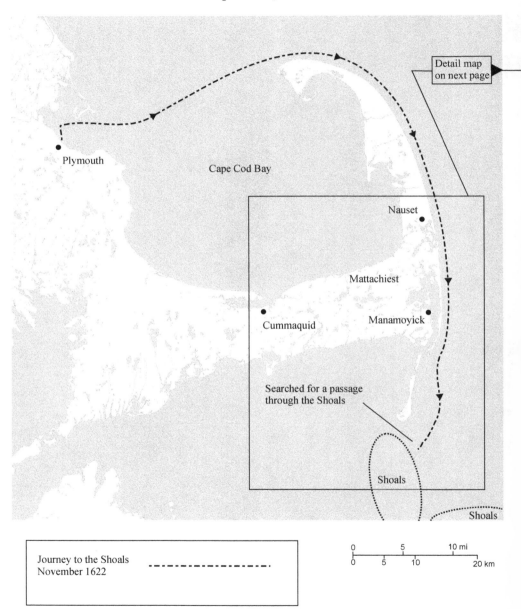

Plymouth

Cape Cod Bay

Detail map on next page

Nauset

Mattachiest

Cummaquid

Manamoyick

Searched for a passage through the Shoals

Shoals

Shoals

Journey to the Shoals
November 1622

0   5   10 mi

0   5   10   20 km

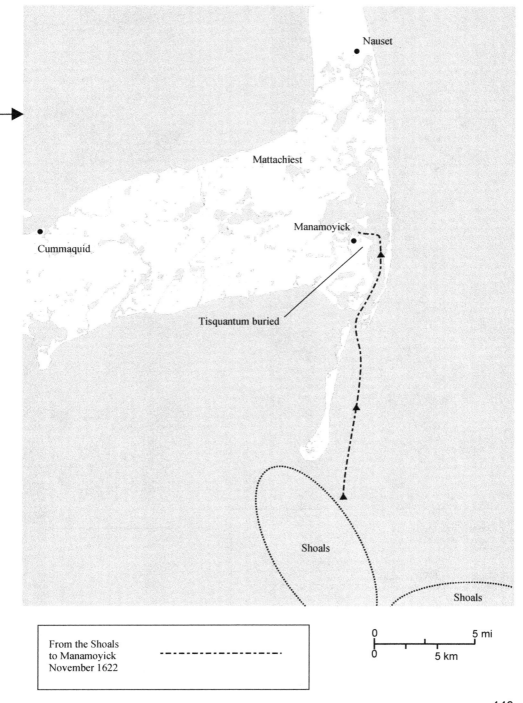

Nauset

Mattachiest

Manamoyick

Cummaquid

Tisquantum buried

Shoals

Shoals

From the Shoals
to Manamoyick
November 1622

0   5 mi

0   5 km

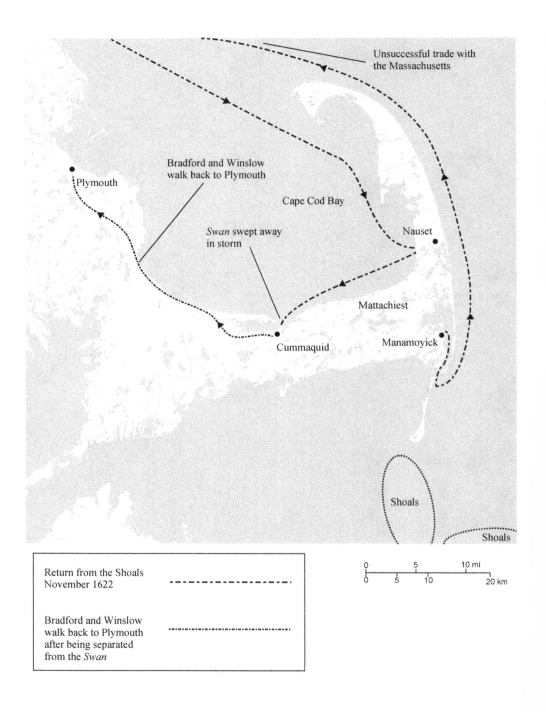

Unsuccessful trade with
the Massachusetts

Bradford and Winslow
walk back to Plymouth

Plymouth

Cape Cod Bay

Swan swept away
in storm

Nauset

Mattachiest

Cummaquid

Manamoyick

Shoals

Shoals

Return from the Shoals
November 1622

Bradford and Winslow
walk back to Plymouth
after being separated
from the *Swan*

0   5   10 mi
0   5   10   20 km

Visit to Sowams
Guests of Sachem Corbitant
Hobomock Reveals the Plot against the Pilgrims

Chapter 53, 54 & 55

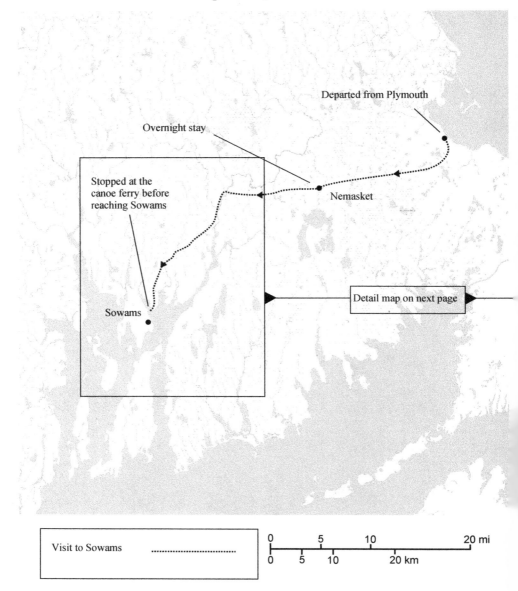

Departed from Plymouth

Overnight stay

Stopped at the
canoe ferry before
reaching Sowams

Nemasket

Detail map on next page

Sowams

Visit to Sowams	....

0   5   10   20 mi

0   5   10   20 km

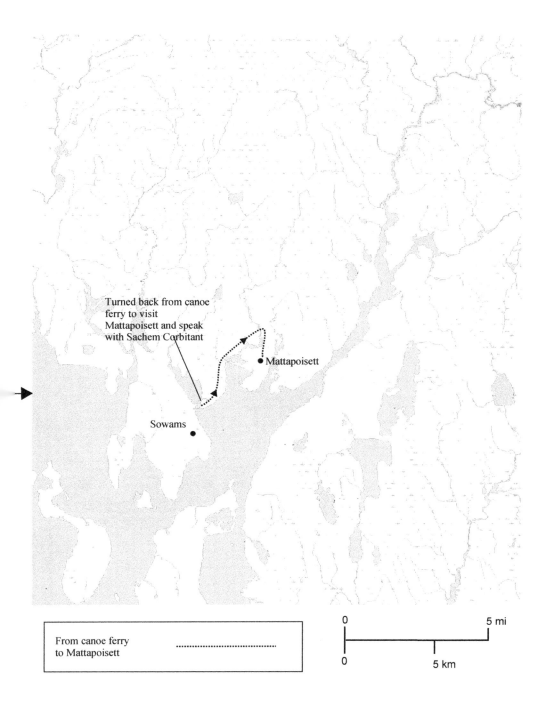

Turned back from canoe
ferry to visit
Mattapoisett and speak
with Sachem Corbitant

● Mattapoisett

Sowams
●

| From canoe ferry to Mattapoisett | .... |

0   5 mi

0   5 km

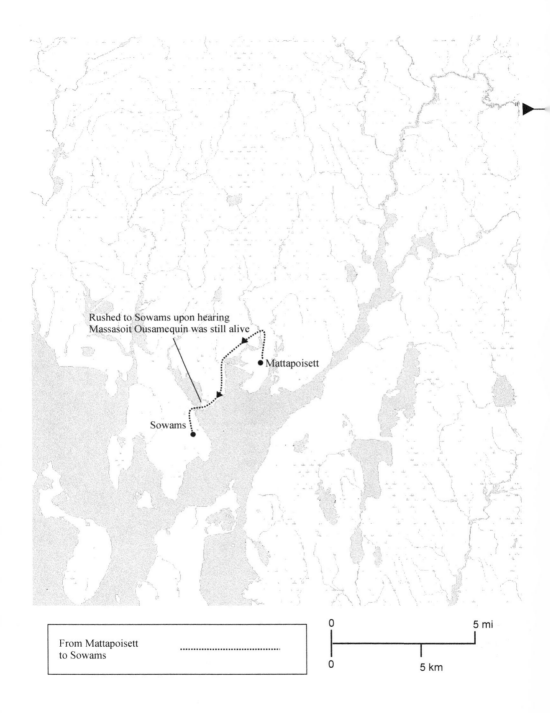

Rushed to Sowams upon hearing
Massasoit Ousamequin was still alive

● Mattapoisett

Sowams ●

| From Mattapoisett to Sowams | .... |

0   5 mi

0   5 km

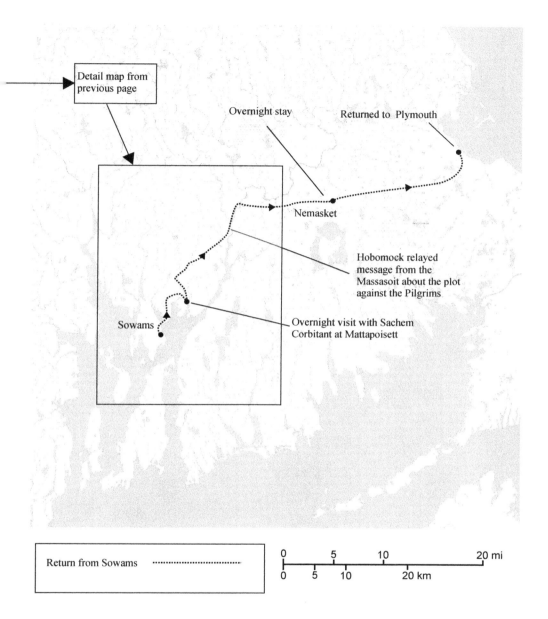

Detail map from previous page

Overnight stay

Returned to Plymouth

Nemasket

Hobomock relayed message from the Massasoit about the plot against the Pilgrims

Overnight visit with Sachem Corbitant at Mattapoisett

Sowams

Return from Sowams

0   5   10   20 mi
0   5   10   20 km

Captain Standish Rescues Weston's Men

Chapter 56

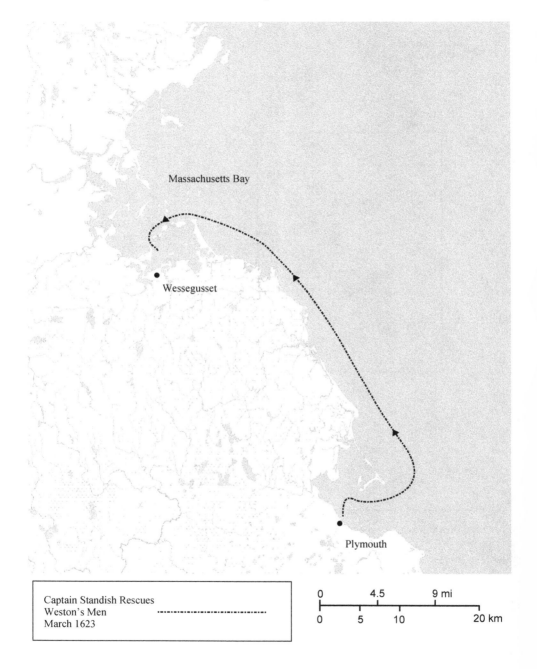

Massachusetts Bay

Wessegusset

Plymouth

| Captain Standish Rescues Weston's Men March 1623 | -- |

0   4.5   9 mi

0   5   10   20 km

Raising the Pinnace

Chapter 74

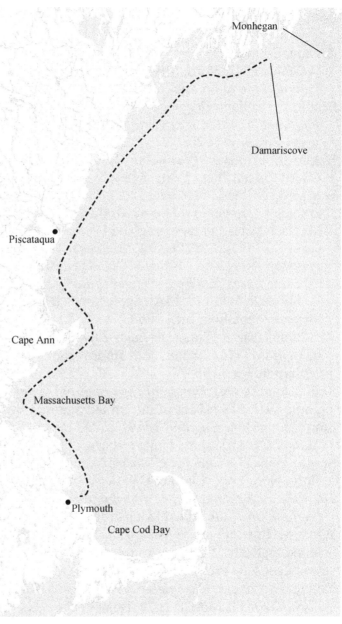

Monhegan

Damariscove

Piscataqua

Cape Ann

Massachusetts Bay

Plymouth

Cape Cod Bay

To Damariscove
to raise the Pinnace
1624

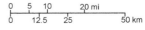

0   5   10   20 mi
0   12.5   25   50 km

Bibliography

Primary Sources

Altham, Emmanuel. *Three Visitors to Early Plymouth*, edited by Sydney V. James Jr. Bedford, MA: Applewoods Books from the publication by Plimoth Plantation, Inc., 1963.

Bradford, William. *Bradford's History of Plymouth Settlement, 1608-1650, Rendered in Modern English by Harold Paget.* New York: E.P. Dutton and Company, 1920.

Bradford, William. *Of Plymouth Plantation 1620-1647*, edited by Samuel Eliot Morison. New York: Alfred A. Knopf, 1970.

Bradford, William. *Of Plimoth Plantation*, edited by Kenneth P. Minkema, Francis J. Bremer and Jeremy D. Bangs. Boston: Colonial Society of Massachusetts and New England Historic Genealogical Society, 2020.

Bradford, William. *Of Plimoth Plantation*, edited by Lisa Brooks and Kelly Wisecup. New York: Literary Classics of the United States, 2022.

De Rasieres, Isaack. *Three Visitors to Early Plymouth*, edited by Sydney V. James Jr. Bedford, MA: Applewoods Books from the publication by Plimoth Plantation, Inc., 1963.

Pory, John. *Three Visitors to Early Plymouth*, edited by Sydney V. James Jr. Bedford, MA: Applewoods Books from the publication by Plimoth Plantation, Inc., 1963.

Smith, John. *A Description of New England*, edited by James Horn. New York: Literary Classics of the United States, 2007.

Smith, John. *New England Trials*, edited by James Horn. New York: Literary Classics of the United States, 2007.

Smith, John. *The General History of New-England*, edited by James Horn. New York: Literary Classics of the United States, 2007.

The Pilgrim Fathers: or The Journal of the Pilgrims of Plymouth, New England, in 1620, edited by George Cheever. USA: John Wiley, 1849.

Winslow, Edward. *Good News from New England – A Scholarly Edition*, edited by Kelly Wisecup. Amherst and Boston: University of Massachusetts Press, 2014.

Young, Alexander. *Chronicles of the Pilgrim Fathers of the Colony of Plymouth from 1602 to 1625*. Boston: Charles C. Little and James Brown, 1841.

Secondary Sources

Ames, Azel. *The May-Flower and Her Log.* Boston and New York: Houghton, Mifflin, 1907.

Bangs, Jeremy Dupertuis. *Pilgrim Edward Winslow: New England's First International Diplomat.* Boston, New England Historic Genealogical Society, 2004.

Bremer, Francis J. *One Small Candle.* Oxford University Press, 2020.

Fraser, Rebecca. *The Mayflower: The Families, the Voyage, and the Founding of America.* New York: St. Martin's Press, 2017.

Hall, David D. *The Puritans: A Transatlantic History.* Princeton and Oxford: Princeton University Press, 2019.

Mack, Jonathan. *A Stranger among Saints.* Chicago: Chicago Review Press, 2020.

Philbrick, Nathaniel. *Mayflower.* New York: Penguin Books, 2007.

Stratton, Eugene Aubrey. *Plymouth Colony: Its History and People, 1620-1691.* Salt Lake City: Ancestry Publishing, 1986.

Tomkins, Stephen. *The Journey to the Mayflower.* New York and London: Pegasus Books, 2020.

Turner, John G. *They Knew They Were Pilgrims.* New Haven and London: Yale University Press, 2020.

Whittock, Martyn. *Mayflower Lives.* New York and London: Pegasus Books, 2019.

Garrett Buhl Robinson is a poet living in New York City.

More information about his books can be found on his website:

www.PoetinthePark.com

Poet in the Park ®

In Humanity I see Grace, Beauty and Dignity.